Underwater Holidays

Underwater Holidays

by Janet Viertel

text by Jack Viertel

today
press

Publishers · GROSSET & DUNLAP · New York
A FILMWAYS COMPANY

Cover photograph: Flip Schulke/Black Star Agency

Copyright © 1978 by Janet Viertel
Published simultaneously in Canada
Library of Congress catalog card number: 76-17406
ISBN 0-448-12087-9 (paperback)

First printing 1978
Printed in the United States of America

For
My children and grandchildren

In Appreciation

This is a book for everyone interested in the underwater world: it is
for people who have never tried snorkeling or diving, but might like to;
for the snorkeler or free diver; and for the scuba diver. Many
professional divers have given me endless help and advice in
preparing and checking the charts and maps in Chapter 3; I am most
deeply indebted to them. I'd like to express my gratitude particularly
to Captain Ed Davidson of Key Marathon, Florida; Bret Gilliam of
St. Croix, Virgin Islands; Dale Huddleston of Hawaii; Jack McKenney
of Los Angeles, California; Dave McLeod of Paget, Bermuda;
Nancy Sefton of Grand Cayman Island; Carl Seyfer of Honolulu,
Hawaii; John Shuck of the Bronx and Bob Gondolfo of Bronxville,
New York; Carl Roessler of San Francisco, California; Lee Turcotte of
Miami, Florida; Joe Vogel of St. Thomas, Virgin Islands; and Gardner
Young of Nassau, The Bahamas. I would like to add my thanks to
Andrew Glickson and Gary Tong who prepared the maps.

Contents

ONE

The Joys of Snorkeling and Diving

For untold centuries man has been seen, from time to time, standing at the water's edge, looking toward the horizon, yearning for adventure, beauty, and a glimpse into the mystery of unknown worlds. If only he'd fallen in! Equipped with a mask, snorkel, and flippers, he might have found everything he was seeking. For the world under the water is certainly as mysterious, as beautiful, and as adventurous as any exotic world across the ocean could ever be. Not only that—it's easier to reach. You don't even need an ocean. There are lakes, caves, sink-holes, rivers, quarries, and ponds in all fifty of the United States and in all countries of the world. These are well worth exploring, and almost anyone can do it. The common image of a "frogman" as a daredevil spearfisherman or a technically sophisticated scientist gliding through the deep is a thing of the past. Of course they still exist; but underwater exploration is now within the province of almost anyone who can swim passably, and a visit to one of the many popular underwater reefs will reveal grandparents, parents, children, and grandchildren, navigating placidly through some of the most stunning and beautiful scenery anywhere on our planet. The skills are easily acquired: the equipment is simple, readily available, and not terribly expensive.

Snorkelers examine a reef in Hanauma Bay on the island of Oahu. (Hawaii Visitors Bureau)

And would-be explorers with poor eyesight can even have their prescription lenses fitted to their masks.

Snorkeling, while it is a delightful activity for most people, is not for everyone. Those with extreme and unusual fear of the water and those who tend to be abnormally claustrophobic or unusually quick to panic should remain well up the beach, along with those who cannot swim at all. Underwater exploration should be comfortable and fun, and there is no point in attempting it if your natural tendencies tell you not to.

If you're comfortable in the water, however, you may well find snorkeling and diving a perfect pastime.

If you tend to get cold while in the water, there are snorkeling areas where the water temperature is in the eighties, and in cooler water you can wear a "wet suit," which will keep you perfectly comfortable. Once you are familiar with the techniques and have accustomed yourself to snorkeling gear, the number of directions your new hobby can take you in is almost limitless. In the beginning, peering through the water at almost anything may be an unusual thrill. Even the sight of a discarded beer can has an extra dimension if you see it under water. And when you begin to explore the incredible natural

A lone fish making its way between majestic strands of elkhorn coral.
(Janet Viertel)

beauty, the mystery and history in the underwater world, it is likely that the world over water will begin to look a little drab by comparison. Coral reefs offer a panorama of color and shape, grace and movement that cannot be described in words and can only be approximated in pictures. The reef world is forever moving; fish dart between stands of majestic antler coral, or glide along the bottom searching for a morsel of dinner; delicately webbed yellow and purple sea fans undulate in the gentle swell. To be a part of this vibrant, living community, even for a short time, can be an emotionally charged experience.

And sight-seeing, even of this spectacular sort, is not the only thing you can enjoy. There are any number of fascinating underwater activities. For the hunter there is the thrill of chasing and spearing fish in their own territory—not from the ease and comfort of a fighting chair. Lobster, conch, scallops, clams, and oysters can also be taken, and these make great beach-picnic fare, as do abalone on the U.S. West Coast. You should spear only what you expect to eat. Regulations must be checked before a fishing expedition is organized, since spearfishing is frowned upon in many places, and restricted in some.

If your instinct is toward adventure, there are thousands of shipwrecks to be explored, many bearing treasure, or at least rumors of treasure.

For the science buff or the research-minded, the sea is an everexpanding field, yielding tremendous finds for the archeologist and marine biologist alike, helping to untangle man's complicated history and the history of all life on Earth. Marine biology is a relatively new field and a most promising one.

Collectors and craft enthusiasts will find a nearly limitless variety of shells and other sea treasures, which can be made up in unusual displays or fashioned into jewelry, mosaics, or nearly anything a creative imagination can conjure up. Collectors of tropical fish may be interested in acquiring specimens for their tanks at home, and in fact, it is quite practical to do so.

Finally, if the undersea world moves you, you may want to bring back photographs of your trip. This

Besides the spectacular coral reefs surrounding the 700 islands of the Bahamas, the remains of sunken ships can sometimes be seen. (Bahamas Tourist News Bureau)

12

is not as easy as toting your camera around Europe on your neck, but the field of underwater photography is challenging and gratifying and may result in beautiful works of art, as well as a chance to share the sights you have seen with others not quite as fortunate.

As you become more involved in the underwater world, you may want to learn scuba diving, which will allow you to go well below the surface carrying an air supply on your back. A thirty-hour training course and certification will equip you with the necessary knowledge, and although the scuba gear is more expensive and somewhat more cumbersome than a mask, snorkel, and fins, the rewards far outweigh the inconvenience.

All of this would be too good to be true if there were no related problems, but like any sport, snorkeling entails some minor problems. Contrary to the opinion of many who have never tried snorkeling, however, the hazards involve the diver, himself, and not the water or its natural inhabitants. Indeed, the biggest single enemy the snorkeler must cope with in the tropics is the sun. Because he lies facedown in the water, sometimes for an hour or more, the water laps over his back and legs, gently cooling him as it refracts the sunlight onto his skin, often causing severe and painful burns. Therefore, I'd advise the snorkeler to wear an old T-shirt and a pair of tights. Never mind how silly you think you look. You'll look a lot sillier with white cream all over you at dinner. Having avoided the sun, your next big danger is your own adventurousness. Most underwater accidents are caused by divers' overconfidence. Do not think you can "try anything" after a couple of test runs in a pool. Be sensible. Don't scuba without sufficient training—it's not as simple as it looks. Don't snorkel in areas where currents and waters are beyond your capacity. Don't scuba or snorkel after drinking, using drugs, or heavy eating. Be careful around boats and water hazards. Perhaps most important—never mistake the sea for your friend; treat it with respect, and it will do the same for you.

There are not many natural hazards in the ocean, and those that do exist are easily avoided. If you can refrain from touching things with which you are not familiar, or panicking at the sight of some large sea creature that may have wandered into your field of vision, you should have no problems. Underwater exploration is simple, and the diverse opportunities it offers should assure many years of enjoyable, even thrilling, experiences.

TWO

All about Snorkeling

Exploring the underwater world in the shallowest of water with complete safety and comfort. The snorkeler is enjoying many sights invisible to his standing companion. (Janet Viertel)

The range of methods for exploring the underwater world is vast and complex, but to begin at the beginning is blissfully simple. Snorkeling can be perfected by anyone who is in normally good health and can swim passably. It is much less strenuous than swimming, and since the best snorkeling is in shallow water, you don't have to be a champion swimmer to feel safe and comfortable.

Even so, most people quite naturally feel slightly apprehensive before their first snorkeling experience. The best hedge against fear is to familiarize yourself thoroughly with your equipment and the proper procedure before embarking, and then to get comfortable in a really placid body of water before doing any real exploration. There isn't much equipment required. In fact, four pieces should get you ready to go, three if you count both of your flippers as one unit. The flippers, if

properly fitted, will never give you any trouble. Water will enter your mask and snorkel from time to time, and no amount of snorkeling experience can prevent this from happening. Nerve-wracking as this sounds, you'll find it a triviality within minutes. You will quickly become proficient at "clearing" the water out of either or both, and in short order you will get so used to doing this you'll do it almost instinctively.

14 PURCHASING YOUR EQUIPMENT

Snorkeling gear is available in a wide range of places, from five-and-dime stores and novelty shops to sporting goods stores and diving supply houses. Avoid the cheaper equipment offered in stores that do not specialize in sporting gear, for in such establishments these items are often really toys; they tend to be unsafe and frequently do not work at all. If there is a dive store in your area, your best bet is to shop there. The salesmen are frequently divers; they can advise you about the features of different models of masks, snorkels, and flippers, and help you choose equipment that will best suit your needs. If the shop sells more expensive equipment, such as wet suits and scuba tanks, so much the better. They will want you to enjoy the sport and get involved enough to require more advanced gear, and so will make every effort to help you feel comfortable with your first purchases. They may even offer you some instruction. If there is no dive store in your area, a reputable sporting goods store will usually have first-rate equipment and salesmen who can be of help. Your equipment should cost you between twenty and thirty dollars.

The most difficult item to choose is your mask. Masks come in a variety of shapes and sizes, but this is not merely a designer's whim. Each mask offers different features, and a salesman can explain the advantages of one over another. The key in choosing a mask is fit. It must follow the contour of your face closely, and for this reason masks are designed in varying shapes. The best way to make sure you have a snug fit is to place the mask over your eyes and nose without using the back strap. Suck in through your nose; the suction should hold the mask tightly to your face. If the mask tends to fall off, air is leaking in, and if air leaks in, water will certainly manage to do the same. Try another. Be certain that your hair is not between your skin and the mask, since this will allow air to leak in.

The dive shop salesman will advise you about the features of different models of masks, snorkels, and flippers. (Janet Viertel)

Your mask should have a back strap that separates into two strands, which fit over the back of your head. This "separated strap" will keep the mask more securely in place. Once you have a mask that fits properly, place the strap across the back of your head above your ears and adjust the length for comfort. It should be tight enough to hold the mask firmly, but not so tight as to cause any pain from pressure.

Some masks come with "purges," which allow you to clear any water from your mask merely by exhaling through your nose. These are convenient but have shorter lives, because after many hours of use the purge itself may begin to leak, and then the mask usually has to be replaced. Other masks have nose pieces that allow you to pinch your nose in order to relieve pressure on your ears. These are also convenient if you plan to go below the surface where ear pressure can occur. A salesman can help you decide which, if any, of these features you want in your mask. To some extent your choice will depend on what types of activity you are interested in.

If you need prescription lenses "welded" into your mask, a salesman can probably advise you about this also. Underwater objects appear larger and closer than they actually are, and having lenses put in your mask can be moderately expensive. Unless you have really poor vision, you may want to try a

few dives without the prescription mask to see whether it is worth the trouble. If your salesman cannot arrange to have the lenses put into your mask, *Skin Diver Magazine* regularly carries advertisements for this service, and you can no doubt find an outfit near you or by mail order that will do the job.

Your next piece of equipment is a snorkel, which is nothing more than a hollow tube with a mouthpiece at one end; the snorkel allows you to draw air from above while you float facedown in the water. There are

as many types of snorkels as there are masks, but again, the basic requirements are simple: the mouthpiece should fit snugly, and the snorkel should be twelve to fifteen inches long. Most snorkels are J-shaped, although some have a flexible rubber center allowing the mouthpiece to hang straight down when it is not in use. These latter snorkels are primarily for scuba divers, who carry a snorkel for auxiliary air. The J-shaped models should be perfectly satisfactory. Do not buy a combined mask and snorkel, a snorkel that has a ball on

The mask should have a back strap that separates into two strands, which fit over the back of your head. (Janet Viertel)

16

The dive shop salesman can help you select flippers that fit properly.
(Janet Viertel)

the end to keep out water, or a snorkel over fifteen inches long. These are all dangerous.

Your final essential purchase is a pair of flippers, or fins. These are sold by size, like shoes, and should fit comfortably. If they are too tight they will cause foot cramps. Like your mask, the stylistic choice you make with your flippers (open or closed toes or heels, floating or not) is less important than the fit. Your choice will depend on your planned activity, and your salesman can advise you.

TRYING ON YOUR EQUIPMENT AT HOME

You won't worry about drowning above water, so put your equipment on and practice using it on land at least once. Assemble all of your purchases in a quiet room, or with someone who is going to help you learn to snorkel, or learn with you, and get comfortable with your gear. Read any material that has come with it, and then try it on.

Put the snorkel in your mouth between your lips and gums. Bite gently on the projecting rubber pieces if your snorkel has these tabs. Hold your nose with one hand so that you cannot breathe through it, and breathe normally through your mouth via the snorkel. Don't gasp—just breathe through your mouth as if the snorkel were not in your mouth. Keep in mind that it is no harder to breathe through the snorkel when you are in the water than it is on land. When you are comfortable using the snorkel, take it out of your mouth and attach it to your mask strap by means of the rubber snorkel tab that comes with the snorkel. Normally the mouthpiece is fastened on the right side of the mask, but you may fasten it on the left if you prefer. (Some snorkels have mouthpieces molded in a slight tilt that will conform to your mouth better if they are fastened to the right of the mask.)

Should the mouthpiece dig into your gums, trim it a little with scissors. When the snorkel is attached, place the mask over your eyes and nose and slip the strap over the back of your head. Check to make sure your hair is not caught between the edge of the mask and your skin. Put the snorkel back into your mouth and breathe normally again. The mask will have effectively sealed off your nose, and you may now walk around the room breathing through your snorkel and peering through your mask. Have a convenient excuse in case of unexpected visitors. When you have become comfortable with the mask and snorkel, you are ready for a dip in open water. There is no need to test your fins, since they are terribly clumsy on land, but they give you grace and much increased power and maneuverability in the water. You should, however, be sure they fit comfortably.

YOUR FIRST OPEN-WATER SWIM

Plan your first swim in a body of water that you have no fear of—a pool or placid inland lake or well-populated beach. Don't swim by yourself. If you have no one to try snorkeling with, get someone who is willing to watch you. Swimming without a "buddy" can be dangerous, and as simple as snorkeling is, you will not want to feel that you are in any danger on your first try. Before using your mask for the first time, wash the face plate thoroughly with detergent and rinse it carefully. This is not something you have to repeat each time you use the mask.

If the water in which you plan to swim is very cold (so cold that you would not normally swim in it), you may want to get a wet suit. These rubber suits can sometimes be rented from dive shops and can certainly be bought, but they are quite expensive for the beginning skin diver. Your best bet is to avoid extra cold water and wet suits on your "learning" dive, even if it means buying your way into the indoor pool of the local health club for the afternoon. After all, this is for pleasure.

The procedure for getting into the water with your equipment is simple and substantially easier if you can go in from the steps of a pool or from a beach, rather than over the side of a boat. First, you must defog your mask, which will prevent its clouding up with vapor as you swim. Wet the mask with water and rinse it. Then spit into it and rub the saliva around thoroughly. When the lens is coated thoroughly, rerinse the mask.

Put the snorkel in your mouth between your lips and gums. (Janet Viertel)

Place the mask over the eyes and nose and slip the strap over the back of the head. (Janet Viertel)

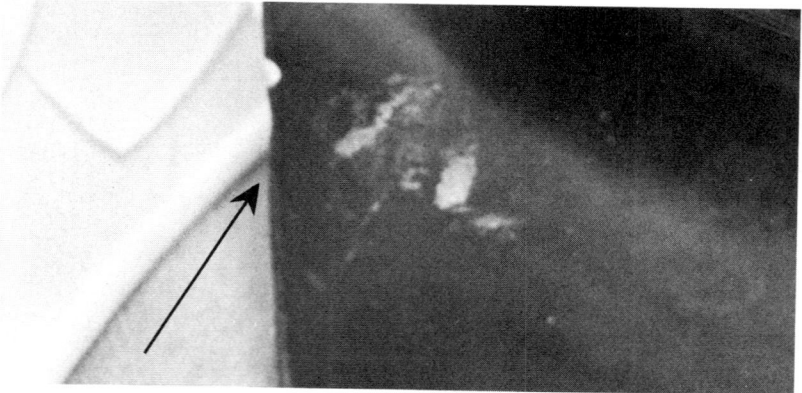

Here a bathing cap is incorrectly placed between the mask and the face. It will break the suction and water will leak into the mask. (Janet Viertel)

If you are swimming in a pool, do not spill this final rinse back into the pool. Instead of this primitive method, you can use commercial preparations available for defogging; rubbing with a cut raw potato will also do the job. The advantage of spit is that you never forget to pack it.

Now slip your mask on your face and straighten the back strap on the back of your head above your ears. Your snorkel should already be attached to the mask, so slip the mouthpiece into your mouth. If you are wearing a bathing cap, be sure it is not between your mask and your face—like your hair, it will break the seal and allow water to seep into your mask. If you are in a pool, the easiest way to get into your fins is to sit on the side or steps. If you are on a beach, put your fins on on land and walk backward into the water. This sounds slightly mad, but it is much easier to walk backward with fins on. Try it and see. When you are more experienced, you will find it is much simpler to walk into the water carrying your flippers in your hand and put them on by raising one foot and then the other as you float facedown, breathing through your snorkel.

Now, you're ready to enter the water. When you get about waist deep, or are standing in the shallow end of the pool, look around you, breathing through the snorkel. If you are sure you are really comfortable, bend over and put your face in the water, keeping your feet on the bottom. Keep breathing easily. You should see your feet, which, due to water distortion, will appear bigger than they are.

Assuming you are having no problems breathing naturally and seeing perfectly, lift up your feet and kick smoothly. You will float easily facedown with your gear on; so if you prefer, you really don't have to kick at all to stay on the surface of the water. Stay in shallow water and keep breathing normally. Keep your hands at your sides or clasped behind your back. You will not need your hands for snorkeling, and later you will want to have them free for collecting, photographing, spearfishing, or whatever your underwater activity may be. For now just let them rest; keep your fins under water and use a gentle flutter kick to get around. If you are at all uneasy, take a rubber tube float with you. Your entire first snorkel can be done in water shallow enough to stand in, and that should help to keep you from being apprehensive.

One can easily put on fins or flippers while sitting on the steps of a pool.
(Janet Viertel)

A potential snorkeler takes her first look underwater. She sees her own feet enlarged by 25 percent. (Janet Viertel)

The snorkeler takes off into shallow quiet water, hands behind back, breathing normally and gently flutter-kicking. (Janet Viertel)

TROUBLESHOOTING

If water gets in your snorkel, the easiest thing to do at the beginning is to lift your head out of the water, take the snorkel out of your mouth, and empty it. Later you can try blowing sharply out of your mouth, which will blow the water out the top end of the snorkel. You may want to practice by taking a deep breath, letting the snorkel fill up with water, and clearing it by blowing out. When you get to be more of an expert, you will be able to roll over on your back and clear out the snorkel in that position. This does a more thorough job, but there is no need to learn it at the earliest stage. Make sure the snorkel points straight up when your head is looking straight down.

If water leaks into your mask, you may clear it, like the snorkel, by lifting your head out of the water and raising the lower edge of the mask away from your face. The water will run out. If your mask has a purge valve you may, without lifting your head out of the water, simply blow out through your nose and the water will empty out. If your mask is leaking continually, even a little, come up and check to see that it is fitted properly and that the back strap is tight. If you can't get the mask to stop leaking, you will want to try another one.

If you are tired, you can do a cork float. This is worth trying just to see how easy it is, even if you are feeling no fatigue. Bend your knees and bring them to your chest. Put your arms around your knees and clasp your hands together. You can float facedown and breathe in this position until you regain energy. If you ever find yourself needing this kind of a rest in the water, you should get out as soon as you have the energy. It is not wise to snorkel or dive if you are fatigued.

Above all, if you are in an outdoor pool or on the open water, be careful of sunburn.

SURFACE DIVING

Surface diving, which is not at all essential in order to enjoy snorkeling, is an easy way to explore somewhat deeper water without all of the training and paraphernalia needed for scuba. It consists of a dive from a floating surface position and an ascent back to the surface all in one breath. First, lying on the surface, take three deep breaths. This "hyperventilation" clears the carbon dioxide from your system and allows you to hold your breath for a longer time. Don't take more than three breaths, however, as too much hyperventilation can cause you to pass out under water. Three breaths are perfectly safe. Take a fourth breath and hold it. Bend at the waist, head downward, let your arms hang down and throw your legs and rear end skyward. Your body should be in a straight line upside down. The weight of your legs in the air will drive you under the surface. As you descend, bring your arms back along your sides. Do not begin to kick until your legs are completely submerged, since this only wastes energy. When you reach the bottom (or are as far down as you want to go), you can swim around exploring all you want, but remember that you need enough air to get to the top again. When you begin your ascent reach one hand above your head and look up. It is easy to get turned around under water, and you will want to make sure you are not headed for a boat bottom or some other obstacle on your way up. As you reach the surface, blow the water out of your snorkel. If you are in a boating area, look around you to make sure no boats are headed toward you.

There is a good chance you will have some ear discomfort on the way down, and this must be relieved as you descend. Ear pain is caused by increased water pressure on the outside of your eardrums, and it is not wise to ignore. It is important to learn to "clear" your ears by equalizing the pressure inside the ear. This can be done by swallowing or moving your jaw. If these methods don't work (and for some people they do not), you will have to equalize by holding your nose; press the rubber flanges—if your mask is so designed—against your nostrils, shut your mouth, and swallow or blow

air into the eustachian tubes, which lead to your ears. To many people, the author included, this method at first seems tantamount to blowing your head off, and it is startling. Actually it is extremely simple, and trying it a few times on land will solve the problem.

Do not wear ear plugs when snorkeling, as they make it impossible to equalize pressure. Certain kinds of bathing caps do the same, and it is better, if possible, not to wear one when planning to surface dive. If you are suffering from a cold or sinus malady, you should not attempt a surface dive, as equalizing is almost impossible if your sinuses are clogged or irritated.

As you become more proficient at surface diving you will want to explore the bottom. Take a pair of work gloves and wear them when holding onto the rocks or taking animals or discarded shells from the water. This will prevent countless scratches, cuts, and other minor wounds. Even with gloves, don't stick your hands into unfamiliar holes or touch anything that you don't recognize. Occasionally a

sharp-toothed animal or stinging coral (see identifications) will surprise you if you are careless.

Leave the water before you are really fatigued. You can build up strength by repeated dives. When you get home, rinse all of your equipment carefully in fresh water and let it dry in a shady area. Store it on a shelf out of extreme heat. Hanging it will eventually cause it to crack.

When you have learned to be comfortable snorkeling and surface diving, you will be ready to begin scuba lessons, if you are interested. Your dive shop will be happy to recommend a good scuba course, or the last chapter of this book will help you to locate a qualified teacher. But even if you never go on to scuba, snorkeling or skin diving can provide you with many years of rewarding activity. It may take you a few trips before you can surface dive, but don't rush it. You're only out there to have fun, after all, and the first steps are extremely easy to accomplish. From your first entry into the water it might take you as little as four minutes until you are snorkeling comfortably; it certainly shouldn't take more than an hour.

THREE

Where to Go

After years of traveling alone, with family, with other adults, and with other families, most of us can safely say that we have logged as many pleasurable hours planning trips as actually enjoying them. In fact, some of the finest trips were never taken and might have been perfectly awful if they had been. Don't stint on dreaming about vacations. There's always a chance you will be faced with rain and a rotten currency exchange when your dreams come true. The following pages are not merely for the dreamer, however. They will give the beginning snorkeler, as well as the experienced scuba diver, some useful facts through descriptions, charts, and maps of the various snorkeling and diving areas of North America, Hawaii, and the Caribbean.

Each place is unique, and by describing the features of each, we hope to help you find the area that is best for you. Special efforts have been made to present this information dispassionately, accurately, and completely, and so far as is known, this is the only compilation of its kind of such data available to the would-be vacationer.

There are fourteen sections listed, from the Bahamas to the Hawaiian Islands, and from Southern Canada to the Yucatan. Each area is covered by some general comments, devoted as much to the flavor of the area as to the diving conditions, as well as maps and charts, relating entirely to snorkeling and scuba. The maps are not drawn to scale, but are merely to be used as aids in finding specific locations within a given area closest to the dive sites, so that you can make appropriate travel plans. Each diving area is numbered on the maps (generally speaking the diving areas are clustered together), and each number may be found on the appropriate chart, together with a factual description of the dive site—its depth, clarity, sights, suitable activities, dangers, etc. In addition, the charts indicate the availability of diving facilities—shops, boats, compressed air, etc. This last information is based on latest available data (1976), but businesses often change hands, as do hotels, and it is impossible to guarantee that a dive shop operating today will still be there when you arrive. For details write to one or more of the dive shops in the area you are going to visit before you make reservations. The listing of dive shops and hotels is by no means complete, and no recommendation is implied.* Dive areas with no facilities whatever, such as the Cay Sal Banks, are listed because they are diveable by boat tour.

Needless to say, the maps and charts cannot cover every existing dive spot. The Bahamas, for instance, consist of 700 islands surrounded by 70,000 square miles of ocean, and good diving is scattered everywhere. Chances are if you get to a well-dived or heavily snorkeled area, the locals will be aware of many spots not listed here and will be able to guide you to them. The Bibliography at the end of the book will help to provide you with more detailed information about the individual areas and about specialized activities.

Lacelike strands of coral and brilliant undersea vegetation lure divers to the warm, crystal-clear waters of the Bahamas. A scuba diver glides silently beneath a branch of staghorn coral. (Bahamas Tourist News Bureau)

---

* Although dive shops and hotels have been extremely cooperative in the preparation of this section, no fees or services, promotional or otherwise, have been rendered to the author or publisher.

24

When you depart on your diving holiday, bring as much of your own equipment as you can. For the snorkeler this means your own mask, fins, and snorkel. If you scuba dive, it is best to have your own regulator and life vest, in addition to snorkeling gear. Most facilities will supply you with tanks, backpacks, weights, and air, and many can fit you with snorkel gear and regulator as well; but you will probably be more comfortable with your own. Bring your own photographic equipment and lots of film. Underwater pictures have a fairly low percentage of success, so you will want to get plenty of shots. In some places underwater cameras are available by rental, but check this before you go.

By no means should you plan to scuba dive without a certification card from one of the following: the National Association of Underwater Instructors (NAUI), the Professional Association of Diving Instructors (PADI), the National Association of Skin Diving Schools (NASDS), or the YMCA (see Chapter 5 for details). For your own protection, no reputable dive shop will fill your tank with air until you show this card. The exception is the "Caribbean resort" dive course that some areas offer, followed by shallow dives with your instructor. These courses are fine but do not qualify you for any further diving. Remember too that certification by any of the above institutions does not qualify you for anything but basic, simple scuba. If you expect to dive caves, ice, deep wrecks, or any other unusual spots, take an advanced course and check yourself out with competent local divers before you try it. Let them teach, advise, and, if possible, accompany you.

Having determined from the charts and maps where you want to go, it is usually advisable to make arrangements through a reputable travel agent. Certain hotels have "dive packages" that include equipment and trips over the reefs. There are also excellent boat trips you can charter through your agent, some of which are listed on the charts. In addition to any reliable travel agency, there are a few that specialize in diving and snorkeling vacations, and they can usually give you the best and most up-to-date advice. In addition, they are constantly putting together trips and tours that you otherwise might not be aware of and that are frequently less costly than individual travel. These agencies—regardless of their home office address—serve customers from all over the country. Three of these specialized and reliable agencies are:

EAST COAST
Atlantis Safaris
P.O. Box 530303
Miami Shores, Fla. 33153
Tel. (305) 754-7480.
(Atlantis offers trips to Bimini, the Turk and Caicos Islands, Mexico, Bonaire, Grand Cayman, Cayman Brac, Curaçao, Belize, Jamaica, San Salvador, Dominican Republic, and Roatan, as well as areas beyond the geographic limits of this book.)
The Happy Wanderer
1428 Midland Ave.
Bronxville, N.Y. 10708
Tel. (914) 237-3322
(This agency arranges travel and hotel reservations wherever you want, and offers trips to Bonaire, St. Thomas, The Cayman Islands, San Salvador, and Bermuda.)

WEST COAST
See and Sea Travel Service
680 Beach St.
Suite 340, Wharfside
San Francisco, Calif. 94109
Tel. (415) 771-0077
(This agency specializes in maximum diving for the avid enthusiast wishing to make four or five dives a day. The tours cover Bonaire, Cozumel, Hawaii, Grand Cayman, Curaçao, and areas beyond the geographic limits of this book.)

Many areas still permit spearfishing, and there are passionate devotees of the sport. (Paul Tzimoulis/Skin Diver Magazine)

NOTES ON THE CHARTS

1. *The depth column*—Often more than one number will appear indicating that there are several depths to which you can dive in the same area. This column will also indicate whether the area is shallow enough for good snorkeling. (Thirty feet in clear water is considered maximum snorkeling depth.)

2. *Visibility and weather columns*—These two factors change constantly in most areas, so information in these columns is to be taken generally. Sadly, most areas are not at their best in winter, when you would most want to go South, until you reach close to South America. Some areas are gin clear part of the year and completely undiveable at other times. In addition to these seasonal changes, tides, pollution, river run-offs, and rough water can cloud up an area at unexpected times.

3. *Dangers column*—There are certain minor dangers that exist for the snorkeler in so many places that they have not been listed. These include sea urchins, fire coral, and the like, and they are covered in Chapter 4. As a general rule, you will stay out of danger by not touching anything unfamiliar. For the diver the largest danger is usually himself. Be sure you are qualified to make the dive you want to make before you embark. Observe all safety precautions. See Chapter 5 for further information. The *dangers* column, in other words, lists only unusual external dangers, such as strong currents, dangerous species of shark, heavily boated areas, etc.

4. Many areas still permit spearfishing, the taking of lobsters, abalone, live shells, etc. However, man is rapidly depleting the seas, and it is suggested that you take only what you can eat. Do not take coral as it disturbs the delicate ecosystem of the reef. Snorkelers and divers everywhere are making a concerted effort to save the beauties of the waters.

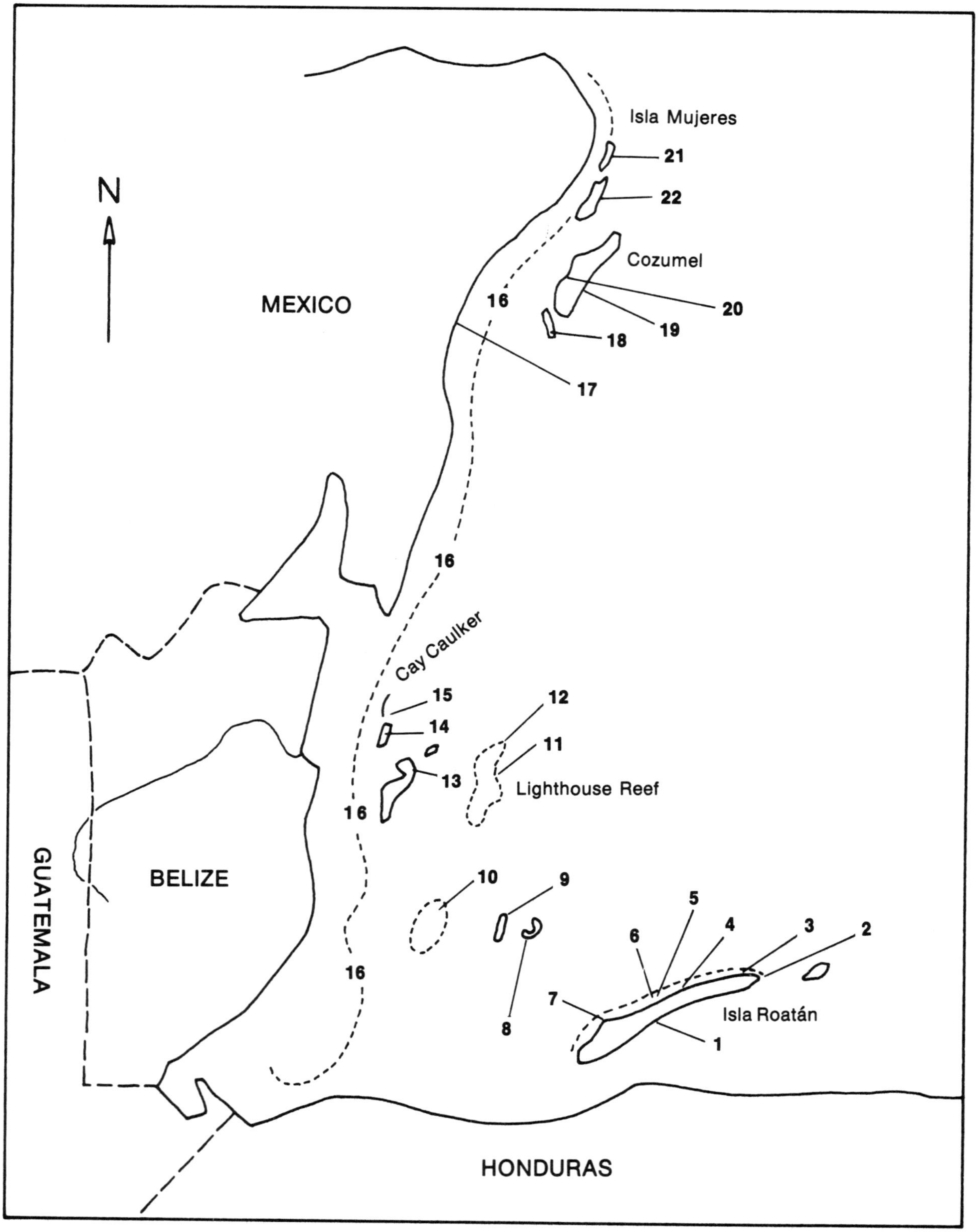

N

MEXICO

Isla Mujeres

21

22

Cozumel

20

19

16

18

17

16

Cay Caulker

15

14

12

11

Lighthouse Reef

13

16

GUATEMALA

BELIZE

10

9

5

6

4

3

2

16

7

Isla Roatán

8

1

HONDURAS

THE YUCATAN PENINSULA

(MEXICO/QUINTANA ROO/ BELIZE/ROATÁN)

The Belize reef is the second largest barrier reef in the world; only the Great Barrier Reef of Australia surpasses it. It runs from north to south along the Mexican territory of Quintana Roo, the country of Belize (formerly British Honduras), and the island of Roatán, which lies north of Honduras. This reef supplies one of the great snorkeling and diving experiences of the world, and in the bargain you get accommodations ranging from the primitive to the luxurious, and the Yucatan Peninsula's famed Mayan ruins, which generate their own tourist business. Amazingly, with all of these attractions, the area is neither overbuilt nor on the verge of collapse from pollution. How long this situation can be maintained is, of course, anybody's guess. It might be mentioned that getting there is no mean feat. You will almost certainly have to take two planes, and depending on which area you are going to, you may take as many as four, plus a helicopter and a jeep ride. At one resort you are actually urged to swim from the dining room back to your bungalow. (Remember to wait forty minutes after eating.)

All of this aside, the area is spectacular in many respects. It is the southernmost spot treated in this book, and the weather and visibility are consistently near perfect, even when the northern Caribbean is comparatively cold and choppy. The snorkeling and diving,

Boats take divers and snorkelers out to where they will see a variety of marvelous sights in Cozumel, Quintana Roo. (Mexican National Tourist Council)

both by boat and from beaches, offer an enormous variety of sights, including caves, wrecks, blue holes, coral gardens, a wide variety of fish, and many unexplored spots for the adventurous diver.

If you have a rather long vacation period, and want some exotic and unusual experiences, you might consider touring the fantastic Mayan ruins for a few days, and then moving on to one of the dive areas to complete your vacation, sunbathing and exploring the water.

Be forewarned that although accommodations and dive facilities are available, they vary tremendously in scope and luxury. Make sure you know what you are getting before you decide to go. A final word of warning: The food and water are unreliable throughout Mexico, although many of the specialties of the area are nearly irresistible to the curious gourmet. Montezuma's revenge, a kind of killer diarrhea that is only fatal to your vacation plans, can be the result. Consider taking some powdered soup on the trip, some tea bags, and paregoric.

The Yucatan Peninsula

ROATÁN

Water Temp.: 80°

Regulations: Spear only what you can eat.

PLACE	NO.	DESCRIPTION	ENTRY AND DISTANCE FROM SHORE	DEPTH	SNORKEL OR DIVE
ROATÁN ISLAND	1	Every imaginable type of reef and drop-off	Both at various spots	Varied	Snorkel or dive
WEST END POINT	2	Series of bays with sandy beaches	Beach or boat Can swim from shore	Surface 20' – 40' – 100'	Snorkel or dive
BEAR'S DEN	3	Coral limestone reef with a series of cave formations starting at 50'	Boat	10' – 20' – 75' to drop-off	Dive
EEL GARDEN	4	Near Bailey's Key—great stretch of sand at 110'	Boat	110'	Dive
THE WALL (drop-off)	5	Drop-off all along n. shore of island. You can dive its whole length of more than 30 mi.	Beach or boat 100' to ½ mi.	Few ft. to drop-off to 110'	Dive
HOLE-IN-THE-WALL	6	Chimney-shaped coral tunnel	Boat ⅓ mi.	Varies 60' – very deep	Dive
HALF MOON BAY WALL	7	Drop-off all along coast	Boat ⅓ mi.	50' and down	Dive

Visibility: 75′ – 120′   **Best Season:** Anytime

SURF OR CALM	HIGH-LIGHTS	FISHING AND PHOTOS	DANGERS	DIVE FACILITY	ACCOMMODATIONS
Calm	Spectacular reefs and fish	No collecting corals or fans	None	All at Anthony's Key Roatán Honduras, C.A.	Anthony's Key Resort Roatán Bay Islands Honduras or U.S. Office P.O. Box 530344 Miami, Fl. 33153 Tel. (305) 754-3812 or P.O. Box 18412 Dallas, Texas 75218 Tel. (214) 328-4244 24 cottages
Calm	Sponges, large fish, fantastic corals	Photos	None	Available at Pirate Den Hotel Sandy Bay Roatán Honduras, C.A.	
Calm	Tunnels, caves	Photos	Don't kick up sand in cave. Take guide.	As above	Pirate Den Hotel Sandy Bay Roatán, Honduras C.A.
Calm	Thousands of garden eels, sting rays	Photos	None	As above	As above
Calm	Corals, sponges, fish	Photos	None	As above	As above
Calm	Coral and unusual chimney	Photos	None	As above	As above
Calm	Sponges, corals, fans	Photos	None	As above	As above

BELIZE

Water Temp.: 84° May to October

Regulations: No spearfishing with scuba. No taking of black coral. Artifacts over 100 years old become property of people

30

PLACE	NO.	DESCRIPTION	ENTRY AND DISTANCE FROM SHORE	DEPTH	SNORKEL OR DIVE
HALFMOON CAY	8	Both shallow reef and drop-off	Boat to Half-moon Cay and then off beach At shore	Shallow 4′ – 8′ and drop-off to thousands	Snorkel shallow Dive deeper area
LONG CAY	9	On edge of 2,000′ drop-off, beginning in 30′	Beach Off shore	Shallow from beach	Snorkel or dive
GLOVER'S REEF	10	Reef 700′ thick and forms a 44-mi. drop-off that surrounds the reef	Beach. Can go by dug-out to reef 5 min.	2000′ drop-off; most diving done at 30′ – 100′	Snorkel or dive
LIGHTHOUSE REEF	11	Four lovely islands	Boat or beach on cays 55 min. from Belize City	Shallow and drop-off	Snorkel or dive
BLUE HOLE	12	An apparently bottomless, vertical undersea cave	Boat	Possibly 3000′; 175 yds. wide	Dive

Visibility: 150′–200′ (March to May)   **Best Season:** Anytime.

of Belize. No lobsters April 15–July 15.

SURF OR CALM	HIGH-LIGHTS	FISHING AND PHOTOS	DANGERS	DIVE FACILITY	ACCOMMODATIONS
Calm	Shallow gardens, conch Deeper side, lobster and caves with grouper; sponges, fish	Photos; spear without scuba	None. Drop-off, experienced. Shark (Some seem harmless)	Belize Divers World Eden Isles P.O. Box 515 Belize City, Belize Mr. Jim Smith Colorado Divers World 557 Milwaukee Denver, Color. 80206 (303) 333-6303	None. Only a lighthouse keeper and 8 people in all
Calm	Fish, lobsters, corals	Photos. Spear only what you can eat; no scuba	None	As above	Glover's Reef Village on Long Cay Belize, British Honduras (small)
Calm but can be rough with S.E. wind	24 species of coral; wreck, fish, fans	Photos; fish as above	None	All at Glover's Reef Village also 7-day cruise trips from Glover's Reef Village to other reefs	24 guests-12 cabins No electricity, flush toilets, or hot water. Lamont Enterprises Box 563 Belize City Belize C.A. Tel. 2548
Calm but can get rough	200′ visibs, great beach-combing, wrecks, fish, reefs	Photos; fish as above	None	Many tours of U.S. go here Keller Lodge Belize River	Many of all sorts and prices Keller Caribbean Sports Lodge on banks of Belize River (30 people only)
Calm	Caverns, stalactites, stalagmites; fish swim upside-down in cavern	Photos	Experienced divers only	As above	On Ambergris Cay Paradise House Hotel P.O. Box 16 Belize City, Belize, C.A. or 9225 Katy Fwy Suite 302 Houston, Texas 77024

BELIZE CONTINUED

32

PLACE	NO.	DESCRIPTION	ENTRY AND DISTANCE FROM SHORE	DEPTH	SNORKEL OR DIVE
TURNEFFE ISLANDS	13	Largest coral atoll. Closest to Belize City. Shipwrecks here.	Boat	Varies	Dive
COCKROACH CAY	14	Shallow reef	Boat	20′ and drop to 2000′	Dive
CAY CAULKER	15	Coral reefs and drop-offs	Boat or beach. 1 mile by boat to main reef.	10′ − 30′ shallow and drop-off	Snorkel or dive
2nd-LARGEST BARRIER REEF IN WORLD	16	Tremendous barrier reef; runs length of Belize	Boat; many islands and cays with beaches 14 mi. from mainland	Shallow to thousands of ft.	Snorkel shallow, dive deep

SURF OR CALM	HIGH-LIGHTS	FISHING AND PHOTOS	DANGERS	DIVE FACILITY	ACCOMMODATIONS
Varies	5 wrecks at n. tip Mauger Cay; 3 wrecks s. tip Cay Bokel	Photos; fish as above	Shark, especially great white	None	No accommodations
Calm	Seafans, antler coral, gorgonia, big fish, hog fish	Photos; spearing as above	Current at drop-off	None	No accommodations
Calm	All reef sights, fish, wrecks, corals	Photos; fish as above	None	All at Eden Isles Sports Hut	Eden Isles Cay Caulker, Belize P.O. Box 515 Belize City, Belize or 711 Fannin St. Suite 1222 Houston, Texas Tel. 713-227-8040 El Pescador Punta Arena Beach San Pedro, Ambergris Cay, Belize, C.A.
Varies	Fantastic corals, fish, marine life	Photos; fishing as above	Diver's experience is important	Varies from place to place. See each area.	Varies Coral Beach Hotel San Pedro Ambergris Cay Belize, C.A. and many others For diving tours: Dive Belize 2513 Metarie Rd. Metarie, La. 70001 Keller Caribbean Sports, Ltd. c/o Go Diving Inc. 4319 Hiawatha Ave. So. Minneapolis, Minn. 55406

SOUTHERN MEXICO   Water Temp.: 84°

Regulations: Speargun fishing is illegal. You must get a tourist card to enter Mexico. See your nearest Mexican Government

34

PLACE	NO.	DESCRIPTION	ENTRY AND DISTANCE FROM SHORE	DEPTH	SNORKEL OR DIVE
AKUMAL	17	Coral reefs, fish and all marine life. Coves of Yalku and Xelha.	Beach and 50 yds.; swim right in front of resort	6'–12'; reefs 18'–20'	Snorkel or dive
PALANCAR REEF COZUMEL	18	A miniature barrier reef, 6 mi. long	2-hr. boat from San Miguel	Shallow side 20'–60'; several thousand feet on deep side	Snorkel or dive
PUENTA MORENA COZUMEL	19	Shallow rocky reef	Drive from San Miguel then off beach at shore	10'–15'	Snorkel or dive
SAN FRANCISCO BEACH COZUMEL	20	Fine snorkeling and beach-combing 12 mi. from San Miguel	Sail and then beach At shore	Shallow	Snorkel
ISLA MUJERES (Women Island)	21	A coral island 5 mi. off tip of Yucatan Peninsula	From beach	Shallow	Snorkel or dive
CANCUN (Kan-Koon) (Not too much is yet known about snorkeling and diving this newly developing area.)	22	An L-shaped island 14 mi. long joined to mainland by a bridge. Great Lagoon 18 square mi.	Beach or boat	Varies	Snorkel or dive

Visibility: 100′ – 200′   **Best Season:** March to May—but anytime is good.

tourist office for all requirements.

SURF OR CALM	HIGH-LIGHTS	FISHING AND PHOTOS	DANGERS	DIVE FACILITY	ACCOMMODATIONS
Inside reef very calm; outside can be rough	Beautiful corals, tropical fish, all marine life, black coral, lobster	Photos	None. Take dive guide outside of reefs.	Club De Yates Akumal Caribe, A.C. 5 de Mayo 131 Sur C. Juarez Mexico or write: Pablo Bush Romero 5820 Burning Tree Dr. El Paso, Texas 79912 Tel. 915-584-3552	Many hotels of varying price Hotel Playa Azul San Miguel, Cozumel Mexico Cabanas Del Caribe El Presidente
Varies	Tremendous coral mounds, grottos, sponges, fish, very blue black coral, sheer drop-offs	Photos	Diver should be experienced; watch current in exposed areas on open side.	As above	As above
Rough, varies	Coral, caves, sea fans, lobsters	Great photos	Rough	None	Privately owned farm to go through to beach. No accommodations
Calm	Shallow coral reef	Photos, beachcombing	None	None at S.F. Beach	See Cozumel Palancar Reef
Can be rough	Colorful fish and lobsters, triton and cone shells. Nearby Cancun Reef and Contoy Island have big fish and caves.	Photos	Strong currents	All at Aqua Mundo Dive Shop	Hotel Zazil-Ha and Bungalows
Varies	Parrot fish, angels, and exotic marine life	Photos	None	Some hotels have equipment	10 hotels now open and more coming. This spot is growing. Write: Cancun Information Bureau 485 Madison Avenue New York, N.Y. 10022 (212) 421-9220

Baja California

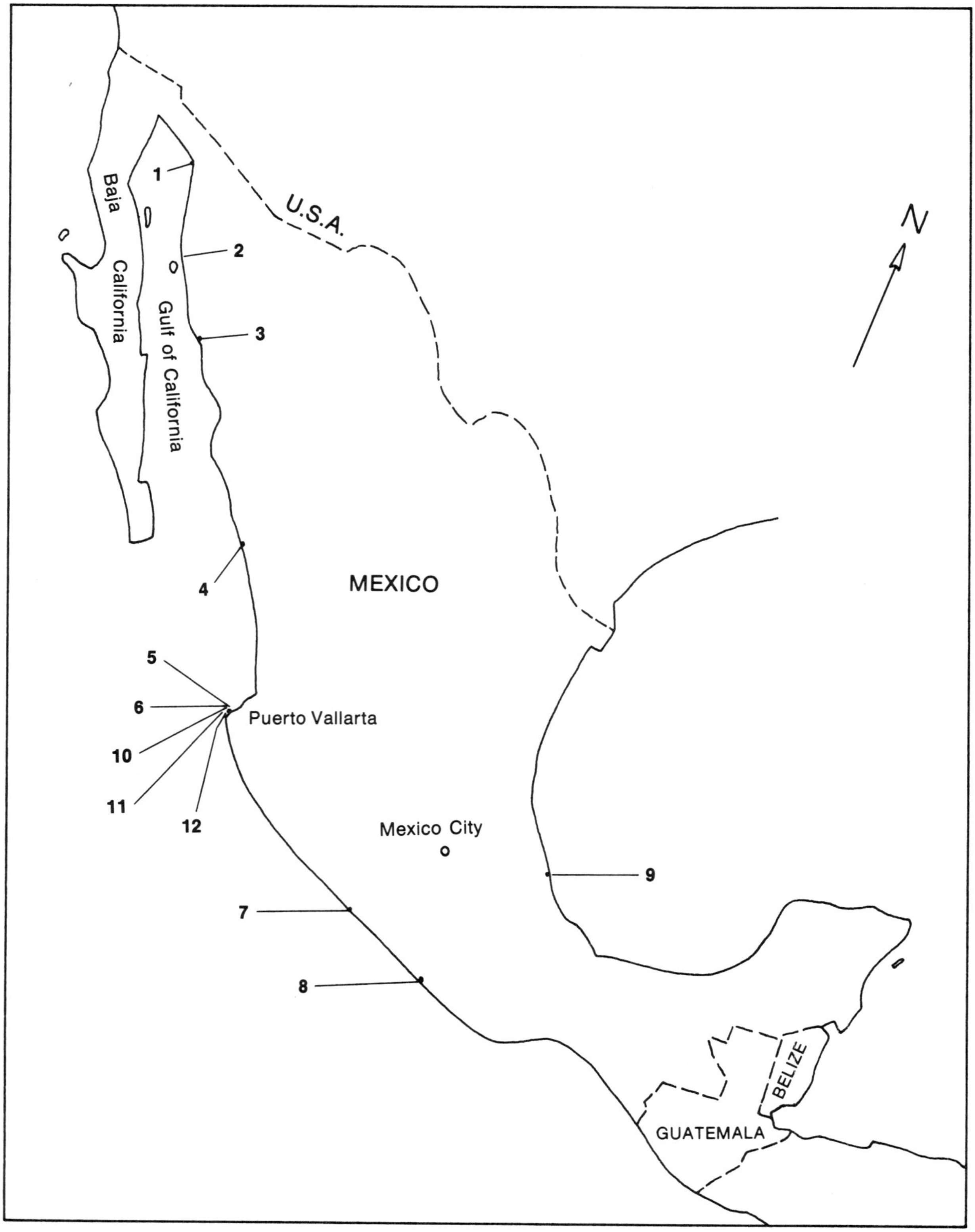

Gulf of California

1

2

3

U.S.A.

N

4

MEXICO

5

6

10

11

12

Puerto Vallarta

Mexico City

9

7

8

GUATEMALA

BELIZE

MEXICO*

Outside of the Yucatan peninsula and Baja California, the diving in Mexico is limited but not nonexistent. For the most part it consists of island offshore diving for seasoned scuba users, and there is little snorkeling. Boat trips take divers to various spots where enormous sea turtles and manta rays, as well as oversized fish, are common sights. Shells may also be collected, and there are several wrecks to be observed. Some dive facilities are available, but people wishing to make this kind of trip are advised to take their own equipment. The seasons and visibility vary substantially, depending on where you are planning to go, so be sure to check the charts before making any plans.

For the casual diver the beach at Mismaloya is quite stunning, and there are sights in shallow water for snorkelers. This area was the site of the filming of *The Night of the Iguana.*

Any trip to Mexico should be preceded by a careful check of the tourist entry regulations and diving laws. People who dive in Mexico tend to be those who have already been to the easily accessible dive spots. If you are up for high adventure, however, Mexico's diving stands a good chance of giving you what you are asking for.

* (Exclusive of Baja and the Yucatan—see separate sections)

Mexico

Water Temp.: 50º – 70º – 80º

Regulations: Speargun fishing is illegal. You must get a tourist card to enter Mexico. See your nearest Mexican Government

PLACE	NO.	DESCRIPTION	ENTRY AND DISTANCE FROM SHORE	DEPTH	SNORKEL OR DIVE
PUNTA PENASCO (summer & fall) (Expert)	1	Fish; reefs made of fossilized shells and sand	Boat	25' – 30'	Dive
KINO BAY (summer & fall) (Expert)	2	Go to Islands of Tiburon, Turner, or San Esteban. Lots of fish	Boat	Varies	Dive
GUAYAMAS (Diving good here all year) (Expert)	3	Lots of fish on reefs farther from shore	Boat	Varies	Dive
MAZATLAN (Do not go June – August; rains.) (Expert)	4	Fish reef	Boat	Varies	Dive
LAS TRES MARIAS (Mariettas) (Do not go June – August; rains.) (Expert)	5	Big fish, boulders, rocks over a coral bottom	Boat	60' – 125' and down	Dive
PUERTO VALLARTA (Winter & fall) (Expert)	6	Jumping-off pt. Must go by boat to nearby towns	Boat Varies 2 – 3 mi.	20' – 80'	Snorkel or dive
ZHUATANEJO (Go anytime) (Expert)	7	Lovely underwater scenery, clear water	Boat Varies 1 mi.	Varies	Dive
ACAPULCO (Go anytime)	8	Great scenery and fish	Boat	Varies	Dive

Visibility: 10′–100′   **Best Season:** See individual listings

tourist office for all requirements.

SURF OR CALM	HIGH-LIGHTS	FISHING AND PHOTOS	DANGERS	DIVE FACILITY	ACCOMMODATIONS
Can be rough	Ledges with fish under them	Photos	Currents, extreme tide changes	Take your own	Fishing camp
Can be rough	Lots of fish, huge game fish	Photos possible	Currents, rough waters	Take your own	1 good motel Posada Del Marin Bahia Kino 1 trailer park
Calm	Manta rays in spring	Photos possible. Poor visibility	None	Dive shop	Many hotels and trailer parks
Varies	Big fish	Photos possible	None	Dive facilities	Several hotels
Varies	Big fish and lots of them	Photos possible	Can be rough	Out of Mazatlan	Many hotels in nearby Puerto Vallarta
Calm	Fish, lobsters, sea life, manta rays	Photos	None	Equipment available dive shop	Many hotels
Calm	Great variety of fish, some nurse shark	Photos, but visibility poor	None	Available here	Many hotels
Varies	Wrecks, caves, lagoons, shells	Photos	Shark	Available here	Large resort, many hotels.

MEXICO CONTINUED

PLACE	NO.	DESCRIPTION	ENTRY AND DISTANCE FROM SHORE	DEPTH	SNORKEL OR DIVE
VERA CRUZ (Best in summer: May – September)	9	Coral reefs at Isla-de-en Medio and many other spots	Boat (short trip) Off shore	Varies	Snorkel or dive
LOS ARCOS	10	Three arched rocks	Boat	10' – 120'	Snorkel or dive
MISMALOYA	11	Tropical fish	Beach At shore	Shallow	Snorkel
YELAPA	12	Reef in a lagoon	Boat	Varies	Snorkel or dive

40

SURF OR CALM	HIGH-LIGHTS	FISHING AND PHOTOS	DANGERS	DIVE FACILITY	ACCOMMODATIONS
Varies	Beautiful fish and reefs, great variety of marine life; wrecks, shells	Photos	None	Some available	Several hotels
Calm	Small tropicals where shallow and bigger fish deeper; shells, rays	Photos, but visibility can be poor	None	At Playa De Los Muertos	At Puerto Vallarta
Calm	Lovely tropical fish in clear water	Photos, but visibility can be poor	None	None	At Puerto Vallarta
Calm	Turtles, fish, shrimp	Photos	None	Snorkel gear at small hotel and at Viva Tours	Thatched Hut Hotel

41

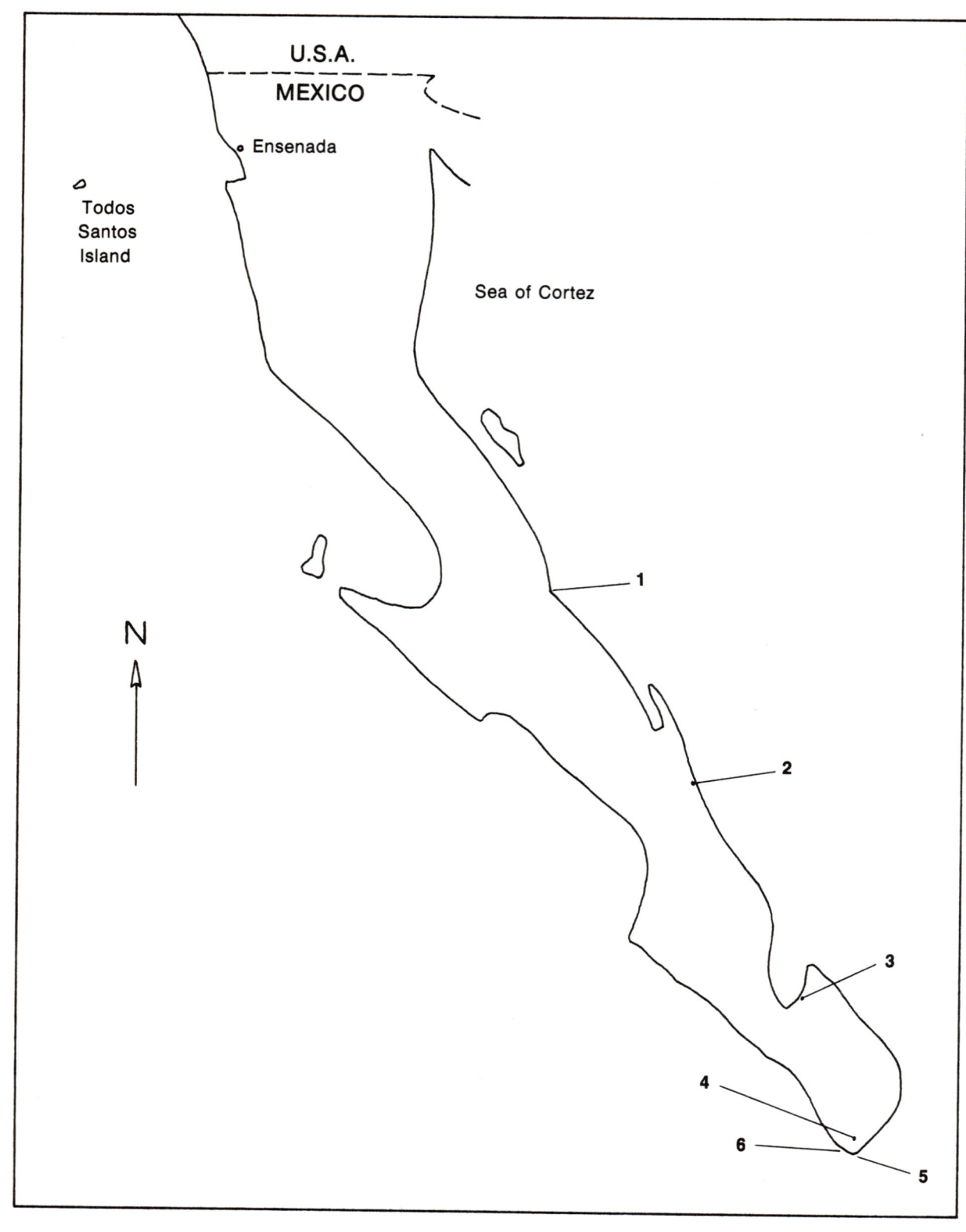

U.S.A.

MEXICO

o Ensenada

Todos
Santos
Island

Sea of Cortez

N

1

2

3

4

6

5

BAJA CALIFORNIA

For the expert diver in search of wild adventure, Baja California should not be overlooked. For years this peninsula, which forms the western coast of the Gulf of California, was impassible without a four-wheel-drive vehicle and a stack of spare tires. A highway has now been paved, and several areas have regular plane service as well—but the peninsula is by no means tamed.

The resort communities of La Paz and San Lucas, at the southern end of Baja, are the most developed areas and offer some organized dive facilities. But the trip from the U.S. border can now be comfortably made by car or camper, and the deserted beaches provide plenty of diving areas and some snorkeling as well. The Gulf of California provides a natural trap for fish migrating northward, and the conditions are ideal for breeding and feeding. As a result there are spots where, it is said, the fish population is so thick that the bottom cannot be seen. Visibility is variable, unfortunately, and depends as much on the plankton population in the water as it does on the weather.

Because of the primitive nature of a trip to Baja, you should be very sure of hotel reservations, gas mileage, and supplies, as the building of facilities has not yet caught up with the highway traffic. However, it is being built up rapidly. Also be sure you have a Mexican tourist card and have met all other Mexican tourist regulations before embarking. This is the real wilderness, folks, but if you like it, then nothing else will do.

Baja California

Regulations: Speargun fishing is illegal. You must get a tourist card to enter Mexico. See your nearest Mexican Government

44

PLACE	NO.	DESCRIPTION	ENTRY AND DISTANCE FROM SHORE	DEPTH	SNORKEL OR DIVE
MULEGE (10 mi. N. of Punta Chivato) Just S. of Bahia Concepcion	1	Beaches and coves for shelling and snorkeling Lagoons for snorkeling and photos	Beach Reefs and off-shore island	Shallow 10'–50'	Snorkel or dive
LORETO	2	Offshore islands with fish	Boat	10'–50'	Snorkel or dive
LA PAZ (Diving at Balondra (15 mi. away)	3	Fish and varied marine life; offshore islands	Beach at Balondra, swim or boat to reef	60'	Snorkel or dive
CABO SAN LUCAS	4	Deep water, many fish, and other forms of sea life	Beach (short swim) Go in from shore	Very deep	Dive
CABO SAN LUCAS End of Cannery Pier	5	Walk out and peer down to see huge school of bait fish packed together	Walk in from rock jetty At end of pier	25'	Snorkel, dive
SHEPARD'S ROCK W. side of bay	6	Shallow water diving with sand falls	Boat Off Shore	Shallow to deep	Dive

Visibility: 20′ – 100′ Depends on plankton bloom and current

Best Season: Water is warmer in South Baja

Tourist office for all requirements.

SURF OR CALM	HIGH-LIGHTS	FISHING AND PHOTOS	DANGERS	DIVE FACILITY	ACCOMMODATIONS
Calm or quick chop due to wind	Big fish	Photos	Currents	La Vita Bueno (boat) sails twice a month for 7-day dive trips	Yes, but since new road has been built they are scarce. Restaurants and gas stations are scarce too, so come with reservations and be careful of supplies. However, it is being built up rapidly including several Holiday Inns.
Calm or chop	Many fish, rocks covered with shellfish	Photos	Currents	As above	
Calm or quick chop	875 varieties fish, marine life, corals, yellowtail, black skipjack	Photos	Strong currents	Excellent. A houseboat cruises islands near La Paz. Rsv. La Paz Skin Diving Service, Box 133 La Paz, Baja Cal.	Hotels here
Fairly calm	Fish, lobsters, shellfish, black coral	Photos	None	Some	As above
Calm	Red snapper, wreck at 90′, sand fall, and dense school of bait fish packed into a ball. Visibility poor.	Photos	None	Unknown	As above
Calm	N. and s. of Shepard's Rock are "Rivers of Sand" for the expert. Begin at 160'. Grottos, fans, tropicals. 4 sandfalls.	Photos	Only for very experienced divers with good guide.	At Cabo San Lucas	As above

46

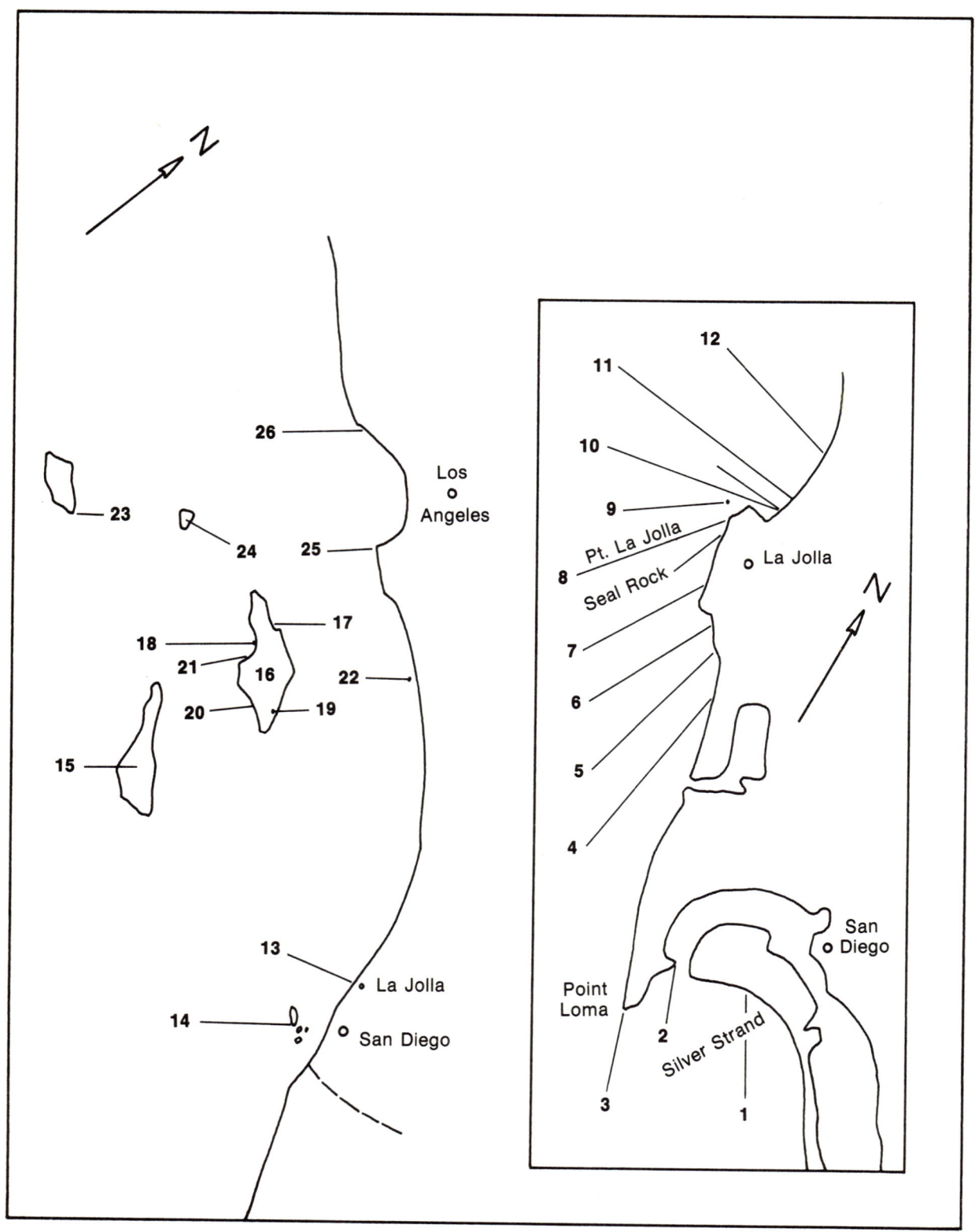

Los
Angeles

26

23

24   25

17

18

21

16

20   19

22

15

13   La Jolla

14   San Diego

12

11

10

9

Pt. La Jolla

8   Seal Rock

7

6

5

4

La Jolla

N

Point
Loma

San
Diego

3

2   Silver Strand   1

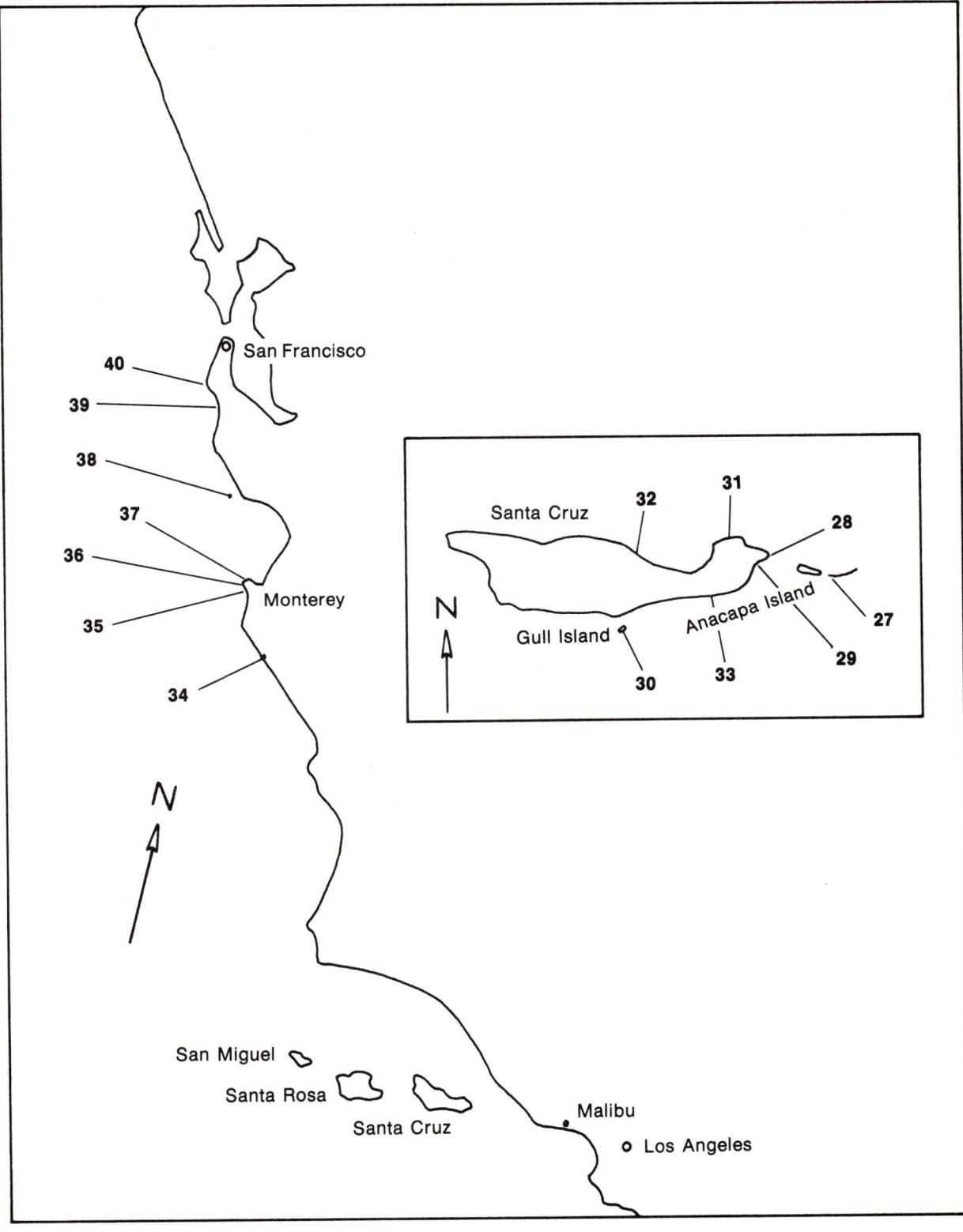

40
39

San Francisco

38

37

36

35

Monterey

34

N

Santa Cruz **32** **31** **28**

N

Gull Island **27**

Anacapa Island

30 **33** **29**

San Miguel

Santa Rosa

Santa Cruz

Malibu

o Los Angeles

A seal seen underwater off Santa Barbara Island. (Jack McKenney/Skin Diver Magazine)

CALIFORNIA

The coast of California, although lacking the attraction of coral reefs, boasts some of the most adventurous and exciting snorkeling and diving available anywhere. Sport diving in the United States really began forty years ago in San Diego, and today 50 percent of the divers in the United States make their homes in California. From Disneyland to the Golden Gate Bridge and the giant redwood forests, the state offers so many well-known attractions for tourists that no attempt will be made to explain its tempting complexities. A travel agent can supply you with details of the various vacation spots.

To a great extent the diving is for sport fishing with spears and spearguns, as well as for abalone and lobster hunting. The water tends to be cool, and the visibility immediately along the coast is sometimes impaired by pollution. Islands off the coast, such as San Clemente, offer clearer water.

During the Depression years a good number of people practiced free diving (snorkel but no scuba) for abalone, and the tradition has remained active. A good deal of strenuous underwater swimming with only snorkel gear seems to please the hardy California divers. Scuba diving here is also more strenuous than in the tropical waters, and a dive course is essential. Even if you are certified from an area other than California, make sure you dive with local people who will be able to advise you about the local beach entries and any possible surge offshore.

Photographing in kelp beds off Catalina Island. (Jack McKenney/Skin Diver Magazine)

Boat diving is easily available from various landings listed in the charts. In addition to charters, many of the landings offer ramps where you may launch your own boat.

The timid snorkeler or diver should, however, by no means rule California off the list. San Diego offers some fine and quiet snorkeling and diving experiences, particularly in tide pools, where enormous varieties of marine life can be observed. The city also boasts a full complement of more challenging dives, as well as excellent spearfishing. In Los Angeles there is a lot of boat diving to the islands— Catalina being a favorite. And off the Monterey Peninsula

there are a variety of dive trips, both for beginners and experienced scuba users. As you go farther north, the water gets colder, but you will want a wet suit for all of the California waters, so this temperature change should not affect you too much.

Despite the absence of coral reefs (the main attraction of Floridian, Caribbean, and Hawaiian waters), California diving offers visitors and natives a satisfying spectrum of dive experiences that includes giant kelp forests, abalone and lobster hunting, excellent spearfishing, tide pools of all varieties, an amusing complement of curious sea lions to follow you around, and even a jade quarry, located off the coast south of San Francisco. Facilities are excellent, and hotels are plentiful and dependable.

California

SAN DIEGO AREA

Water Temp.: 56°–70°

Regulations: Regulations for the taking of fish, abalone, scallops, etc., are too long to be included here. Get California Sport

PLACE	NO.	DESCRIPTION	ENTRY AND DISTANCE FROM SHORE	DEPTH	SNORKEL OR DIVE
SILVER STRAND	1	Kelp beds	Beach at shore, but boat is better because of surf.	25'	Dive
N. ISLAND JETTY	2	Area for capturing shellfish	Near jetty	Varies	Dive
POINT LOMA (Experienced)	3	Great kelp beds with fish and abalone	Boat (land area is Navy Park Land) 15 min.	25'–45' 70'–110' on outside	Dive
TOURMALINE	4	Off 5100 La Jolla Blvd. Sandy beach end of Tourmaline St.	Stairs to beach At shore	10' for ¼ mi.	Snorkel or shallow dive
BIRD ROCK	5	End of Bird Rock Ave.; boulders, grassy	Beach	Shallow near shore	Dive
HALFMOON BAY	6	N. of Bird Rock at end of Bird Rock Ave.	Beach At shore	15'	Snorkel or dive
SEAL ROCK CASA COVE ½ mi. S. of Pt. La Jolla	7	Calm tide, pools, large reef off sea wall with many kinds of marine life	Beach At shore	8'-15' Farther out, 30'-40'	Snorkel or dive

Visibility: 25' – 100'   **Best Season:** Fall, but always quite good

Fishing Regulations from Dept. of Fish & Game, 1416 9th St., Sacramento, Ca. 95814, or your local sport or dive shop.

SURF OR CALM	HIGH-LIGHTS	FISHING AND PHOTOS	DANGERS	DIVE FACILITY	ACCOMMODATIONS
Rough	Lobster in Oct.; rockfish, halibut	Fishing	Big surf	Diving Unlimited 1148 Delavan Dr. San Diego, Ca. 92102	Many at all prices, including camp grounds and trailer parking
Varies	Lobster, especially at night; crabs, rockfish	Fishing	Strong current, dirty water; watch tides	New England Divers 3860 Rosencrans St. San Diego, Ca. 92110 Many launching ramps for your own boat	As above
Calm	Kelp bed, abalone, rock scallops, fish, lobster, sponges, sea anemones	Fishing; photos, Visibility 20' – 30'	Big swells, kelp	Diving Locker Stores 1020 Grand San Diego, Ca. 92109 also at: 155 So. Hwy 101 Solana Beach, Ca. 92075 and 348 E. Grand Ave. Escondido, Ca. 92025	As above
Varies	Halibut in summer; corbina and croaker	Fish; Visibility 5'	Rough surf, dive calm days only; watch for surfers		As above
Varies	Fish, small lobsters, green abalone	Fishing; photos	Heavy waves, watch for diver fatigue	As above	As above
Calm	Abalone, lobster	Lobster, abalone; photos at Nicklins Rock 1 mi. out	None	As above	As above
Calm	Lovely marine life, lobster, abalone	Photos	None	As above	As above

SAN DIEGO AREA CONTINUED

52

PLACE	NO.	DESCRIPTION	ENTRY AND DISTANCE FROM SHORE	DEPTH	SNORKEL OR DIVE
POINT LA JOLLA (Alligator Head)	8	Shallow reefs, thick kelp	Beach 60 yds.	30'	Snorkel or dive
QUASTS HOLE	9	Reef	Boat ¼ mi.	60'	Dive
LA JOLLA COVE LA JOLLA CAVES	10	Large park, clear water. Enter from Ellen Browning Scripps Memorial Park on Cave St.	Beach and grass park At shore	20 to 100 yds. 35 to 200 yds. offshore	Snorkel or dive
LA JOLLA CANYON (Expert if in the Canyon)	11	(¾ mi. S. of Scripps Pier) Drop-off starting very shallow	Beach at foot of Calle Frescata St. 200 yds.	10'–30'– 150'–1000'	Dive
SCRIPPS CANYON (Expert only)	12	(½ mi. N. of Scripps Pier) Deep canyon with much animal and plant life	Boat 20-30 min.	30'–60'– 1000'	Dive
CASA COVE (La Jolla)	13	Enter Coast Blvd. S. of lifeguard headquarters. Reefs, fish, colorful algae	Stairs to a sandy beach 10'	To 35'	Snorkel or dive
CORONADOS ISLANDS (Mexico)	14	Four small rocky islands with cold water, great visibility, and many spots to dive	Boat 19 min. from San Diego	30'–100'	Snorkel or dive
SAN CLEMENTE ISLAND	15	Kelp, fish, abalone	Boat 60 mi. (overnight)	10'–150'	Snorkel or dive

SURF OR CALM	HIGH-LIGHTS	FISHING AND PHOTOS	DANGERS	DIVE FACILITY	ACCOMMODATIONS
Calm	Kelp, fish (bass and yellowtail)	Fishing; photos	None	See page 51	Many at all prices, including camp
Varies	Fish, reef	Photos	None	As above	As above
Calm: rough in N. or N.W. swell	Reef, caves, fish, lobsters, morays, sea fans	Great photos; no spearing; visibility 15'–30' Abalone and lobsters may be taken in season	Current in caves at times. Entry and exit can be difficult when rough.	As above	As above
Varies	Marine life, many small fish, rays, squid in winter	Photos if visibility is good	Muddy water below 150'; larger rips during Big Surf	As above	As above
Calm	Steep drop, many fish	Great photos if water is clear	Diver must be expert; electric rays, shark	As above	As above
Calm to 2' surf	Fish, abalone, kelp, lobster	Photos; visibility 10'–20', good for close up work	Kelp; roughness at S. end of beach	As above	As above
Varies	Sea life, huge sea bass, thick kelp beds	Mexican law governs spearfishing; photos; cannot take lobster, abalone, garibaldi	Current surf-surge; do not go in caves	As above	As above
Calm in lee of island	Kelp, fish, abalone, lobster	Spearfishing; photos excellent	Separation from boat by currents; quick drop-off to 150'	Diving Unlimited 1148 Delavan Dr. San Diego, Ca. 92102 Runs trip	As above

53

SANTA CATALINA ISLAND   Water Temp.: 50°–70°

Regulations: See San Diego area.

54

PLACE	NO.	DESCRIPTION	ENTRY AND DISTANCE FROM SHORE	DEPTH	SNORKEL OR DIVE
SANTA CATALINA ISLAND	16	An island with many dive spots (very popular)	Boat L.A. 2-3 hrs.	To 600'+	Snorkel or dive
ISTHMUS AREA Facing L.A. Harbor on Catalina	17	Face of cliffs with caves and sea life	Boat At shore	To 130'	Snorkel or dive
LEE ON WEST SIDE (back-side)	18	Lobsters, caves	Boat	Aver. 40'	Dive
CITY OF AVALON DIVING RESERVE	19	An area reserved for divers. N. of Avalon	Boat	35'–80'	Dive
CATALINA West Side (back-side)	20	Kelp beds	Boat	50'	Dive
CATALINA West Side (back-side)	21	Rocks, kelp	Boat	50'	Dive

Visibility: 25′ – 100′   **Best Season:** Fall and winter

SURF OR CALM	HIGH-LIGHTS	FISHING AND PHOTOS	DANGERS	DIVE FACILITY	ACCOMMODATIONS
Varies	Kelp, marine life, caves, crevices, fish, abalone, lobster	Fishing or photos	See below	Ferries go to Catalina. You can stay overnight. Catalina Cruise Lines Berth 95, Box 511 San Pedro, Ca. 90731 or	Many. For complete list write Avalon-Catalina Island Chamber of Commerce P.O. Box 217 Avalon, Ca. 90704 Tel. 213-547-5030 or Avalon 723
Calm, clear	Abalone, caves, kelp	Catching abalone; Photos, visibility 50′ – 100′	Boat traffic	Catalina Cruise 330 Golden Shore Blvd. Long Beach, Ca. 90802 OR L.A. dive shops have charters, see below You can fly.	Also docks and moorings for boats; camping by special permit; camps and picnic spots but must have permit except for city of Avalon. Permits from Catalina Cove and camp agency
Calm in coves	Abalone, fish, lobsters, caves	Spearfishing; abalone	None	Catalina Divers Supply in Avalon has supplies and maintains a raft with a compressor at diving reserve.	
Calm	Fish, kelp, 3 wrecks, sunken airplane	No spearing in reserve; good photos of wrecks	None	CHARTER BOATS "Truth" 22 St. Landing San Pedro Roy Hauser	As above
Varies; rough	Lobster, abalone	Collecting lobster and abalone	Rough water; watch for swells	Golden Dubloon 22 St. Landing San Pedro Eddie Tsukimura	As above
Varies; rough	Huge lobster, sheephead, bass, abalone	Spearfishing; collect lobster, abalone	Rough water; watch for swells	Boats at Norm's Landing Aquatic Ctr #2 312 N. Harbor Blvd Santa Ana, Ca. 92703 or check other landings in L.A. area	As above

LOS ANGELES AREA   Water Temp.: 50°–70°

Regulations: See San Diego area.

56

PLACE	NO.	DESCRIPTION	ENTRY AND DISTANCE FROM SHORE	DEPTH	SNORKEL OR DIVE
LAGUNA BEACH TIDE POOLS	22	Tide pools are common on S. Calif. coast. (It is a shallow pool— more or less on shore.)	Beach At shore wade over rocks	8′–10′ or in ocean 10′–40′	Snorkel or dive
SAN NICOLAS ISLAND (many different dive spots)	23	Shoals with kelp beds	Boat	20′–80′ and down	Dive
SANTA BARBARA ISLAND (many dive spots)	24	Plateaus with kelp, eelgrass, abalone, and fish; rocks	Boat	To 90′	Snorkel or dive
PT. VICENTE PALOS VERDES	25	Good fishing ground for scallops and lobster; rocky; kelp	No beach; 100 yds. from shore	40′	Snorkel or dive
LEO CARRILLO BEACH (Malibu)	26	Good fishing ground for lobster, abalone, and fish	Beach 200–300 yds.	35′	Snorkel or dive

Visibility: 25′ – 100′   **Best Season:** Spring and fall

SURF OR CALM	HIGH-LIGHTS	FISHING AND PHOTOS	DANGERS	DIVE FACILITY	ACCOMMODATIONS
Calm	Fish, anemones, algae, kelp, abalone, varied marine life	Photos; fishing abalone	Rocks and coral—wear gloves	New England Divers 11830 W. Pico Blvd. West L.A. 90015 Tel. 213-477-5021	Many of all prices in area
Can be calm or white water	Kelp, many fish, lobster, sea lions, killer whales, black abalone, shells	Spearing; photos excellent	Waves; killer whales; swells; current	Sunland Sports Lodge 8677 Wilshire Blvd. Beverly Hills, Ca. 90211 Tel. 213-652-4990	As above
Calm or swells	Abalone, lobster, fish	Spearing; photos	None; some swells	Laguna Seasports 7066 Van Nuys Blvd Van Nys, Ca. 91405 Tel. 213-787-7066	As above
Rough 2′ – 6′ waves	Reefs, scallops, lobster	Fishing; photos	Surge; heavy surf; rocky entry	and at 18503 Hawthorne Blvd Torrance, Ca. 90504 Tel. 213-542-8609 and at 3335 Motor Av. West L.A., Ca. 90034 Tel. 213-559-7771 These shops organize tours to offshore islands.	As above
Rough 4′ – 8′ waves	Kelp, reefs, abalone, lobster, fish	Fishing and collecting only	Rip tides; strong current; heavy surf	As above	As above

SANTA CRUZ ISLAND

Water Temp.: 50°–70°

Regulations: See San Diego area.

58

PLACE	NO.	DESCRIPTION	ENTRY AND DISTANCE FROM SHORE	DEPTH	SNORKEL OR DIVE
ANACAPA ISLANDS (3 islands) (Many different dive spots)	27	Reef, fish, wreck	By boat but beach when you get there; 13 mi. from mainland 10' from shore	3' – 150'	Snorkel or dive
SMUGGLER'S COVE	28	A cove with a sandy bottom; west tip is good.	Boat 2½ – 3 hrs. from mainland	Varies	Snorkel or dive
YELLOW BANKS	29	Kelp beds; offshore reefs (visibility unreliable)	Boat 2½ – 3 hrs. from mainland	90'	Dive
GULL ISLAND	30	A large rock 200 yds. from Santa Cruz	Boat 2½ – 3 hrs. from mainland	10' – 70'	Snorkel or dive
POTATO BAY	31	Anchor in bay; Potato Rock is 200 yds. outside bay (visibility about 50')	Boat 2½ – 3 hrs. from mainland	15'- 85'	Dive
PELICAN BAY	32	Inlet with sandy bottom	Boat 2½ – 3 hrs. from mainland	40'	Dive
ALBERT'S ANCHORAGE	33	Giant kelp forests with some fish in clear water	Boat as above, then beach	Varies	Snorkel or dive

Visibility: 25' – 100'   **Best Season:** Spring and fall; visibility poor in winter and summer.

SURF OR CALM	HIGH-LIGHTS	FISHING AND PHOTOS	DANGERS	DIVE FACILITY	ACCOMMODATIONS
Calm	Fish, reefs, wrecks, lobster, abalone	Spear or photos; visibility varies; fall is excellent	Current, rocks	Charters to Santa Cruz and Anacapa. Call Port Hueneme: 805-488-4715 Cisco Landing: 805-486-7346 Santa Barbara: 805-969-4651 805-969-4608	All along Calif. coast; many and varied
Calm	Kelp, fish	Photos	None	Aqua Venture 2172 Pickwick Dr. Camarillo, Ca. 93010 805-484-1594	As above
Varies	Fish, anemone, scallops, starfish, nudibranchia, abalone, lobster	Photos	Current at times	You must get permission to go ashore, but you can dive from a boat freely. See charters above, your local dive shop, or come in your own boat, if large enough.	As above
Varies	Abalone, lobster, blue coral	Photos; visibility excellent; abalone, scallops, lobsters	Current, surge	As above	As above
Can be rough	Nudibranchia anemones, rock scallops, sea lions	Photos	None	As above	As above
Calm	Kelp, crabs, squid	Photos	None	As above	As above
Calm	Giant kelp forests, few fish	Photos; not too many fish	None	As above	As above

MONTEREY PT. LOBOS AREA   Water Temp.: 50°–70°

Regulations: See San Diego area.

60

PLACE	NO.	DESCRIPTION	ENTRY AND DISTANCE FROM SHORE	DEPTH	SNORKEL OR DIVE
JADE COVE Located: Los Padres Nat'l Forest on Carmel–San Simeon Hwy (U.S.1) 65 mi. S. of Monterey and 40 mi. N. Morro Bay. It is between Plasket Pt. N. and Crevice Channel S. (Very experienced divers only)	34	A series of coves at the bottom of a steep climb down 180' cliff to look for jade	Beach At shore	5'–30'	Snorkel or dive
BLUEFISH COVE (3 mi. S. of Carmel) Pt. Lobos State Park Reserve	35	A group must be granted permission to dive. Launch boat at Whaler's Cove to take you to Bluefish Cove. A scenic dive in marine gardens	Boat At shore	35'	Dive
MONASTERY BEACH	36	Rocky area with kelp and marine life	Beach At shore	50'	Mostly diving; limited snorkeling
LOVER'S POINT	37	Reefs with fish	Beach At shore	5'–35'	Snorkel or dive
GREYHOUND ROCK	38	Fish and abalone area	Boat 1 hr., then beach At shore	20'	Snorkel or dive

Visibility: 25′–75′   **Best Season:** Summer

SURF OR CALM	HIGH-LIGHTS	FISHING AND PHOTOS	DANGERS	DIVE FACILITY	ACCOMMODATIONS
Rough, white	Kelp forests, schools small fish; green canyon walls; you can find jade but cutting is so expensive it is not worth it	You can bring up what jade you can carry; no machinery	Surf, tides, currents, steep climb, insects	Bamboo Reef Enterprises 2110 Winchester Blvd. Campbell, Ca. 95008 att: Bob Kelly 408-374-8411 Ed Brawleys Seven Seas Skin Diving Ctr 598 Foam St. Monterey, Ca. 93940 408-375-8926 408-375-1377	All along Calif. coast, varied and many
Calm	Kelp, crabs, rockfish, anemones, all marine life; sea lions, great colors	No fishing or collecting; photos, especially macro photos (Close up photography with special equipment)	Cold current, hard entry	As above	As above
Rough 2′–6′ waves	Kelp, fish, marine life	Visibility 20′–30′; spearing and photos	Hard entry, deep water	As above	As above
Calm	Fish, reefs	No spearing; photos	None	As above	As above
Calm; can chop	Fish, kelp, caves, marine life	Fishing; close-up photos	Sea urchins	As above	At Carmel

SAN FRANCISCO AREA

Water Temp.: 56° – 65°

Regulations: See San Diego area

62

PLACE	NO.	DESCRIPTION	ENTRY AND DISTANCE FROM SHORE	DEPTH	SNORKEL OR DIVE
MOSS BEACH	39	Kelp with marine life	Beach or go by boat 20 min. At shore	20'	Snorkel or dive
POINT SAN PEDRO	40	Wreck of the *Drumburton* and other wrecks still not found	From beach or down 75' handhold/ foothold cliff trail, then 200 yds. to wreck 1000 yds. from beach; 200 yds. beyond rocks	Shallow	Snorkel or dive

Visibility: 10'-15'   **Best season:** Summer and early fall

SURF OR CALM	HIGH-LIGHTS	FISHING AND PHOTOS	DANGERS	DIVE FACILITY	ACCOMMODATIONS
Calm; occasional chop	Rockfish, abalone, kelp, caves	Close-up photos; limited fishing	Sea urchins	Bamboo Reef Enterprises 584 4th St. San Francisco, Ca. 94107 415-362-6694 or same at 1111 University Ave.	Many along coast of Calif.
Surging water	Wrecks, urchins, crab, algae	10'–15' visibility	Strong surge; murky waters	Berkeley, Ca. 94702 415-548-7560 Anchor Shack Diving Centers 571 Jackson St. Hayward, Ca. 94544 415-886-4656 also 5775 Pacheco Pacheco, Ca. 94553 415-825-4960	As above

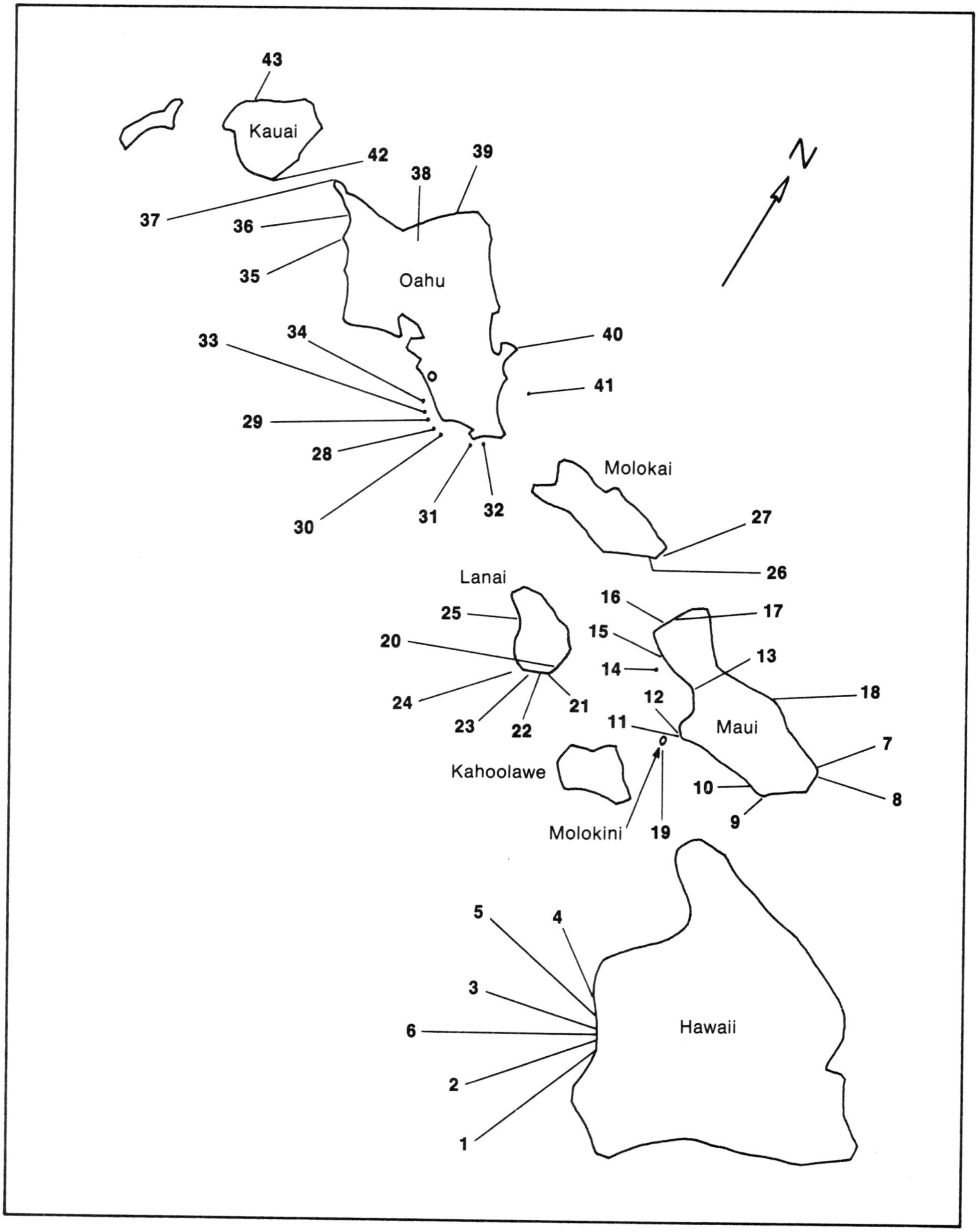

43

Kauai

42

39

38

N

37

36

35

Oahu

33

34

40

41

29

28

30

31

32

Molokai

27

26

Lanai

25

16

17

20

15

13

14

24

12

18

23

22

21

11

Maui

7

10

8

Kahoolawe

9

Molokini

19

5

4

3

6

Hawaii

2

1

HAWAII

The six islands of Hawaii (Kaui, Oahu, Molokai, Lanai, Maui, and Hawaii) are the closest Pacific equivalent to the Caribbean diving scene. Although in some respects Hawaiian diving is less spectacular than tropical diving in the East, for the careful observer there is every bit as much to see, and much of it, in fact, can only be seen here. The underwater terrain is determined more by the lava flow from Hawaii's famous volcanoes than by coral formations, and as a result there are caves, canyons, and tunnels to explore, many of them encrusted with sea animals and plants, tube worms, nudibranchs, and anemones, which provide a feeding ground for the myriad small but brightly colored and unusual reef fish (see Fish Identification Chart). Spearfishing is good in several areas where large fish abound. There are size and weight limits on underwater capture, which should be observed. For the collector, Hawaii offers a shellfish population that can hardly be surpassed, and various kinds of cones, cowries, helmets, tritons, and augers are common.

Diving is both by boat and from the beach, with a good deal of shallow-water snorkeling recommended. The road systems to get you from one dive site to another are excellent, as are the dive facilities, including a recompression chamber at Pearl Harbor. With the islands connected by regular air service, it is perfectly possible to

Jewellike tropical reef fish and exotically colored coral clusters lure the underwater sportsman all year round in Hawaii. (Hawaii Visitors Bureau)

dive all six during one vacation, but make reservations well in advance, since Hawaii is one of the most popular resort areas in the world. For West Coast residents it is far and away the most sensible type of "tropical" vacation, the Caribbean being too distant.

Air and water are warm, and the water visibility, while variable, is usually clear in one spot when it is murky at another. However, a word of warning: Hawaii is justly famous for its surfing, and there is a reason for this. The waves can be high, and the currents strong. Hawaii does not and cannot guarantee the safety conditions on any public beach on the islands, or that emergency phone service will be operative. Visitors are urged not to snorkel or dive at any beach before inquiring as to the tide situation and assuring themselves that a life-

guard is on duty. During the winter months the sea becomes especially unpredictable and riptides are frequent. This is particularly true on the north and west shores of Oahu, but extreme caution should be exercised in all locations.

Otherwise, Hawaii is a fragrant, lovely spot, where diving can become a part of a vacation filled with other activities, including sightseeing, sunbathing, golf, tennis, and shopping for local crafts. Of course, if diving is your only interest in visiting the islands, you will not be disappointed, and with a little island hopping you can get in an enormous amount of unusual and satisfying underwater activity.

Hawaii

ISLAND OF HAWAII
Water Temp.: 71°–80°

Regulations: No spearing of lobster. Check size limit of fish and lobster. Spearfishing governed by length or weight—check

PLACE	NO.	DESCRIPTION	ENTRY AND DISTANCE FROM SHORE	DEPTH	SNORKEL OR DIVE
CITY OF REFUGE NATIONAL PARK	1	Bay, lava reef	Boat ¼ mi.	10′–30′–40′	Snorkel or dive
KEALAKEKUA BAY	2	A small, deep bay	Boat 6 mi. by boat from dock	20′ and down	Snorkel or dive
THE ARCHES	3	Beautiful archways	Boat 4 mi. from dock	20′–40′–50′–60′	Snorkel or dive
RED HILL	4	Unusual area once part of a volcanic cinder cone	Boat 1½ mi. from dock	40′–90′	Dive
LAVA RIDGE COVE	5	Long narrow lava ridges	Boat 1½ mi. from dock	10′–20′	Snorkel or dive
KEAUHOU CLIFF	6	Large granite chunks	Boat	25′–50′	Snorkel or dive

ISLAND OF MAUI
Water Temp.: 71°–80°

Regulations: See regulations for Island of Hawaii.

PLACE	NO.	DESCRIPTION	ENTRY AND DISTANCE FROM SHORE	DEPTH	SNORKEL OR DIVE
HANA BAY BEACH PARK	7	A beach snorkel and a beautiful tide pool	Walk along rocky cliffs and enter from rocks or off old dock Off shore	3′–4′ 10′–15′	Snorkel

Visibility: Often 100'   **Best Season:** Spring and summer. Kona Coast best in a.m.

locally. Closed season on lobster, May, June, July, August. Certification as diver required for scuba equipment and airfills.

SURF OR CALM	HIGH-LIGHTS	FISHING AND PHOTOS	DANGERS	DIVE FACILITY	ACCOMMODATIONS
Calm	Fish, coral, lava boulders	Photos only	None	Skin Diving Hawaii P.O. Box 2064 Kailua Kona, Hawaii 96740 Tel. 808-329-3977	All at every price
Calm	Corals and marine life, red pencil urchins, tropical fish, lobsters	Great photos	None	Hawaiian Divers P.O. Box 572 Kailua Kona Hawaii 96740 Tel. 808-329-3407	As above
Calm	Lava arches 30'–40' in diameter; tropical fish caves at 50'	Great photos	Be careful of wave action	Cruise Boat Fairwind Charters att: Mike Dent Box J Keahou Bay Kona, Hawaii 96740	As above
Calm	Flat lava mesas, caves, fish, rare tropical fish	Photos	None	As above	As above
Calm	Many fish	Photos	None	As above	As above
Calm	Many fish, parrots, squirrel fish, coral formations with rivers of black sand caves	Photos	None	As above	As above

Visibility: Often 100'   **Best Season:** Spring and summer; (mid-Sept. to mid-Oct.)

SURF OR CALM	HIGH-LIGHTS	FISHING AND PHOTOS	DANGERS	DIVE FACILITY	ACCOMMODATIONS
Calm; can chop if windy	Similar to a tide pool with lovely fish and reef	Photos if you can do it. Free diving	None. Keep away from rocks in Big Surge areas	None at Hana. See West Coast Maui	Hotel Hana Kai Island of Maui Hawaii 96713 and many others at various prices.

ISLAND OF MAUI CONTINUED

PLACE	NO.	DESCRIPTION	ENTRY AND DISTANCE FROM SHORE	DEPTH	SNORKEL OR DIVE
HAMOA BEACH (reserved for guests of Hotel Hana Maui)	8	Lava reefs and fish; sand beach; turtle grounds	Beach and rocks along left side 30′ from shore	To 30′ can be shallower if no surge	Snorkel or dive
LA PEROUSE BAY MAKENA (hard drive unless with jeep)	9	Reef with many and varied fish	Boat 30 min. from Maalea Bay, then beach. 100 feet from beach. Good snorkeling next to cliffs on east side.	10′–40′	Snorkel or dive
MAKENA AHIHI BAY (Ahihi is a marine refuge)	10	Much lava, rock, and reef	Boat or off shore 50′ 100 yds.	20′–50′ shallow by rocks	Snorkel or dive
CHARLIE YOUNG BEACH	11	Fish, reefs, shallow rocks	Beach 100 yds.	10′–25′	Snorkel from shore
KAMAOLE PARK	12	Fish, sandy beach with rocks on both sides	Beach Off shore 50′–60′ from rocks	Shallow	Snorkel
HEKILI POINT OLOWALU	13	Reef S. of point	Beach or boat 150 yds.	10′–25′	Snorkel or dive
AU AU CHANNEL (Experienced)	14	Relatively shallow channel	Boat	85′–300′ Best at 110′	Dive
SHERATON AND KAANAPALI AIRSTRIP	15	Rock cliffs, Sheraton reef and airstrip	Beach 75–100 yds.	10′–30′	Snorkel or dive

68

SURF OR CALM	HIGH-LIGHTS	FISHING AND PHOTOS	DANGERS	DIVE FACILITY	ACCOMMODATIONS
Calm to rough	Fish, reefs, turtles	Spearfish; photos	None. Currents run strong in front of reef	None See West Coast Maui	Hotel Hana Maui Island of Maui Hawaii 96713 Tel. 808-536-7522 Mr. Tony R. de Jetley
Usually calm; early morning best	Fish, reefs, artifacts	Photos; spearfishing	None	Dale Huddleston Central Pacific Divers 780 Front St. Lahaina, Maui, Hawaii 96761 Tel. 808-661-4661	Many at varied prices
Calm	Fish, reef, good visibility; lots of tropical fish	Photos	None	Al Weizer Dive-n-Sport Kihei, Maui 99753 188 Noe Tel. 808-879-1412 Trips to La Perouse	As above
Usually calm; wind in afternoon	Fish; many net fishermen go out in this area. Fun to watch	Photos if no wind	None	Hawaiian Pacific Divers of Maui 10 Market St. Wailuka, Maui 96793 Tel. 808-244-5910 Bob Chambers	As above
Calm	Fish and shells (augers, miters, cones)	Photos; do not collect shells	None	Sea Hawaii P.O. Box 98 Lahaina, Maui, Hawaii 96761	As above
Usually calm; winds come through canyon (blow off here)	Reef fish, especially butterflies	Spearfishing; photos	None. Watch offshore winds	As above	As above
Varies; wind in afternoon	Black coral	Photos	Strong currents, lots of wind	As above	As above
a.m. good; windy p.m.	Many schooling fish at Sheraton	Photos	Currents, offshore wind	As above	As above

ISLAND OF MAUI CONTINUED

70

PLACE	NO.	DESCRIPTION	ENTRY AND DISTANCE FROM SHORE	DEPTH	SNORKEL OR DIVE
NAPILI BAY	16	Skin dive from shore	Beach Around rocky areas	10′ – 25′	Snorkel or dive
HONOLUA BAY (Soon to be restrictive to divers.)	17	A large bay with easy entry	Beach or boat 150 yds.	15′ – 30′	Snorkel or dive
WAILUA	18	Good diving in good weather	Boat or rocky shore Around rocks along shore to 100 yds.	15′ – 50′	Snorkel or dive
MALOKINI Crater Lagoon	19	Lava reefs with fish and caves	Boat 30 min.	To 300′	Snorkel or dive (snorkel from shore)

ISLAND OF LANAI

Water Temp.: 74º – 78º

Regulations: These are excellent areas. No shelling. No spearing. No coral collecting.

PLACE	NO.	DESCRIPTION	ENTRY AND DISTANCE FROM SHORE	DEPTH	SNORKEL OR DIVE
HOLUPOE BEACH	20	Beautiful sand beach and bay; snorkeling and diving area	Beach or boat From beach to center of bay	2′ – 35′	Snorkel or dive
THE FIRST CATHEDRAL	21	Reef, filled with caves and grottos	Boat 100 yds from shore	30′ – 100′	Snorkel or dive
KNOB HILL AND 2nd CATHEDRAL	22	Long lava ridges covered with coral; huge cave in 2nd cathedral	Boat 100-150 yds. from shore	15′ – 110′	Snorkel or dive
THIRD FISHING HUT	23	Big lava arch, reef, shallows up to shore	Boat 50′ – 200 yds from shore	15′ – 110′	Dive; can snorkel close to shore

SURF OR CALM	HIGH-LIGHTS	FISHING AND PHOTOS	DANGERS	DIVE FACILITY	ACCOMMODATIONS
Calm	Shells on beach after high seas; lava ridges	Photos	None	See page 69	See page 69
Usually calm	Great fish and shallow snorkeling	Photos when clear	Big surf, stay out	As above	As above
Surgy	Big fish	Photos	Big surf	As above	As above
Calm	Fish, reefs, artifacts, caves	Photos	Current; sharks	As above	As above

Visibility: To 100'   **Best Season:** Spring and summer

Mostly calm, especially a.m.	Fishes, schools of porpoise	Photos only	None	See Maui	Not on Lanai
Depends on weather, can chop	Shells, caves, grottos, big fish, lobsters	Great photos	None; shore current	As above	None
Usually calm; can chop when windy	Huge schools of French grunt at 2nd cathedral Lava ridges; big fish	Photos only	Current along shore	As above	None
Surge in close	French grunts, lava arches	Great photos	Currents	As above	None

ISLAND OF LANAI CONTINUED

PLACE	NO.	DESCRIPTION	ENTRY AND DISTANCE FROM SHORE	DEPTH	SNORKEL OR DIVE
FIN ROCK	24	Ridges and pinnacles off shore from cliffs	Boat 100 yds. from shore	To 75'	Snorkel or dive
KAUMALA PAU DROP-OFF	25	Deep ledge in front of harbor	Boat; can swim to drop-off 150 yds.	35'–140'	Dive

72

ISLAND OF MOLOKAI   Water Temp.: 74º–78º

Regulations: See those for Lanai.

PLACE	NO.	DESCRIPTION	ENTRY AND DISTANCE FROM SHORE	DEPTH	SNORKEL OR DIVE
PAUWALU HARBOR	26	Long fringing reef	Beach—but long surface swim; boat better 30'–½ mi.	10'–60'	Snorkel or dive
MOKUHOONIKI ROCK (Expert)	27	Area off a rock with big fish; a super spot	Boat 1 hr.	To 125'	Snorkel or dive

SURF OR CALM	HIGH-LIGHTS	FISHING AND PHOTOS	DANGERS	DIVE FACILITY	ACCOMMODATIONS
Calm	Many schooling tropicals; holes, reefs, fish, bright tube corals	Great photos	None	See page 69	See page 69
Calm	Holes, fish, moray eels	Excellent for photos	None	As above	None

Visibility: Often to 100'   **Best Season:** Spring and summer

Windy; look for clearest water	Fish (especially big parrots), turtles	Visibility poor	Big surf reversing along shore currents	No dive shop, but a compressor. Contact: Larry or August Rawlins at Chevron Station in Kaunakakai	Moderate-priced accommodations on Molokai
Rough; 4'-12' waves	Fish, shark, rays, giant sea bass	Photos only, 100' visibility	Rough surf; shark; currents	There may be a shop on Molokai now. Central Pacific Divers 780 Front St. Lahaina Maui Hawaii 96761 Tel. 808-661-4661 Dale Huddleston runs trips fairly regularly.	As above

ISLAND OF OAHU

Water Temp.: 74° – 78°

Regulations: See those for Lanai.

74

PLACE	NO.	DESCRIPTION	ENTRY AND DISTANCE FROM SHORE	DEPTH	SNORKEL OR DIVE
HONOLULU E. DIAMOND HEAD	28	Lava reefs	Boat	Varies	Dive
100-FOOT HOLE (Expert only)	29	8' tunnel going through a 35' lava rock formation	Boat 15–30 min. from dock 1 mi.	85'	Dive
FANTASY REEF	30	Lava reef	Boat 30 min. from dock 1 mi.	20'–100'	Dive
HANAUMA BAY (Underwater Park)	31	Underwater preserve	Beach 50'	10'–40'	Snorkel or dive
SANDY BEACH (Expert only)	32	1 mi. E of Hanauma Bay	Beach At shore; drop-off ½ mi. out	35'–90'	Dive
WAIKIKI WRECK BUOY	33	½ mi. straight out Waikiki Beach	Boat 10 min. ½ mi.	12'–30'	Snorkel or dive
MAGIC ISLAND	34	Outside Ala Wai boat harbor	Boat 5 min.	20'–80'– 120'	Snorkel or dive
MAKAHA	35	Archways and caves	From beach; boat for farther out	30'–80'	Dive
MAKUA	36	Caves, tunnels, 70' verticle chimney	Beach or boat. 400 yds. from shore.	30'–50' drop-off to 120'	Snorkel or dive

Visibility: 20′–120′   **Best Season:** Summer

SURF OR CALM	HIGH-LIGHTS	FISHING AND PHOTOS	DANGERS	DIVE FACILITY	ACCOMMODATIONS
Calm	Fish, shells	Spearfish; photos; shell collecting	None	Dan's Dive Shop 1382 Makaloa St. Honolulu, Hawaii 96814 Tel. 808-946-7333 Carl H. Seyfer	Many at all prices
Calm	Fish, reefs, coral, grottos	Photos; spearfish; visibility good	A strong current can occur	South Sea Aquatics 1125 Ala Moana Blvd. Honolulu, Hawaii 96814 Tel. 808-538-7724 Ken Taylor	As above
Calm	Fish, reef, coral, sponge, shells, turtles	Photos; spearfish; excellent visibility	None	Skin Diving Hawaii Ala Wai Marina 1651 Ala Moana Blvd. Honolulu, Hawaii 96815 Tel. 808-941-0548 Sally Noxon	As above
Calm, clear; Oct.-Mar. can vary	Fish, shells, corals, reefs	Photos only	None; don't kick rocks		As above
Surf	Corals, lobster, shells, fish	Spearfish	Heavy surf; strong currents	As above	As above
Varies	Small corals, sandy canyons, small fish	Photos; visibility 20′-50′	None	As above	All at every price
Calm if weather good	Navy anchor, flat corals, wreckage, small black coral	Photos, wide-angle lens; visibility poor	None	As above	As above
Calm if weather good	Shells, lobsters, small fish	Photos, visibility excellent	None	As above	As above
Usually calm	Good shells, lobsters, fish	Spearfishing; lobstering; shelling; photos, visibility 150′	Sharks, but do not seem to bother divers; take a guide	As above	As above

ISLAND OF OAHU CONTINUED

PLACE	NO.	DESCRIPTION	ENTRY AND DISTANCE FROM SHORE	DEPTH	SNORKEL OR DIVE
KAENA POINT (Expert only)	37	Rough fishing area	Boat 200 yds.	60' – 120'	Dive
WAIMEA BAY	38	1½-hr. drive from Waikiki	Beach or boat 300 yds.	15' – 45'	Snorkel or dive
PUPUKEA	39	1½ mi. E. Waimea; protected cave for picnc and snorkel; lava mourds	Beach 50'	15' – 45'	Snorkel or dive
MOKU MANU	40	An island 1 mi. off Kaneohe Marine Corps Air Station	Boat ¼ mi.	30' – 60' and 70' – 120' – 250'	Snorkel or dive
RABBIT ISLAND (MANANA ISLAND)	41	1 mi. off Sea Life Park; inshore area sandy. Area around island colorful	Boat ½ mi.	35' – 130'	Dive

76

ISLAND OF KAUAI

Water Temp.: 78°

Regulations: See those for Lanai.

KOLOA POIPU	42	Beautiful reef	Beach At shore	to 35'	Snorkel or dive
HAENA POINT END OF ROAD	43	Beautiful reef	Beach At shore	10' – 50'	Snorkel or dive

SURF OR CALM	HIGH-LIGHTS	FISHING AND PHOTOS	DANGERS	DIVE FACILITY	ACCOMMODATIONS
Rough	Great fish	Spearfishing for big game	Rough water; strong currents	As above	As above
Calm summer; swells in winter and surf	Fish	Fishing; photos, visibility 30'–70'	Surf in winter	All at Waikiki	All at all prices
Calm summer; can be rough winter	Caves, tunnels, spotted moray eels, shrimp, fish, etc.	Photos; spearfishing	Watch for morays and scorpion fish. Surf in winter	As above	As above
Rough	Coral formations, big fish, plateaus, black coral	Spearfishing; photos, good visibility; big game	Shark	As above	As above
Calm if weather is good	Shells, fish	Spearfishing; good photos	Currents, surge	As above	As above

Visibility: 20'–150'   **Best Season:** Spring and summer

SURF OR CALM	HIGH-LIGHTS	FISHING AND PHOTOS	DANGERS	DIVE FACILITY	ACCOMMODATIONS
Calm	Fish, starfish, shells, reef	Spearfishing; photos	None	Mike and Larry Sea Sage Diving Ctr. 4544 Kukui St. Kapaa, Kauai, Hawaii 96746	Rooms available; can be inexpensive
Varies from calm to 10' waves	Lobsters, eels, fish, coral heads, shells	Spearfishing; photos	Current in channel	All facilities at Island Marine Dive Shop 4257 Rice St. Lihue, Kauai, Hawaii 96746 Kauai Skin Diving Co. near Poipu Tel. Koloa 808-742-1641	As above

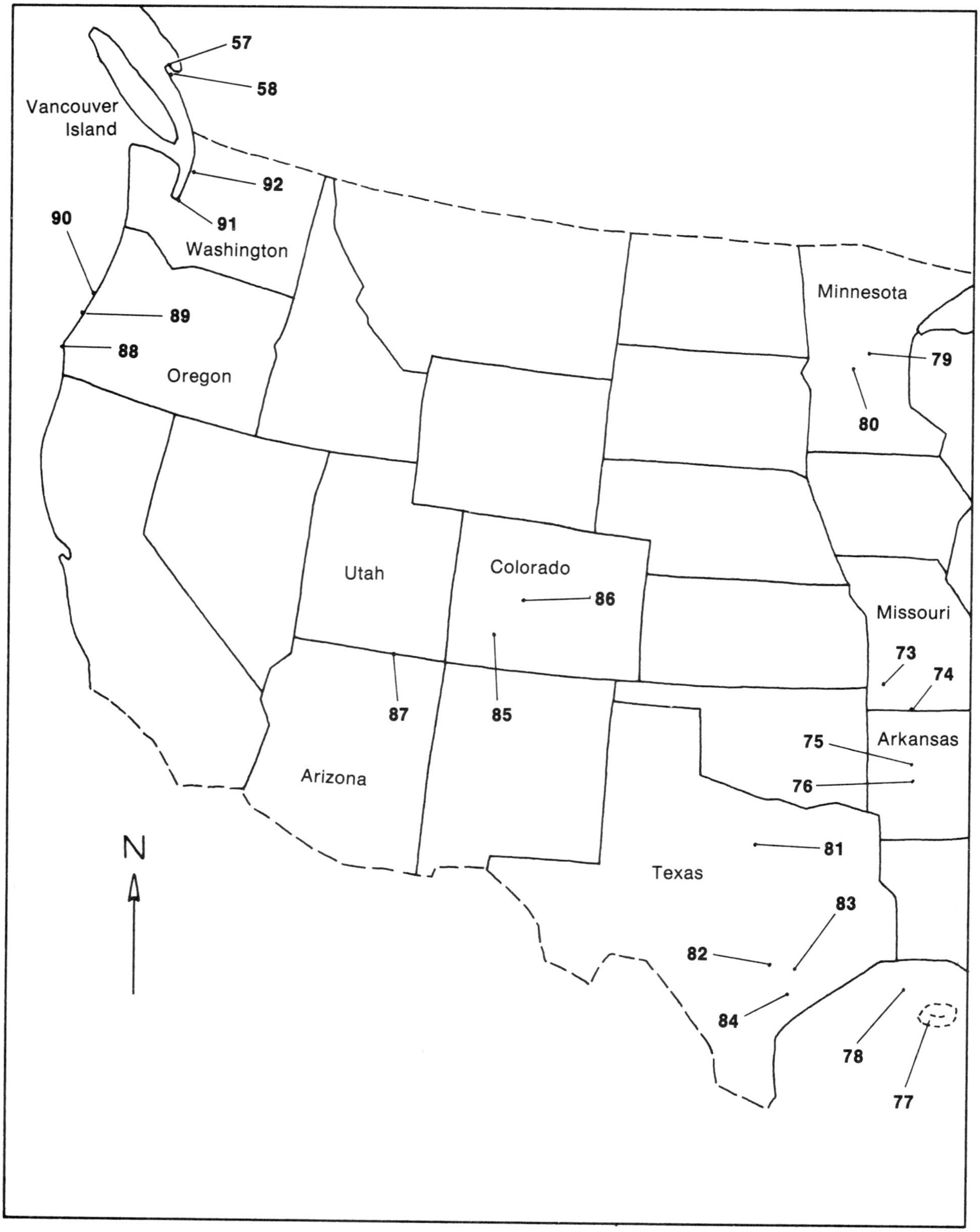

57

58

Vancouver
Island

92

90

91

Washington

89

88

Oregon

Minnesota

79

80

Utah

Colorado

86

Missouri

73

74

87

85

Arizona

75

Arkansas

76

N

81

Texas

83

82

78

84

77

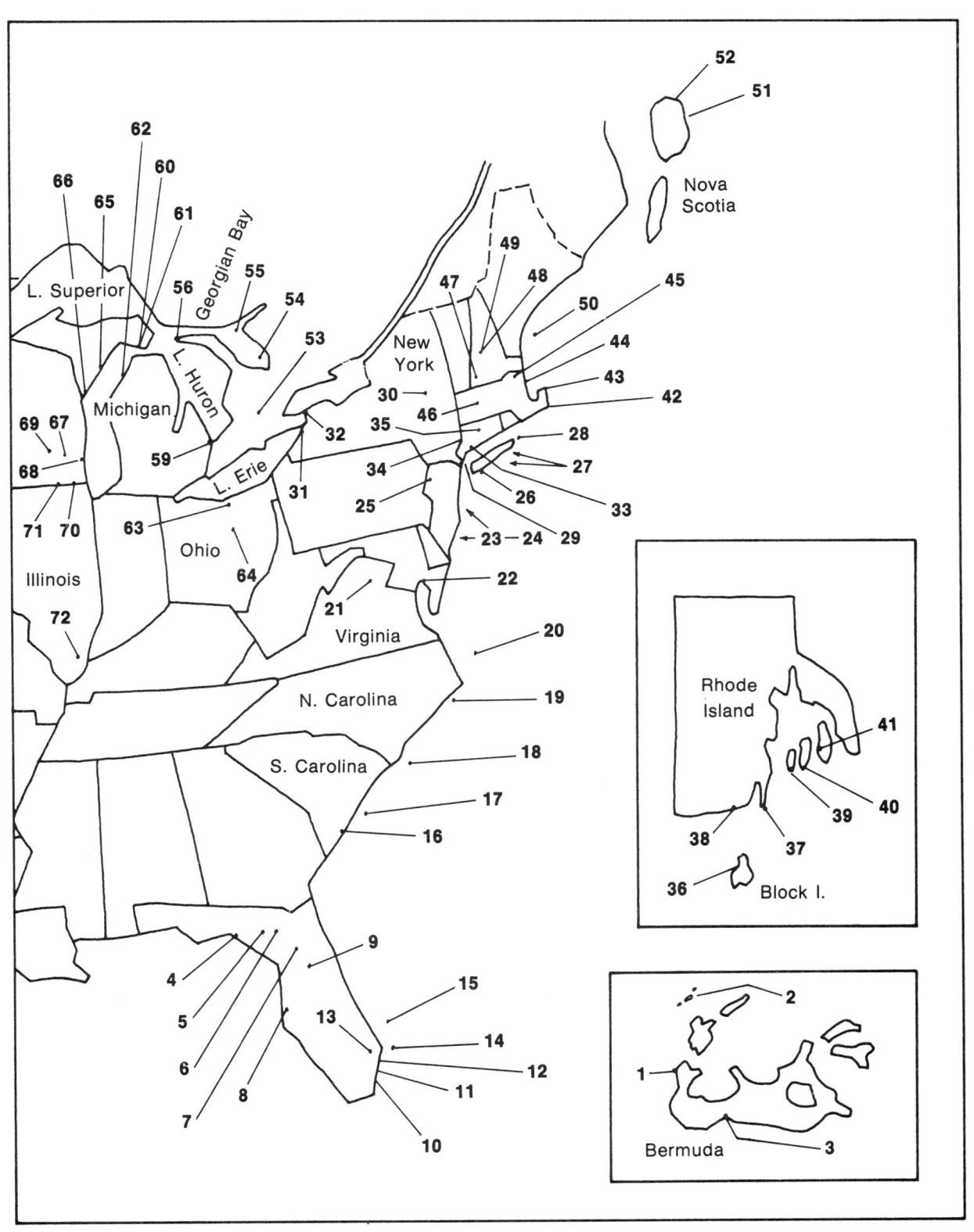

52
51
Nova
Scotia

62
66
60
65
61
Georgian Bay
55
L. Superior
56
54
49
53
48
47
50
45
New York
44
30
46
43
42
Michigan
L. Huron
32
35
28
69 67
34
27
68
59
L. Erie
31
25
26
33
71 70
63
23 — 24   29
Illinois
Ohio
64
22
72
21
Virginia
20
N. Carolina
19
S. Carolina
18
17
16

Rhode Island
41
40
38   37
39
36   Block I.

4
5
6
8
7
9
15
13
14
12
11
10

2
1
Bermuda
3

A group of young divers preparing for a slush dive on Lake Sunapee, New Hampshire. (Judy La Porte)

BERMUDA,* THE UNITED STATES, AND SOUTHERN CANADA

Well, there's no place like home. The mainland of the United States may not offer much in the coral reef – tropical fish department, but whatever else you want, the U.S. has it. From the springs of northern Florida, where you can play with friendly sea cows, to the coast of Washington, where you can wrestle an octopus, the forty eight mainland states offer an unbelievable variety of intriguing underwater experiences. There are caves, wrecks, ice, slush, photo spots, and fishing grounds; in short, plenty of snorkeling and diving. Naturally, you cannot "dive the mainland" in a week or two the way you can "dive the Cayman Islands." The country is so spread out and offers so many types of diving that a book this size can barely scratch the surface. The charts merely highlight only some of the better-known snorkeling and diving spots across the country. Wherever you are, there is probably a reputable sporting goods or dive store that can fill you in on the local dive sites—hundreds of which we have not been able to include.

If you are planning a trip and want to orient it toward diving, you might consider one of the following:

THE FLORIDA SPRINGS
This is freshwater diving in a warm climate. The springs weave across northern Florida, leading in and out of caves, lakes, and rivers. Water is clear, fish abound, and in the winter the water in some of the areas is populated with friendly sea cows, relatives of the seal, which will engage in games of hide and seek, which they always win in the end.

THE GREAT LAKES
There are 1,200 shipwrecks here, in all kinds of condition, many of them unexplored, many more undiscovered. The wrecks are frequently the home of schools of fish, which can be taken by spear while you are exploring. Naturally this is better suited to the warmer seasons of the year.

THE MICHIGAN AND WISCONSIN LAKE COUNTRY
These lakes abound with freshwater fish and rock formations, and frequently offer up treasures from past civilizations. The country surrounding the lakes is beautiful and a good vacation spot for a party including some nondivers. Water tends to be cold, but a wet suit solves this problem nicely.

THE LOUISIANA OFFSHORE OIL RIGS IN THE GULF OF MEXICO
For exhilarating but tough diving and big-game spearfishing, the oil rigs of Louisiana have become famous. The underwater portions of the rigs have attracted a varied fish population that grows to enormous size on the food provided by marine life clinging to the rigs. The diving is deep and the current can be a problem, but if you're up to it, it's an unforgettable experience.

THE PACIFIC NORTHWEST COAST
This area offers the unusual sport of octopus wrestling, about which the less said the better. However, for large game fish the area is on a par with Louisiana. Again, one copes with cold water with a wet suit.

BERMUDA
For a display of tropical reef life somewhat more northerly than the Caribbean, Bermuda offers the snorkeler and diver clear water, wrecks, reefs, a pleasant climate, and a charming island. This is a delightful and ever-popular vacation spot.

CANADA
The Canadian lakes and northern waters offer a limitless supply of ice-diving spots as well as a good regular diving ground in the summer when the water is cold, but still liquid.

For the vacationing beach-lover the Caribbean or Hawaiian Islands and the Florida Keys, as well as the Bahamas, are without doubt the top snorkeling and diving spots; but for the real underwater enthusiast the United States offers curiosities, adventures, and a general variety that no other place can boast of. Look around your own neighborhood. There's probably a mysterious nearby spot below the surface awaiting your attention.

* (Exclusive of California and the Florida Keys)

Bermuda, the United States,

BERMUDA

Water Temp.: 60°–80°

Regulations: No spearfishing.

PLACE	NO.	DESCRIPTION	ENTRY AND DISTANCE FROM SHORE	DEPTH	SNORKEL OR DIVE
S.W. BREAKER (temp. 60°–80°)	1	Spectacular reef; fish will eat out of diver's hand	Boat 20 min.	25'–30'	Snorkel or dive
N.W. BARRIER REEF	2	Beautiful reef; shipwrecks	Boat 1 hr.	25'–30'	Snorkel or dive
PAGET	3	Shallow reefs off Paget	Beach At shore	Very shallow	Snorkel or dive

FLORIDA

Water Temp.: 68°–78°

Regulations: Vary. Be sure to check. There are state regulations and county regulations.

PLACE	NO.	DESCRIPTION	ENTRY AND DISTANCE FROM SHORE	DEPTH	SNORKEL OR DIVE
NATURAL BRIDGE SPRING (S. Tallahassee, 6 mi. from (Woodville)	4	Water runs underground forming a natural bridge (park area). Springs and sink holes	Walk in from shore	40'	Snorkel or dive
ICHETUCKNEE RIVER (E. of Branford; park area; state owned)	5	Several springs plus a 3-mi. run to bridge on U.S. 27. (Snorkel or tube all the way.) Takes 3 hrs. Wet suit!	Walk in from shore	13' at cave floor at start	Snorkel
DEVIL'S EYE SPRING (next to Jenny and July Springs, on Sante Fe River. E. Branford)	6	Made of 3 boils (surface disturbance) with a round limestone shaft	Walk in from shore	6'–20'–50'	Snorkel or dive, or cave for expert cave diver

and Southern Canada

Visibility: Varies   **Best Season:** Visibility better in winter; temperature better in summer.

SURF OR CALM	HIGH-LIGHTS	FISHING AND PHOTOS	DANGERS	DIVE FACILITY	ACCOMMODATIONS
Usually calm; can be rough	Fish, spectacular reef formations	Photos only; visibility 60' – 150'	None	Dave McLeod's Skin Diving Adventures The Gables Guest House Paget, Bermuda	Many at various points.
Usually calm; can be rough	Reef, fish, wrecks	Photos only	None	As above	As above
Calm; can vary	Fish, corals	Photos	None	As above	As above

Visibility: Varies   **Best Season:** Late fall, winter, spring, early summer

Calm	Area site of Civil War battle; relics	Photos	None, but watch currents	None	At Tallahassee
Calm, slow current	Relics. Slow long float carried by water; scenic!	Neither	None	Dale Stone, Ichetucknee Bus Run. Rentals and bus will pick you up when run is over. P.O. Box 475 Branford, Fla. 32008 Tel. 904-935-1671	Ichetucknee Campgrounds ½ mile W. Ichetucknee Bridge Box 246 Branford, Fla. 32008 Tel. 904-935-1086 Les and Onice Peden
Calm	Cave 3' high 18' wide to a room "Devil's Dungeon"	Neither	None except cave	Not Known	Trailer Park at Highsprings, Fla.

FLORIDA CONTINUED

PLACE	NO.	DESCRIPTION	ENTRY AND DISTANCE FROM SHORE	DEPTH	SNORKEL OR DIVE
SILVER GLEN SPRINGS (E. of Ocala in Ocala National Forest)	7	Spring with 2 boils	Beach At shore	28'	Snorkel only
CRYSTAL RIVER SPRING (in town of Crystal River, 1 mi. W. of U.S. 19)	8	A beautiful spring, snorkel or dive; 100' visibility	Boat (rentals) 15 min. boat trip	5'–30'–55'	Snorkel or dive
ALEXANDER SPRINGS National Forest Recreation Area	9	Huge spring fed from a cave	Beach At shore	27'	Snorkel or dive
BISCAYNE NATIONAL MONUMENT Elliott Key	10	Corals and fish, wrecks	Boat 6 mi.	To 12'	Snorkel; can dive deeper at nearby Pacific Reef
POMPANO BEACH (S.E. 12 St.)	11	Shallow area with fish and marine life	Beach 80 yds.	12'–15'	Snorkel or shallow dive
BOCA BEACH	12	Ledge with coral	Beach 10'	4'–10'	Snorkel

84

SURF OR CALM	HIGH-LIGHTS	FISHING AND PHOTO	DANGERS	DIVE FACILITY	ACCOMMODATIONS
Calm	Relics, fish, scenic	Photos	None	Atlantic Scuba Academy 20 N. Atlantic Ave. Daytona Beach, Fla. 32018 Tel. 904-253-7558	Trailer and tent camping area
Calm	Many fish, plus manatees (sea cows) in winter; artifacts	Photos excellent; no spearfishing	None	Aqua Peer Dive Shop, Crystal River, Fla. 32629 Tel. 904-795-2776	In nearby towns
Calm	Lily pads, fish, fossils, flora, artifacts	Photos great; no spearfishing	Shallow cave; do not enter	Atlantic Scuba Academy 20 N. Atlantic Ave. Daytona Beach, Fla. 32018 Tel. 904-253-7558 Herb's Dive Shop, 2434 S. Atlantic Ave. Daytona Beach, Fla. 32018	Camping, trailers, tent sites
Usually calm, but rough in north wind	3 wrecks, fish, lobsters, soft corals	Spearing and photos; no collecting	Water skiers; Pacific reef can be stormy	Cutler Ridge Diving Center 20850 S. Dixie Hwy Miami, Fla. 33157 Tel. 305-251-2710	Many ashore
2'–3' waves; varies with wind	Fish, soft corals, shells	Spearing, photos	At times heavy surf	Aquatic Gateways Diving Center 15 N. Federal Hwy Pompano Beach, Fla. 33062 Tel. 305-782-5768 Matt and Steve Dee	Many
Varies with winds	Fish, urchins, shells	Photos No spearing	At times heavy surf	As above	Many

FLORIDA CONTINUED

86

PLACE	NO.	DESCRIPTION	ENTRY AND DISTANCE FROM SHORE	DEPTH	SNORKEL OR DIVE
PALM BEACH (Near Palm Beach inlet of Lake Worth)	13	Fish of all sorts, turtles, shells, lobsters	At dock	Varies; about 25'	Snorkel or dive
PALM BEACH Open Ocean, Breakers Reef	14	Outcroppings of rock; many fish; drift dive hanging on to rope behind boat (anchor rope—not on bottom)	Boat ¾ mi. 15–20 min.	50'–85'	Dive
BETHEL SHOALS (out of Sebastian Inlet)	15	Fishing grounds	Boat 13 mi. S.E. of Sebastian Inlet	50'	Dive

S. CAROLINA
Water Temp.: 45°–75°

Regulations: Check locally.

PLACE	NO.	DESCRIPTION	ENTRY AND DISTANCE FROM SHORE	DEPTH	SNORKEL OR DIVE
COOPER RIVER (Summer)	16	A river with artifacts	20'	30'	Snorkel or dive
ARTIFICIAL REEF (Summer)	17	Artificial reef that attracts marine life and fish	Boat, 2 hrs.	45'	Dive

SURF OR CALM	HIGH-LIGHTS	FISHING AND PHOTOS	DANGERS	DIVE FACILITY	ACCOMMODATIONS
Calm	Fish, parrots, damsels, tarpon, lobsters, etc.	Photos; 75'–100' visibility at times	None	Norine Rouse Buccaneer Yacht Club 142 Lake Dr. Palm Beach Shores, Fla. 33404 (on shore of Lake Worth) Tel. 305-844-2466	Many
Varies	Many fish, barracuda; wrecks sunk as artificial reefs; lobsters, crabs, shells	Photos; visibility can be excellent	Currents	Colonnades Under Sea Center 2525 Lake Dr. Riviera Beach, Fla. 33404 Tel. 305-844-5291	Many
Varies	Fish (jack, tuna, barracuda, pompano, dolphin, etc.)	Spearfishing	Rough in inlet	In Orlando for information contact: Scotts Swim & Scuba School 3465 Edgewater Dr., Orlando, Fla. 32804 Tel. 305-425-8811 or Jim Hollis Scuba World 5107 E. Colonial Dr. Orlando, Fla. 32807 Tel. 305-273-3373	Many

Visibility: 20'   **Best Season:** Summer.

Swift current	Artifacts	None; visibility 20'	Current	The Wet Shop 5121 Rivers Ave. Charleston, S.C. 29405	Many
Moderate seas	Fish	Spearing, photos; visibility 20'	Tide current	As above	Many

N. CAROLINA

Water Temp.: 60º – 70º

Regulations: Diver's flag mandatory. For diving wrecks get permit: State Office of Archives and History, 109 E. Jones St.,

PLACE	NO.	DESCRIPTION	ENTRY AND DISTANCE FROM SHORE	DEPTH	SNORKEL OR DIVE
FRYING PAN SHOALS (Summer to Oct.) (Expert)	18	Over 900 ships wrecked here! Many are unexplored Duke University Marine Lab published the **Oceanographic Atlas of the Carolina Continental Margin** by J.G. Newton, O.H. Pilkey, and J.O. Blanton. This is available for $4.50 plus 4% sales tax and postage from the State Department of Natural and Economic Resources, Mineral Resources Section, Raleigh, North Carolina 29611.	Boat up to 12 miles, but you can swim to some wrecks from shore.	Varies	Dive
RADIO ISLAND (Morehead City)	19	Fish and wrecks	Boat 1–2 hours; beach there	30'–70'	Snorkel or dive
NAG'S HEAD Outer Banks	20	Fish and wrecks	Beach 50 yards	150'	Snorkel or dive

VIRGINIA

Water Temp.: 30º – 70º

Regulations: No spearfishing.

PLACE	NO.	DESCRIPTION	ENTRY AND DISTANCE FROM SHORE	DEPTH	SNORKEL OR DIVE
HAYMARKET QUARRY	21	Good sightseeing quarry with rock and grass	Beach At shore	10'–100'	Snorkel or dive

88

Visibility: 20′–50′   **Best Season:** Summer to October.

Raleigh, N.C. 27611

SURF OR CALM	HIGH-LIGHTS	FISHING AND PHOTOS	DANGERS	DIVE FACILITY	ACCOMMODATIONS
Varies greatly	Wrecks and fantastic fish life; artifacts & relics (be sure to check N. Carolina law regarding salvage)	Spearing, photos	Seas, wrecks	Morehead City & Wilmington have dive shops that charter to the wreck sites. E.J. & W. Bicycle & Sports Shop, 2204 Handell St., Morehead City, N.C. 28557 Aqua World, Inc. 4001 Wrightsville Ave. Wilmington, N.C. 28401 Tel. 919-799-4886	Many in nearby cities.
Varies; calm to white water	Munitions on wreck; fish	Spearing, photos	Explosion of munitions on wreck	In Norfolk, Va. & Aquahaven Skin Diving School Oak Park Shopping Ctr. 5212 Hollyridge Dr. Raleigh, N.C. 27612 Hatteras & Morehead City, N.C.	Many, varied
Calm 1′–2′ waves	Wrecks, fish	Spearing, photos	Currents along shore		Many

Visibility: To 30′   **Best Season:** Summer

Calm	Fish, cliffs, sunken cars	Photos	None	Ski & Dive Shop 1545 N. Quaker Lane Alexandria, Va. 22302 Tel. 703-683-2220	Many

MARYLAND

Water Temp.: 30°–70°

Regulations: Check locally.

90

PLACE	NO.	DESCRIPTION	ENTRY AND DISTANCE FROM SHORE	DEPTH	SNORKEL OR DIVE
CHESAPEAKE BAY PT. LOOKOUT KENT ISLAND TANGIERS ISLAND	22	Many wrecks here in varying locations. Much diving here.	Boat	Varies	Dive

NEW JERSEY

Water Temp.: 30°–70°

Regulations: Check locally.

JERSEY SHORE WRECKS (Experienced)	23	Wrecks, artifacts	Boat	To 125'	Dive
JETTIES ALONG SHORE	24	Various fish and forms of marine life	Beach 100'	To 20'	Snorkel or dive
HAMBURG QUARRY (Rte. 517)	25	A quarry; Apr.-Nov.	Grassy shore At shore	50'	Snorkel or dive

Visibility: To 40' **Best Season:** Summer

SURF OR CALM	HIGH-LIGHTS	FISHING AND PHOTOS	DANGERS	DIVE FACILITY	ACCOMMODATIONS
Varies	Wrecks of *Hannibal, Victoria, Davidson, Texas,* etc.; oysters, crabs, fish, artifacts	Check local regulations for spearing	Caught in wrecks	Diver's Den, Inc. 8105 Harford Rd. Baltimore, Md. 21234 Tel. 301-668-6866 Scuba Hut, Inc. 418 Crain Hwy S.W., Glen Bornie, Md. 21061 Tel. 301-761-4520	Many

Visibility: To 30' **Best Season:** Summer

SURF OR CALM	HIGH-LIGHTS	FISHING AND PHOTOS	DANGERS	DIVE FACILITY	ACCOMMODATIONS
Calm to rough	Fish, wrecks, artifacts	Spearing; photos	Very experienced divers only	Princeton Aqua Sports 306 Alexander St. Princeton, N.J. 08540 Tel. 609-924-4240 and others in Beach Haven, Edison, E. Hanover, Green Brook, Laurence Harbor, Lincoln Park, Livingston, Manahawkin, Ramsey, Rochelle Park	Many
Calm to rough	Fish, crabs, lobsters, starfish	Spearing; photos	Tides, boats, rough beach entry		Many
Calm	Crystal-clear water	30' visibility	None; divers must be certified	The Quarry Rte. 517 Hamburg, N.J. 07419 Tel. 201-827-7630	In nearby towns

NEW YORK

Water Temp.: Cold to 72°

Regulations: Check locally.

92

PLACE	NO.	DESCRIPTION	ENTRY AND DISTANCE FROM SHORE	DEPTH	SNORKEL OR DIVE
LONG ISLAND JONES BEACH (W. end Jones Beach State Park)	26	Jetty, 1 mi. long; curves from ocean to bay	Boat (diving from state beach forbidden) At jetty	25′	Snorkel or dive
LONG ISLAND ROCKAWAY PT. FIRE ISLAND JETTY SHINNECOCK INLET AND BAY and along sunken jetty from Rockaway to Montauk	27	Diving for fish, lobsters, clams (much pollution); wrecks	Boat; but from some areas beaches give access	Varies	Snorkel or dive
MONTAUK PT. (on E. tip of L.I. S. shore; 2½ hrs. N.Y.C.)	28	Great fish; 4 mi. W. Montauk Lighthouse from Ditch Plains to tip of Montauk	Rock beach or boat 500′–600′	30′–35′	Snorkel or dive
LARCHMONT AND PLAYLAND BREAKWATERS	29	Rocky breakwaters with fish	Boat from Larchmont 10 min. At Playland breakwater is 50 yds. from shore.	4′–35′	Snorkel or dive

Visibility: To 30′   **Best Season:** Summer, warm weather

SURF OR CALM	HIGH-LIGHTS	FISHING AND PHOTOS	DANGERS	DIVE FACILITY	ACCOMMODATIONS
Varies	Bass, lobsters; E. of jetty is wreck of *Tobay* (15′–25′ deep)	Visibility 15′	Shark, boats	Launch for own boat and rentals at many marinas	Many
Can be rough or calm	Many fish of all sorts; lobsters, even sturgeon	Spearing	Shark, rough, boats,	Cougar Sports 3470 Webster Ave. Bronx, N.Y. 10467 Tel. 212-881-5636 Allen Sport Shops 249 N. Ave. New Rochelle, N.Y. 10801 Tel. 914-235-3430	Many
Can be rough	Visibility 2′–30′; great fish: bass, blacks, bonito, pollack, blues	Spearing; photos (fish at dusk on an outgoing tide)	Shark, rough, boats, tides, fishermen's lines	The Dive Shop 110 W. Main St. Bay Shore, N.Y. 11706 Tel. 516-665-2526	Many
Calm	6′ visibility, fish	Spear and collect; visibility too poor for photos	None	Diver's Way 596 Sunrise Hwy. Bay Shore, N.Y. 11706 Tel. 516-665-7990 Central Skindivers 160-09 Jamaica Ave. Jamaica, N.Y. 11432 Tel. 212-739-5772 Richard's Aqualung Ctr. 233 W. 42 St. New York, N.Y. 10036 Tel. 212-947-5018 World Wide Divers, Inc. 155 E. 55 St. New York, N.Y. 10022 Tel. 212-688-2510 and others	Many

NEW YORK CONTINUED

PLACE	NO.	DESCRIPTION	ENTRY AND DISTANCE FROM SHORE	DEPTH	SNORKEL OR DIVE
LAKE GEORGE (there is diving in other interior lakes too)	30	A clear, long, narrow lake in the Adirondacks	From shore; boat is better	Varies; to 50'	Snorkel or dive
NIAGARA RIVER	31	A river containing fish, wrecks, artifacts	Boat; drift dive	25'	Dive
LAKE ERIE (Buffalo)	32	Lake with fish, wrecks, artifacts	Boat 5 min.	25'	Dive

CONNECTICUT   Water Temp.: 36° – 75°

Regulations: Check locally.

PLACE	NO.	DESCRIPTION	ENTRY AND DISTANCE FROM SHORE	DEPTH	SNORKEL OR DIVE
PENFIELD REEF (Westport) & BEDFORD'S PT. (Fairfield)	33	L.I. Sound with fish	Fairfield by boat 8 min.; Westport from shore 50 – 100 yds.	15' – 20'	Snorkel or dive
CANDLEWOOD LAKE	34	A lake with fish and marine vegetation	Beach At shore 100'	30' – 60'	Snorkel or dive
GUASAPAUG LAKE	35	A lake with fish	Beach 300'	25'	Snorkel or dive

94

SURF OR CALM	HIGH-LIGHTS	FISHING AND PHOTOS	DANGERS	DIVE FACILITY	ACCOMMODATIONS
Calm	Artifacts from Revolutionary War; perch, bass, carp	Photos	None	Check at Bolton Landing on Rte 9N	Many
Calm	Fish, wrecks, artifacts	Photos only; 8'–15' visibility	Current, boats	Niagara Scuba Sports 2048 Niagara St. Buffalo, N.Y. 14207 Tel. 716-875-6528	Many
Can be rough	Fish, wrecks, artifacts	Photos only; 0'–15' visibility	Boats		Many

Visibility: 8'–15'   **Best Season:** Summer

Calm	Rocks, fish (tautog and flounder), lobster	Spear; visibility (1'–10') too poor for photos	Current; dive at slack tide	Orbit Marine Sports Ctr. 3273 Fairfield Ave. Bridgeport, Conn. 06605 Tel. 203-333-3483 Noel Voroba	Many
Calm	Fish	Visibility 15'–20'	None	A-1 Diving Ctr. 863 Meridian Rd. Waterbury, Conn. 06705 Tel. 203-755-9772	Many
Calm	Fish, marine growth	Visibility to 25'	None	and others in East Haddam, Manchester, Plainville, Vernon, W. Haven, W. Hartford	Many

95

RHODE ISLAND

Water Temp.: 10°–70°

Regulations: Check locally for lobster-gathering regulations.

96

PLACE	NO.	DESCRIPTION	ENTRY AND DISTANCE FROM SHORE	DEPTH	SNORKEL OR DIVE
BLOCK ISLAND	36	An island S. of Rhode Island with lots of fish, sea life, and wrecks	Beach here; boat from mainland Varies; generally accessible	Varies	Snorkel or dive
PT. JUDITH	37	Long breakwater wall; 68° in summer with many fish	Beach or boat 45 min. 50'	18'	Snorkel or dive
EAST MATUNUCK	38	Long break wall	Beach or boat 45 min. 10'	12'	Snorkel or dive
FT. WEATHERALL (Jamestown)	39	Dive off a fort with artifacts	Beach At shore	23'	Snorkel or dive
KING'S BEACH	40	Off a beach with fish and marine life	Beach 100'	35'	Snorkel or dive
FORT ADAMS	41	An area near a fort	Beach 50'	35'	Snorkel or dive

Visibility: 10′–70′   **Best Season:** Summer

SURF OR CALM	HIGH-LIGHTS	FISHING AND PHOTOS	DANGERS	DIVE FACILITY	ACCOMMODATIONS
Calm to rough	Lots of fish, lobsters, crabs, scallops, eels, and wreck of *The Light-Burn;* other wrecks 10 mi. from here.	Fish or photos	None, but boats	See Rhode Island and Long Island. None on Block Island	Many at varied prices
Inside wall calm, outside rough	Fish of all kinds, shells, lobsters	Spearing and excellent photos	None	Aqua Sports Center 16 Douglas Pike Rte. #7 Smithfield, R.I. 02917 Tel. 401-231-1232 R.&D. Labbe	Many
Inside wall calm, outside rough	Fish, many shells, lobsters, marine life	Spearing and photos; good visibility	None	Viking Camera & Dive Shop 111 Bellevue Ave. Newport, R.I. 02840 Tel. 401-847-4179 and others	Many
Calm	Cannon balls, shell cases WWI, fish of all sorts	Spearing and photos; good visibility	None		Many
Calm except in strong s. wind	Fish, plant life	Spearing and photos	None		Many
Calm	Lots of fish, wooden wreck with artifacts	Spearfishing; photos, but visibility only 10′–15′	None	As above	As above

MASSACHUSETTS

Water Temp.: 33°–70°

Regulations: Check locally.

98

PLACE	NO.	DESCRIPTION	ENTRY AND DISTANCE FROM SHORE	DEPTH	SNORKEL OR DIVE
LONG POINT	42	An area off a beach with fish, wrecks, etc.	Beach or 15 min. by boat or 15 min. by oversand vehicle 20'–30' from beach	To 125'	Snorkel or dive
HERRING COVE BEACH	43	An area off a beach with fish and sea life	Beach or 30–40 min. by boat; 2–3 min. by oversand vehicle 30'–50'	15'–30'	Snorkel or dive
FOLLY COVE (Gloucester)	44	Folly Cove a beach and cove with lovely fish and marine life	Beach At shore	To 50'	Snorkel or dive
CATHEDRAL ROCKS (Rockport)	45	A calm area with beautiful fish and marine life	At shore	To 75'	Snorkel or dive
DEERFIELD RIVER	46	A river with fish and artifacts	Shore 50 yds.	30'	Snorkel or dive

Visibility: 0' – 20'   **Best Season:** Summer

SURF OR CALM	HIGH-LIGHTS	FISHING AND PHOTOS	DANGERS	DIVE FACILITY	ACCOMMODATIONS
Calm on harbor side	Fish, wrecks, sea clams, lobster, crabs, etc.	Spear certain species only; photos	None; watch small tide currents	Marine Specialties, Inc. 235 Commercial St. Provincetown, Mass. 02657 Tel. 617-487-1730	Many
Calm, but choppy to rough in late afternoon	Fish, sea clams, lobster, crabs, etc.	Spear certain species only; photos	None; watch for chop	New England Divers Tozer Rd. Beverly, Mass. 01915 Tel. 617-922-6951	Many
Calm, usually	Fish, rocks with kelp and seaweed, lobsters, hermit crabs, moon snails, shrimp, etc.	Spearfishing; photos	Barnacle-encrusted rocks	Guide: Fred Calhoun P.O. Box 291 Boston, Mass. 02117 and others	Many
Calm, usually	Fish, rocks, lobsters, kelp, weed, shells, shrimp	Spearfishing; photos	Barnacle-encrusted rocks	As above	Many
Calm	Fish, artifacts	Spearfishing; photos (visibility 20')	Boats	None	In area

NEW HAMPSHIRE

Water Temp.: 30°–60°

Regulations: Check locally.

100

PLACE	NO.	DESCRIPTION	ENTRY AND DISTANCE FROM SHORE	DEPTH	SNORKEL OR DIVE
SPOFFORD LAKE (Spofford, N.H.)	47	A lake with fish	Beach 100 yds.	40'	Snorkel or dive
LAKE SUNAPEE (N. of Great Island)	48	A lake with fish, rocks, old bottles, anchors, etc.	Boat ½ mi.	To 75'	Snorkel or dive
LAKE SUNAPEE GEORGE'S MILLS	49	A lake with fish	Beach At shore	To 35'	Snorkel or dive

MAINE

Water Temp.: 30°–60°

Regulations: Check locally.

ISLES OF SHOALS OFF KITTERY	50	A group of islands 10 mi. offshore with clear water, fish life	Boat	40'–50'	Dive

NOVA SCOTIA

Water Temp.: 40°–65°

Regulations: Check locally.

GUYON ISLAND WRECKS OFF CAPE BRETON ISLAND	51	3 wrecks	Boat 50-200 ft.	50'–70'	Dive
MAN-O'-WAR WRECK (Cape Breton Island)	52	Dive on French Man-O'-War, sunk July 1758	Boat Inside Louisbourg Harbor	30'	Dive

Visibility: 0′ – 20′ **Best Season:** Summer

SURF OR CALM	HIGH-LIGHTS	FISHING AND PHOTOS	DANGERS	DIVE FACILITY	ACCOMMODATIONS
Calm	Fish	Photos only (visibility 20′)	Boats	None	In area
Calm, unless a very windy day	Fish and artifacts. Slush diving when ice breaks up! Jump from one floe of ice to the next.	Photos only	None (Use a diver's flag)	Wayne and Judy La Porte Box 53 Rte. 103 Newbury, N.H. 03255 Tel. 603-763-5353	Many and varied; camping too
Calm	Fish, antique bottles	Photos (limited)	None (Use a diver's flag)	As above	As above

Visibility: 0′ – 20′ **Best Season:** Summer

Varies to rough	Many fish, scallops, artifacts	Spearfishing; photos	Cold, rough water	Charter from Cougar Sports 3470 Webster Ave. Bronx, N.Y. 10467 Tel. 212-881-5636 Northeast Divers 40 Broadway Bangor, Me. 00401 Tel. 207-947-4413	Many in State of Maine

Visibility: 50′ – 70′ **Best Season:** June, July, Aug, Sept, Oct. (You will need a wetsuit.)

Calm, but do not dive when rough	The wrecks of *The Afghan Prince* (1918) and *The Langleeridge;* fish	Fishing possible; good photos (50′–70′ visibility)	Urchins, jellyfish, wreck hazards; not serious if careful	Cape Breton, Ltd. P.O. Box 130 Louisbourg, N.S. BOA. 1M0 Tel. 902-733-2840 Dive shops with rental equipment in area	Fleur de Lis Motor Inn Louisbourg, N.S. Restaurant: The Lobster Kettle Louisbourg, N.S. Camping areas
Calm; waves 1′–2′	There are 5 man-o'-war wrecks in area in Louisbourg harbor	Photos only	Urchins, jellyfish, wreck hazards; not serious if careful		

ONTARIO

Water Temp.: 40° – 65°

Regulations: Check locally. In Ontario, spearfishing—or even having a spear within 100 yards of water—means confiscation of

102

PLACE	NO.	DESCRIPTION	ENTRY AND DISTANCE FROM SHORE	DEPTH	SNORKEL OR DIVE
ST. MARY'S	53	A stone quarry (there are several near here)	Lawn to concrete, deck to water At shore	Varies	Snorkel or dive
WAUBAUSHENE ISLANDS CHRISTIAN, HOPE AND BECKWITH (Best Jul. & Aug. but O.K. May – Oct.)	54	Bay diving, many shipwrecks	Beach at Hope Island; go by boat 7 mi.	25' – 35' (approx.)	Snorkel or dive
GEORGIAN BAY (Best Jul. & Aug. but O.K. May – Oct.)	55	Many shipwrecks	Boat	Varies	Dive
TOBERMORY (at end of Bruce Peninsula)	56	Diving on many shipwrecks	Boat	20' and deeper to 250'	Dive

BRITISH COLUMBIA

Water Temp.: 40° – 50° Summer

Regulations: Check locally.

PLACE	NO.	DESCRIPTION	ENTRY AND DISTANCE FROM SHORE	DEPTH	SNORKEL OR DIVE
WHYTE CLIFF PARK (Vancouver area)	57	Area with fish and marine life	At shore	30'	Snorkel or dive
SECHELT PENINSULA (Vancouver area)	58	Sea life and wrecks	Beach	30' – 100'	Snorkel or dive

Visibility: 50′–70′   **Best Season:** June, July, Aug, Sept, Oct. (You will need a wetsuit.)

all gear, your car, and possibly prison.

SURF OR CALM	HIGH-LIGHTS	FISHING AND PHOTOS	DANGERS	DIVE FACILITY	ACCOMMODATIONS
Calm	Fish life, old autos, pumping machinery	Photos in Apr. & May (visibility 40′)	None	Sub Mariners Diving Equipment 962 Wilson Ave. Toronto, Ontario Tel. 416-630-2590	Many in area
Calm	Shipwrecks, fish (perch, bass, chubb)	Photos	None	Must trail own boat to Cedar Point	As above
Calm	Shipwrecks, fish	Photos	Boats, jutting rocks	As above	As above
Varies	At least 50 wrecks, fish	Photos (visibility 20′–80′); Do not remove artifacts	Wreck hazards	Facilities in area. Dive boats operate out of town to wrecks.	Many accommodations on Bruce Peninsula and in Tobermory. Tents and campers. Parking.

Visibility: 30′–100′   **Best Season:** Summer

Calm	Fish, anemones, starfish, sea cucumbers, octopus	Photos only	Drop offs	Diving Locker 1398 Main St. N. Vancouver, B.C. Tel. 604-985-1616 or 2745 W. 4 St. Vancouver, B.C. Tel. 604-736-2681	Many in area
Calm, few currents	Fish, anemones, starfish, sea cucumbers, wrecks	Photos; spearfishing	Currents	As above	As above

MICHIGAN

Water Temp.: 35° – 60°

Regulations: Check locally

104

PLACE	NO.	DESCRIPTION	ENTRY AND DISTANCE FROM SHORE	DEPTH	SNORKEL OR DIVE
ST. CLAIR RIVER	59	Wreckage clutter	At shore	To 60′	Snorkel or dive
LAKE CHARLEVOIX	60	Shallow dive over a wreck	Beach or boat 3 min. ¼ mi.	30′	Dive
LAKE SUPERIOR: GRAND TRAVERSE BAY, WEST ARM	61	Fish, wrecks, artifacts	Beach 15 – 300 yds.	to 600′; dive 35′ – 60′	Snorkel or dive
LAKE SUPERIOR: MANITOU ISLANDS	62	Fish, wrecks, artifacts	Beach; but go by boat from mainland 15 mi. 10 – 20 yds.	35′ – 110′ – 400′	Snorkel or dive

OHIO

Water Temp.: 40° – 72°

Regulations: Check local regulations.

PLACE	NO.	DESCRIPTION	ENTRY AND DISTANCE FROM SHORE	DEPTH	SNORKEL OR DIVE
LAKE ERIE (Cleveland area)	63	A lake with wrecks, fish, artifacts	Beach Along shore	30′ – 60′	Dive (very limited for snorkeling)
WILDWOOD LAKE QUARRY, BASCAN QUARRY, many others	64	Quarries with fish, walls, sometimes car wrecks	At many beaches Along walls	30′ – 40′ for some	Dive (very limited for snorkeling)

Visibility: 5'–30'　　　　　　　　**Best Season:** Summer

SURF OR CALM	HIGH-LIGHTS	FISHING AND PHOTOS	DANGERS	DIVE FACILITY	ACCOMMODATIONS
8–10–knot current	Debris	Photos	Current obstructions	Scuba North, Inc. 13258 W. Bayshore Dr.	In area
Calm	Shallow wreck	Photos only	Wreck hazards	Traverse City, Mich. 49684 Tel. 616-947-2520 Underwater Specialists G4084 Corunna Rd. Flint, Mich. 48504 Tel. 313-732-0920	In area
Calm to rough	Fish, wrecks, artifacts	Spearing rough fish; photos	None	Spuds Underwater Outfitters 2579 Union Lake Rd.	Many in area
Calm to rough	Fish, wrecks, artifacts	Spearing rough fish; photos	None	Union Lake, Mich. 48085 Tel. 313-363-2224	Many in area

Visibility: 30'　　　　　　　　**Best Season:** Summer

Varies from calm to 8' waves	Fish, artifacts, wreck	Spearing; limited photos	Storms	For excellent details of Ohio diving write for "Diving in Ohio," $1, to following places: Sub-Aquatics Inc. 10333 Northfield Rd.	Many in area
Calm	Fish, walls, some marine life	Photos	None, but check locally	Northfield Village, Ohio 44067 or at 8855 East Broad St. R.R. 1, Reynoldsburg, Ohio 43068 or Buckeye Diving Schools 46 Warrensville Ctr. Road Bedford, Ohio 44146 Tel. 216-439-3677	Many in area

WISCONSIN

Water Temp.: Cold in north to 74° south

Regulations: Diver's flag required. Spearfishing license required. Check locally for strict regulations.

PLACE	NO.	DESCRIPTION	ENTRY AND DISTANCE FROM SHORE	DEPTH	SNORKEL OR DIVE
ST. MARTIN ISLE (off end of Door County between Green Bay and Lake Michigan)	65	3 shipwrecks (there are over 300 in this area, many unexplored). Door County refers to death's door for ships.	Boat 2 hrs. from docking area at Ellison Bay	100'	Dive
WHALEBACK SHOALS (off end of Door County between Green Bay and Lake Michigan)	66	3 wrecks (same area as #65) Many wrecks in area. Much quiet water too.	Boat 1 hr.	18'	Snorkel or dive
GREEN LAKE (90 mi. N.W. of Milwaukee) Try area at Sugarloaf or Norwegian Bay	67	Lovely lake, beautiful plants and algae; fish and interesting terrain	Shore 10'	10'–275'	Snorkel (Sugarloaf) or dive
RACINE QUARRY	68	An interesting parklike situation on an old quarry. Many activities, trenches, and areas to explore.	Beach 40'	55' varies	Snorkel or dive
DEVIL'S LAKE (N. of Madison)	69	A beautiful clear lake with glacial formations	At lake shore	35'–70'	Snorkel or dive
LAKE GENEVA (70 mi. N.W. of Chicago)	70	A lovely lake with summer temp. 75°. Dive deep at Blackpoint Shallow Narrows at Fontana	Beach, but must dive from boat June 15–Sept. 15	To 142'	Dive only
PEARL LAKE (Beloit)	71	A delightful lake for diving that is an old sand quarry	Beach 20'	To 40' and 90' N. of clubhouse	Snorkel or dive

Visibility: Best in April; 15'–30'   **Best Season:** Summer

SURF OR CALM	HIGH-LIGHTS	FISHING AND PHOTOS	DANGERS	DIVE FACILITY	ACCOMMODATIONS
Varies; waves usually over 6'	Wrecks, artifacts, fish	Spearing rough, fish; best visibility in April	Open water, can be high waves	On the Rocks Rt. 1 Box 164 Ellison Bay, Wisc. 54210 (all year) Ice diving in winter	Lodge: On the Rocks Rt. 1 Box 164 Ellison Bay, Wisc. 54210
Variable waves; can be 6'	Wrecks, artifacts, fish	Spearing rough, fish; photos	Open water	As above	As above
Calm to choppy	Fish (carp, trout, etc.), old bottles	Visibility good for photos; spearing rough, fish	None	In town of Green Lake. Also, Wisconsin State Divers Underwater World 122 W. B'way Waukesha, Wisc. 53186 Tel. 608-547-1115	In area
Calm	Fish, cars, junk, heavy equipment	Photos (Visibility 10'–20' summer)	None	Ice Diving Ski & Dive 16005 S. Harlem Av. Tinley Park, Ill. 60477 Tel. 312-429-0822	In area
Calm	Fish (bass, trout)	Photos only	None	Airin Baraboo R.J. Boyd Scubalab 5900 Anthony Pl. Madison, Wisc. 53716	In area
Calm	Fish, wrecks, old bottles from .870s	Spear with license; photos	Boats	Petrie Scuba Lab 1406 Emil St. Madison, Wisc. 53713 Tel. 608-257-7811	In area
Calm	Fish of all sorts	Photos	None	Fontana Army/Navy 251 State St. Madison, Wisc. 53703 Tel. 608-257-5043	In area

ILLINOIS

Water Temp.: Cold winter to 52° summer

Regulations: Check locally.

108

PLACE	NO.	DESCRIPTION	ENTRY AND DISTANCE FROM SHORE	DEPTH	SNORKEL OR DIVE
DEVIL'S KITCHEN (within 20 mi. of Carbondale)	72	A dive area with various fish. (Also many strip mines in area)	Beach At shore	Varies, shallow to deep	Snorkel or dive

MISSOURI

Water Temp.: Cold winter to 52° summer

Regulations: Check locally.

PLACE	NO.	DESCRIPTION	ENTRY AND DISTANCE FROM SHORE	DEPTH	SNORKEL OR DIVE
CIRCLE MINE AT ORANGO NEAR JOPLIN (Expert)	73	An abandoned mine 9 square blocks, 300' deep	Shore down a rocky incline	Varies to 300'	Dive
TABLE ROCK LAKE (Indian Point)	74	A man-made lake 58 mi. long with 857-mi. shoreline. With fish and artifacts.	Beaches At shore	15' – 20'	Snorkel or dive

Visibility: 10′ – 20′   **Best Season:** Summer

SURF OR CALM	HIGH-LIGHTS	FISHING AND PHOTOS	DANGERS	DIVE FACILITY	ACCOMMODATIONS
Calm	Fish, trees, plant life, turtles	Spearing rough, fish; photos	Deep water	Watershed Dive Shop 1028 E. Walnut Carbondale, Ill. 62901 Undersea Diving Supply 2942 W. 95 St. Evergreen Park, Ill. 60642 Tel. 312-425-0822 and others in Aurora, Chicago, Elmwood Park, etc.	In area

Visibility: 10′ – 20′   **Best Season:** Summer

Calm	Tunnels, icy water	Neither	Underground drifts, crumbling ledges	Not known	In area
Calm	Fish, wreck, crayfish, arrow heads	Spearing and photos	Fishing lines, boats	John the Diver, Inc. S.R. 1 Box 459 Branson, Mo. 65616 Tel. 417-338-2224 West End Diving Ctrs, Inc., 11004 Manchester Rd. St. Louis, Mo. 63122 Tel. 314-822-3005	In area

ARKANSAS
Water Temp.: Cold winter to 52° summer

Regulations: Check locally.

110

PLACE	NO.	DESCRIPTION	ENTRY AND DISTANCE FROM SHORE	DEPTH	SNORKEL OR DIVE
HEBER SPRINGS BOAT DOCK (Bluffs opposite)	75	Area at foot of bluff with fish	Boat 5 min.	To 200'	Snorkel or dive
PETER CREEK	76	A creek with fish	Boat At shore	10'–250'	Snorkel or dive

LOUISIANA
Water Temp.: 39°–70°

Regulations: Check locally.

PLACE	NO.	DESCRIPTION	ENTRY AND DISTANCE FROM SHORE	DEPTH	SNORKEL OR DIVE
OFF-SHORE OIL RIGS (Expert)	77	The wide area off Louisiana where oil rigs' pumps attract huge fish.	Boat 50 mi. out, 5 hrs; can vary 13–100 mi.	300'+	Dive
FLOWER GARDENS IN GULF OF MEXICO (Summer only)	78	Beautiful reefs with fish. East and west	Boat 110 mi.	Tops of reefs 35'–80'	Dive

MINNESOTA
Water Temp.: 39°–70°

Regulations: Check locally.

PLACE	NO.	DESCRIPTION	ENTRY AND DISTANCE FROM SHORE	DEPTH	SNORKEL OR DIVE
SERPENT LAKE (Crosby, Minn.)	79	A lake with much to explore	Beach At shore	10'–95'	Snorkel or dive
GULL LAKE CHAIN (Brainerd)	80	Lakes with much to explore. Several calm bays	Beach At shore	10'–105'	Snorkel or dive

Visibility: 10′–20′   **Best Season:** Summer

SURF OR CALM	HIGH-LIGHTS	FISHING AND PHOTOS	DANGERS	DIVE FACILITY	ACCOMMODATIONS
Calm	Fish, rocks	Spearfishing and photos	None	Heber Springs Boat Dock P.O. Box 148 Heber Springs, Ark. 72543	In area
Calm	Rocks, bluffs, fish	Spearfishing and photos	None	See above	In area

Visibility: 5′–30′   **Best Season:** Summer

SURF OR CALM	HIGH-LIGHTS	FISHING AND PHOTOS	DANGERS	DIVE FACILITY	ACCOMMODATIONS
Calm or rough	Many large fish (rays, snapper, amberjack, angels)	Spearfishing	Boats, currents, silt, jellyfish	Temento's A.P. Auto Supply 435 Sala Ave. Westwego, La. 70094 Tel. 504-341-1031	Throughout La.
Calm or rough	Manta rays, brain and star coral, shells, huge tame fish	Do not spear. Photos	Shark, but do not seem dangerous if not spearing	For this trip see Louis Shaefer Aqua Safaris Box 1096 Freeport, Texas 77541	In Texas

Visibility: 5′–30′   **Best Season:** Summer

SURF OR CALM	HIGH-LIGHTS	FISHING AND PHOTOS	DANGERS	DIVE FACILITY	ACCOMMODATIONS
Calm, but can vary to 1′ waves	Fish, artifacts, drop-offs	Spearfishing; photos	None	Sports Craft Inc. Rte. 7 Brainerd, Minn. 56401 Tel. 218-829-1901	In area
Bays calm. Lake can have 2′–3′ waves.	Fish, anchors, equipment, old relics	Spearfishing; photos	Boats	As above	In area

TEXAS

Water Temp.: 60°–80°

Regulations: Check locally.

PLACE	NO.	DESCRIPTION	ENTRY AND DISTANCE FROM SHORE	DEPTH	SNORKEL OR DIVE
POSSUM KINGDOM LAKE AT MORRIS SHEPPARD DAM (off State Hwy 16, 100 mi. W. of Dallas)	81	A lake with forests and fish (dam and Buffalo Creek best). Very popular	Boat few min. from scuba pt.	100'	Dive
LAKE TRAVIS	82	A man-made lake 65 mi. long with caves and fish	Boat	To 225'	Dive
JACOB'S WELL (Expert cave) 40 mi. from Austin (Check to see if still available at dive facility)	83	A well with clear water and 3 chambers	At shore	65'	Dive
CANYON LAKE AUSTIN (60 mi. S. of Lake Travis)	84	Small lake, man-made; 80-mi. shore; caves, fish	Boat Few min.	193'	Dive

COLORADO

Water Temp.: 47°

Regulations: Check locally.

PLACE	NO.	DESCRIPTION	ENTRY AND DISTANCE FROM SHORE	DEPTH	SNORKEL OR DIVE
TWIN LAKES GRAND LAKE (near Evergreen, center of 3 diving spots)	85	A lake with some fish (cold)	Beach at Grand Lake 10'	Varies	Dive or snorkel at Grand Lake
JEFFERSON RESERVOIR	86	A deep, cold reservoir with trout	Beach on N. end 10'	200'	Snorkel or dive

Visibility: Varies   **Best Season:** Spring, Summer, Fall.

SURF OR CALM	HIGH-LIGHTS	FISHING AND PHOTOS	DANGERS	DIVE FACILITY	ACCOMMODATIONS
Calm	In Apr. buffalo fish make annual run; other fish: gar, carp	Spearfishing	None	Texas Skindiving Schools 4320 N. Lamar Austin, Texas 78756 Tel. 512-453-7676	In area
Calm	Fish, caves, ledges	Spearfishing	None	and others in N. Dallas, Houston, Arlington, Beaumont	In Austin
Calm	Explore 2 of 3 chambers	Photos	3 chambers dangerous	As above	As above
Calm	Fish, caves, canyons, submerged forests	Spearfishing	None	As above	Launching, camping, and trailer. In Canyon City are motels, etc.

Visibility: Varies   **Best Season:** Spring, Summer, Fall

Calm but wind storms can cause swells	Sand, rocks, trout	Spearfishing; photos	Cold (wet suits and hot water suits)	O. Gaines Hill Aquatic Research & Diving Co. R.R. 3 Box 89A Evergreen, Colo. 80439 Tel. 303-674-4449 Tel. 303-237-0322	In area
Calm, but wind storms can cause swells	Trout, lures, sand, rocks	Spearfishing; photos with strobe (visibility can be good)	Cold (wet suit or hot-water suit)	Same as #85	In area

UTAH

Water Temp.: 60º–80º

Regulations: Check locally.

PLACE	NO.	DESCRIPTION	ENTRY AND DISTANCE FROM SHORE	DEPTH	SNORKEL OR DIVE
LAKE POWELL (best in Sept.)	87	160-mi.-long lake, man-made. Can be 80º in summer. Magnificent underwater scenery of cliffs and caves	Boat	Varies	Dive

OREGON

Water Temp.: 48º–60º

Regulations: Check locally.

PORT ORFORD	88	Ocean snorkeling, diving from a beach.	Beach or 30–45 min. by boat from Coos Bay 10'	25'–150'	Snorkel or dive
COOS BAY	89	A bay near the ocean	Beach 10'	To 60'	Snorkel or dive
WINCHESTER BAY	90	A bay near the ocean with a jetty	Beach 10'	To 60'	Snorkel or dive

WASHINGTON

Water Temp.: 43º–50º

Regulations: Check locally.

GALLOPING GERTIE BRIDGE (Tacoma Narrows Bridge)	91	Dive in the area where Tacoma Narrows Bridge collapsed. Rich in marine life. Night diving	Enter water ½ mi. s. of bridge and drift to bridge on ebb tide or boat At shore	To 120'	Snorkel or dive
EDMUNDS CITY UNDERWATER PARK (13 mi. N. on U.S. Hwy 5. Go W. on 104.)	92	An area where you can see marine life, fish, octopus	Beach 300' at mid-tide	10'–40'	Snorkel or dive

Visibility: Varies   **Best Season:** Spring, Summer, Fall

SURF OR CALM	HIGH-LIGHTS	FISHING AND PHOTOS	DANGERS	DIVE FACILITY	ACCOMMODATIONS
Calm	Many fish (carp, bass, trout), grottos, caverns, caves	Spearing; photos (visibility 25'–30')	None	Tank Refills Canyon Tours, Inc. Box 1597 Page, Ariz. 86040 Tel. 602-645-2433	Very few. There are marinas and trailer parks and boat launching ramps. Also boat rentals

Visibility: 3'–70'   **Best Season:** Spring, Summer, Fall

SURF OR CALM	HIGH-LIGHTS	FISHING AND PHOTOS	DANGERS	DIVE FACILITY	ACCOMMODATIONS
Calm in summer, rough in winter	Fish, anchors, wrecks, crabs	Spearfishing; photos	None (lots of urchins)	Northwest Divers Supply Inc. 852 S. B'way Coos Bay, Ore. 97420 Tel. 503-267-3723 Bill McCarty	In area
Calm in summer, rough in winter	Fish, anchors, wrecks, crabs	Spearfishing; photos	None		In area
Calm in summer, rough in winter	Fish, anchors, wrecks, crabs	Spearfishing; photos	None, but watch current at turn of tide	As above	In area

Visibility: 25'   **Best Season:** Summer

SURF OR CALM	HIGH-LIGHTS	FISHING AND PHOTOS	DANGERS	DIVE FACILITY	ACCOMMODATIONS
Can chop and have current	Plant and animal life, big fish, octopus, crabs, starfish	Spearfishing; photos; octopus wrestling	Currents	New England Divers 11009 First Ave. So. Seattle, Wash. 98116 Tel. 206-CH6-8156	In area
Calm	Wreck, rockfish, cabezon, lingcod, octopus	Photos only	Ferry boats; keep away from landing S. of wreck.	As above	In area

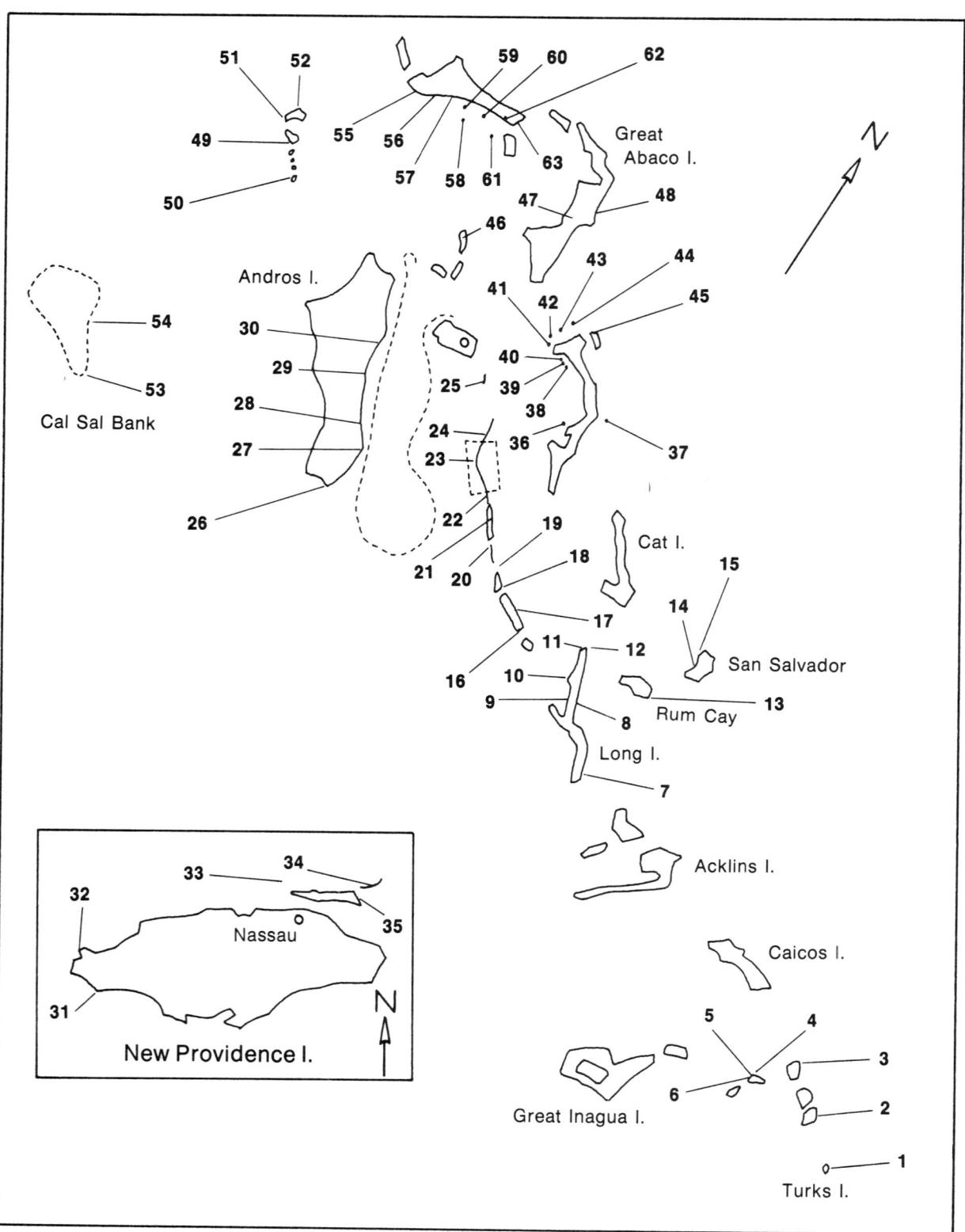

51 52
49
50
55 56 57 58 61 63
59 60 62
Great Abaco I.
47 48
46
43 44
41 42 45
Andros I.
54
30
29
25
40
39
38
36 37
28
27
24
23
26
22
21 20 19
18
Cat I.
17
16 11 12
10
9 8
15
14
San Salvador
13
Rum Cay
Long I.
7
Acklins I.
Caicos I.
5 4
3
6
2
Great Inagua I.
1
Turks I.

33 34
32 35
Nassau
31
New Providence I.

Cal Sal Bank
53

THE BRITISH WEST INDIES AND BAHAMA ISLANDS

Turtles are found under and on top of the water. (Lee Turcotte/Atlantis Safaris)

The Bahamas is such a large area—it comprises 700 islands—that almost no matter what kind of diving or snorkeling vacation you are after, the chances are you will find it here. The island atmospheres range from the noisy, exciting night life of Nassau and the gambling casinos on Grand Bahama to the exotic, nearly deserted solitude of the Exuma chain. There are plush hotels and deserted beaches with no facilities except the boat that brought you there. There are endless lovely reefs to explore, fish to watch and photograph, shells (preferably no longer alive) to gather, wrecks to discover and wrecks that have been discov-

ered, caves, blue holes, turtles basking on the surface of the water, and manta rays dancing and turning under the surface.

The Underwater Explorer's Club on Grand Bahama Island is one of the most complete facilities in the world, and it even includes a dive museum and a two-storied training pool. Anyone can become a member upon arrival and participate in the many daily reef trips run by the club. (See Bahamas Chart for details.)

While the Bahamas offer many fine resort areas and hotels, the visitors interested in maximum underwater experiences would probably most enjoy a tour of some part of the Bahamas by boat—using the boat as a headquarters, sleeping and eating on it and exploring many reefs and areas of enormous interest not accessible from any one island. From many of the hotels there is not particularly good beach snorkeling. (See the Bahamas Chart dive facilities for boat charters—or inquire at the marinas of the larger islands.)

For the wreck-diving enthusiast the Bahamas are superb. There are over 1,600 wrecks, only about 25 percent of them currently discovered. All kinds of treasure from junk to rare coins have been found here, some of it by vacationing divers.

Certain kinds of winds can cause rough water. But usually a rough area on one side of an island indicates a calm on the other, so if you are flexible about exactly what you are willing to explore on a given day, you should get in plenty of diving and snorkeling.

In addition to currents, there is only one other major hazard in the Bahamas—the reefs themselves. There is a reason for the 1,600 shipwrecks. Make sure you are sailing with an experienced captain, and don't attempt to sail the

Divers examine one of the many spectacular coral reefs of the Bahamas.
(Bahamas Tourist News Bureau)

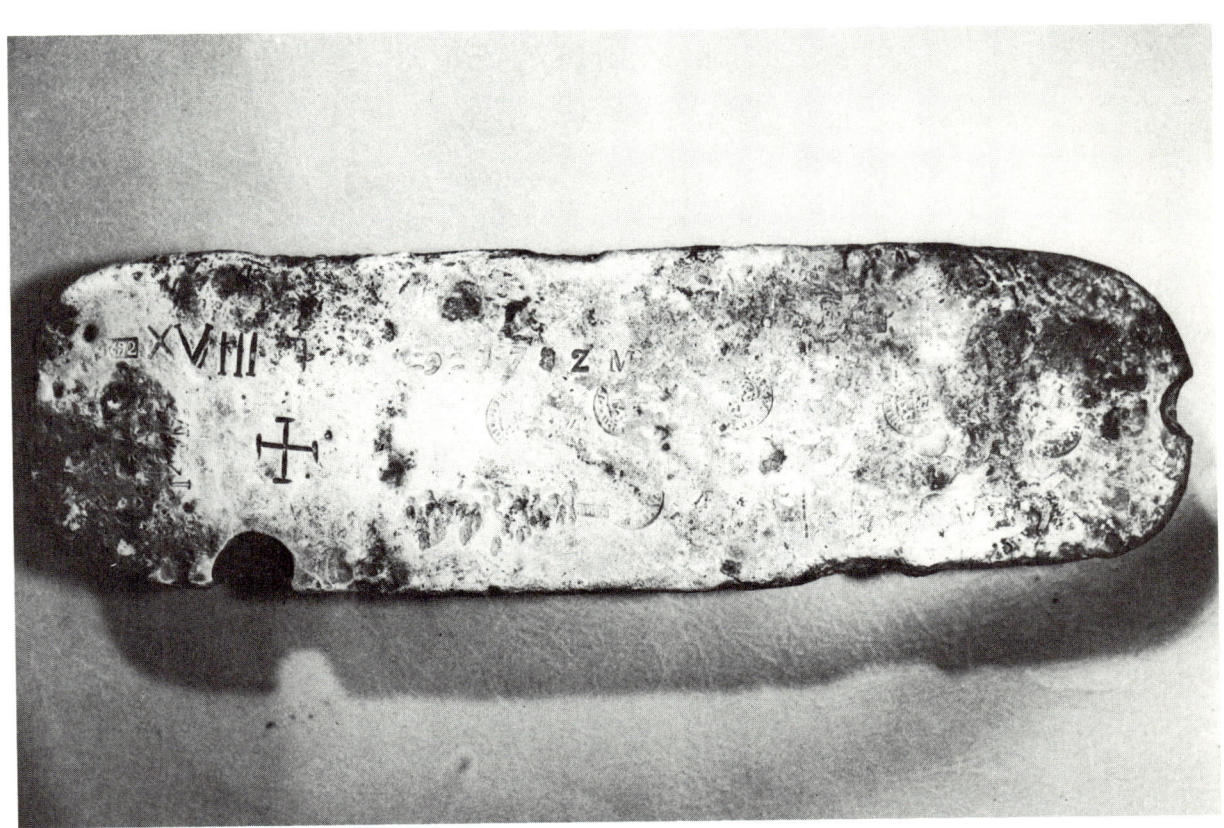

A $25,000 silver bar taken from the wreck of a Spanish galleon off Great Abaco Island in the Bahamas in January 1952. Markings indicate the bar was intended for Philip, King of Spain in the seventeenth century. (Bahamas News Bureau)

area yourself unless you have a good working knowledge of the shallow reefs of each area.

Considering the magnificent wall at Andros Island, the many thrilling spots of the Exuma Cays, and the excellent facilities on many of the islands, as well as the range of deep and shallow skin and scuba diving available, the Bahamas is an area well worth exploring.

NOTE ON THE BAHAMAS CHART:
The first few listings on the Bahamas Chart are part of the British West Indies, and therefore not governed by Bahamian spearfishing laws. The Cay Sal Banks, which are part of the Bahamas, are generally reached by boat from the Florida Keys. (See next section.)

The British West Indies and

The British West Indies

Water Temp.: Averages 78°

Regulations: Spearfishing permitted in Turks and Caicos (British West Indies). In rest of Bahamas: Spearfishing is illegal with

PLACE	NO.	DESCRIPTION	ENTRY AND DISTANCE FROM SHORE	DEPTH	SNORKEL OR DIVE
GRAND TURK ISLAND	1	Drop-off length of W. side of island. 30–40 good locations	From shore	0′–25′– 3600′ on west	Snorkel or dive
SALT CAY	2	Reef off N.W. point	From shore	Shallow	Snorkel
SOUTH CAICOS	3	A beach and excursions to Belle Sound Coral Gardens at the Admiral's Reef (500 yards from hotel)	Beach or boat At shore	Varies	Snorkel or dive
PROVIDENCIALES	4	17-mi. barrier reef	Boat	35′–40′– 100′	Snorkel or dive
PROVIDENCIALES WRECK	5	A wreck off N.W. point	Boat	5′–10′	Snorkel or dive
PROVIDENCIALES DROP-OFF	6	W. side of island, 10 mi. from hotel, a drop off	Boat	45′–6000′	Dive

Bahama Islands

Visibility: 100' – 200'   **Best Season:** May to August, summer best

scuba. Check specific local laws, or Ministry of Trade & Industry, Dept. Agriculture & Fisheries, P.O. Box 28, Nassau, Bahamas

SURF OR CALM	HIGH-LIGHTS	FISHING AND PHOTOS	DANGERS	DIVE FACILITY	ACCOMMODATIONS
Calm	E. side of island is Barrier Reef. Drop-off ½ mile out. Caves, fish, wreck, lobsters	Photos (visibility 150' – 200'), spear-fishing	Urchins, shark; (but only in a limited area off north point)	Phil Pruss Pepcor Ltd. Underwater Adventures Grand Turk, B.W.I. Underwater Research, Ltd. Grand Turk, B.W.I.	Salt Raker Inn P.O. Box 1, Grand Turk, B.W.I. Hotel Kittina, P.O. Box 42, Grand Turk, B.W.I. Turk's Head Inn P.O. Box 58 Grand Turk, B.W.I.
Calm	Reef fish	Photos; spear-fishing	None	None	Mt. Pleasant Guest House (small)
Calm	Dive for conch and lobster	Photos; spear-fishing	None	Scuba available; dive instructor at hotel	The Admiral's Arms (small)
Calm	Fans, coral, sponge, many fish	Photos; spear-fishing	None	Provo Turtle Divers, Ltd. Art Pickering	For accommodations write: Donna Wolfe Third Turtle Inn 2633 Lantana Road Lantana, Fl. 33640
Calm	Wreck of British man-o'-war	Photos; spearfishing	None	As above	As above
Calm	Friendly fish, sponges, fans, corals, black coral	Photos	For experienced divers only. Narcosis	Dive Tours: Gardner Young Underwater Tours, Ltd. P.O. Box 5693 Nassau, Bahamas	As above

BAHAMA ISLANDS

Water Temp.: Averages 78°

Regulations: See above.

122

PLACE	NO.	DESCRIPTION	ENTRY AND DISTANCE FROM SHORE	DEPTH	SNORKEL OR DIVE
LONG ISLAND Wreck of German freighter near Guana Cay	7	Wreck of World War I freighter *Blanchevar*	Beach 200 yds.	25'	Snorkel or dive
LONG ISLAND House Reef "Poseidon's Point"	8	Marvelous protected reef	From shore	To 45'	Snorkel or dive
LONG ISLAND Barracuda Heads	9	Coral caves and channels	Boat	55'	Dive
LONG ISLAND Grouper Village	10	Large coral heads and tame grouper that can be hand-fed	Boat	40'–80'	Dive
LONG ISLAND schooner wreck ¼ mi. n. of Grouper Village	11	Wreck dive; ship was sunk to make artificial reef	Boat ¼ mi.	65'	Dive
LONG ISLAND WALL (Experts only) 1 mi. from Cape Santa Maria Beach	12	Spectacular drop-off	Boat 5 mi.	100' & down to 1200' or 2000'	Dive
RUM CAY WRECK (S.E. end of island)	13	Wreck of Battleship *Conqueror*	Boat from Stella Maris on Long Island 3–4 hrs. ¼ mi. off Rum Key	30'–40'	Dive

Visibility: 100′–200′   **Best Season**: May to August

SURF OR CALM	HIGH-LIGHTS	FISHING AND PHOTOS	DANGERS	DIVE FACILITY	ACCOMMODATIONS
Calm	Shipwreck	Photos	None	Toni Rankin at Stella Maris Inn	Long Island has a well-known resort: Stella Maris Inn Box 105, Stella Maris Post Office Long Island, Bahamas att: Georg and Gaby Friese
Calm	Marvelous corals	Photos	None	As above	As above
Calm	Channels, tropical fish, barracuda, caves with marine life	Photos	None	As above	As above
Calm	Corals 60′–80′ diameter; tame grouper, reef fish, huge snapper	Photos	None	As above	As above
Calm	36′ wooden hull; 2-masted schooner wreck; great marine life	Great for photos	None	As above	As above
Calm or chop; depends on winds	Verticle cliff of living corals; sponges, fish, marine life	Excellent visibility for photos	Shark, but don't seem dangerous	As above	As above
Swells	Cannonballs, winches, wreck debris, corals, fish	Photos	None	At Stella Maris or charter tour	As above

BAHAMA ISLANDS CONTINUED

PLACE	NO.	DESCRIPTION	ENTRY AND DISTANCE FROM SHORE	DEPTH	SNORKEL OR DIVE
SAN SALVADOR Drop-off (Cockburn Town)	14	Lovely prolific barrier reef	Beach, but boat to reef ½ mi.	20' – 35'	Snorkel or dive
SAN SALVADOR Grouper Gully	15	Live, lovely coral reef	Beach near shore	25' – 140'	Snorkel or dive
STOCKING ISLAND Off Exuma	16	Reef right off lovely white beaches	Boats leave Great Exuma several times a day for Stocking Island At shore	Varies	Great snorkeling between Great Exuma and Stocking Island
LILY CAY (Off Exuma)	17	Coral reef	Boat	45'	Easy snorkeling N. of Lily Cay and dive
GUANA CAY (off Exuma)	18	Coral reef	Boat	20' – 30'	Snorkel or dive
HAUNTED ARCH on inside of rudder-cut	19	A small island with an 8' arch that cuts through the island	Boat Under shore	3'	Dive
LITTLE FARMER'S CAY	20	Coral reefs	Boat	20' – 30'	Snorkel or dive
THUNDERBALL GROTTO AT STANIEL CAY	21	Giant vaulted cave. 7 entrances. *Thunderball* was partly filmed here.	Boat Near a small island	Varies	Snorkel into cave at low tide.

SURF OR CALM	HIGH-LIGHTS	FISHING AND PHOTOS	DANGERS	DIVE FACILITY	ACCOMMODATIONS
Calm	Coral, pinnacle, black coral, great fish	Photos	None	At Riding Rock Inn	Riding Rock Inn Resort San Salvador, Bahamas Donald and Anna Garbutt
Calm	Staghorn coral, fish, esp. grouper	Photos	None	As above	As above
Calm	Corals, sand flats, sponges, fish, lobsters, Blue Hole (a long tunnel mystery cave)	Photos	None, but tides	At Out Island Inn Georgetown Exumas or charter Hotel Peace and Plenty Box 55 Georgetown, Exuma Bahamas Norman's Cay Club P.O. Box N. 8164 Nassau, Bahamas (on Norman's Cay)	Many accommodations on Great Exuma Out Island Inn Georgetown, Exuma att: Paul Feyer Phone 215 or charter Gardner Young Underwater Tours, Ltd. P.O. Box 5693 Nassau, Bahamas Hotel Peace and Plenty Box 55 Georgetown, Great Exuma, Bahamas
Calm	Coral heads, 35'–45'; lobsters, fissures, channels	Photos	None		
Calm	Great forests of elk and stag-horn, corals, lobsters	Photos	None		
Surge	Weird moaning sound	Neither	Tides, huge surge back and forth. Do not go too near.	Boat	None
Calm	Elkhorn, corals	Photos	Tides	Boat	None
Calm but current at tide changes	Soft blue glow in cave, sponges, corals, brilliant colors, black coral, fish	Photos	Watch current at tide changes.	At Staniel Cay, Yacht Club	At Yacht Club Staniel Cay Exuma, Bahamas or by marine radio telephone c/o Motor Vessal "Mizpah" via Miami or Nassau

BAHAMA ISLANDS CONTINUED

PLACE	NO.	DESCRIPTION	ENTRY AND DISTANCE FROM SHORE	DEPTH	SNORKEL OR DIVE
CONCH CUT	22	S. boundary of land and sea park	Boat	Varies	Snorkel or dive
EXUMA CAYS LAND AND SEA PARK	23	Lovely bird and marine sanctuary	Boat	2' and down	Snorkel or dive
WAX CAY CUT	24	N. boundary of land and sea park	Boat	Varies	Snorkel or dive
1560 BALLAST STONE WRECK	25	At n. end Highborne Cay, remains of wreck	Boat	30'	Snorkel or dive
ANDROS PATCH REEFS (75 mi. S. of Andros)	26	Unchartered coral reef	Boat	35' – 40'	Snorkel or dive
ANDROS the wall off Small Hope Bay	27	One of the world's great drop-off reefs	Boat 1 mi.	70' – 165' – 5000'	Dive
ANDROS REEF	28	The reef at the top of the wall	Boat 2 miles from small Hope Bay dock. 1 mile from shore	120' – 165'	Dive
ANDROS Love Hill Channel	29	Shallow coral reef	Boat 10 min. 1 mi.	12' – 15'	Snorkel or dive
ANDROS Wreck of the Cutty Sark	30	Topsail schooner wreck	Boat 1 mi.	Shallow, partly above water	Excellent snorkeling

SURF OR CALM	HIGH-LIGHTS	FISHING AND PHOTOS	DANGERS	DIVE FACILITY	ACCOMMODATIONS
Calm	Reefs, fish, grouper, lobster, conch	Photos	Tide rip on oceanside	Boat only Boat charters to Exumas: Gardner Young Underwater Tours P.O. Box 5693 Nassau, Bahamas Tel: 2-3285 & other charters	None
Calm	Sea gardens, drop-offs, corals, fish	Photos	None		None
Calm	Reefs, fish, grouper, lobster, conch	Photos	Tide rip on oceanside	As above	None
Current	45' long pile of ballast stones	Photos	Current, tide	As above	None
Calm	Reef fish, angel fish, huge ocean fish, crabs, turtles, corals	Photos	Shark	Boat	None. See Lance Lenart Miami Beach, Fl.
Calm	Reef at top of wall incredibly beautiful. Fantanstic sponges, corals, fish	Photos	For the experienced only; narcosis; shark	At Small Hope Bay Lodge Andros Beach Hotel Club Caribee (Andros Reef Inn) Andros Aqua Center N. Andros Island c/o 2685 E. Silver Springs Blvd. Ocala, Fl. 32670	Small Hope Bay Lodge P.O. Box 1131 Nassau, Bahamas Andros Beach Club boats, charters San Andros Inn and Tennis Club San Andros, Andros, Bahamas or at 2701 East Sunrise Blvd. Fort Lauderdale, Fl. 33304 Tel. 305-563-6476
Calm	Living corals of fantastic colors	Photos	None		
Calm	Coral, fish, sand channels, beautiful colors	Photos	None		
Calm	Wreck to climb on staghorn coral gardens	Photos	None	As above	As above

BAHAMA ISLANDS CONTINUED

PLACE	NO.	DESCRIPTION	ENTRY AND DISTANCE FROM SHORE	DEPTH	SNORKEL OR DIVE
NEW PROVIDENCE ISLAND Goulding Cay and Drop off	31	Coral reefs and drop-off (Site of original *20,000 Leagues Under the Sea* filmed in 1917 and redone by Disney)	Boat 10 min. from Lyford Cay marina	10'—60' Drop-off to 1000'	Snorkel or dive
NEW PROVIDENCE ISLAND Lyford Cay Drop-off and Black Coral Forests	32	Verticle drop-off in un-usually blue water	35 min. by boat	40'—80'—1800'	Dive
WRECK OF THE MAHONEY (Between N. end Salt Cay and E. end Paradise Island)	33	Shipwreck	Boat	20'—30'	Snorkel or dive
ROSE ISLAND	34	Coral reef, fish, shells	Boat 40 min.	To 30' at shore and 70' on outer ledge	Snorkel or dive
ROSE ISLAND (S. side Sea Gardens)	35	Pleasant reef	Boat	20'	Snorkel or dive
SIX SHILLING CAYS (20 mi. N. of Exumas)	36	Coral reefs; many civil war blockade runners wrecked here.	Boat	To 40'	Snorkel or dive
ELEUTHERA Boiling Hole	37	In 20'—25' of water with a sand bottom is Hole (40' long, 20' wide, 15' deep).	Boat	20' to sand; 15' more to bottom of Hole	Snorkel over, but must dive to go in
ELEUTHERA Pimlico Islands Junkyard	38	Coral reef	Boat	55'—85'	Dive

SURF OR CALM	HIGH-LIGHTS	FISHING AND PHOTOS	DANGERS	DIVE FACILITY	ACCOMMODATIONS
Calm	Coral heads, elk-horn, staghorn, rose, lettuce, fish, black coral at drop-off	Photos	None (Narcosis)	Gardner Young Underwater Tours, Ltd. P.O. Box 5693 Yacht Haven Nassau, Bahamas Tel. 2-3285	Many and varied
Calm	Sponge, black coral, large fish	Photos	Shark (rarely)	As above	As above
Calm	Ship was built about 1880. Sunk while being towed, after partially sinking at dock	Photos	None (current at ebb tide)	As above	As above
Calm	Fish, corals, shells (conch, helmet, tulips, olive shells)	Photos	None	As above	As above
Calm	Sea fans, grouper, unusual urchins	Photos	None	As above	As above
Calm	Wreck, anchors, coral, fish	Photos	Strong tides	By boat	None
Calm, but now and then sulphur water boils out of Hole.	Mobs of fish; reef fish, snapper, grouper, nurse shark, huge amberjack	Not Known	Shark up to 12′ but do not seem dangerous	Current Club N. Eleuthera Island, Bahamas Rogues Cove Eleuthera	Current Club N. Eleuthera Island, Bahamas contact: Bay Travel, Inc. 2435 East Coast Highway Corona Del Mar, Ca. 92625 Tel. 714-675-4320
Calm	Corals, fans, sponges, fish	Photos	None	Arawak Cove Club Box 5155 Gregory Town Eleuthera, Bahamas	

BAHAMA ISLANDS CONTINUED

130

PLACE	NO.	DESCRIPTION	ENTRY AND DISTANCE FROM SHORE	DEPTH	SNORKEL OR DIVE
ELEUTHERA Current Rock, Split Reef, Coral Head	39	Rock with a steel tower and navigation light. High coral heads around the rock, one with a deep split	Boat 20 min.	50′	Dive
ELEUTHERA (W. of Current Rock) Flower garden	40	Large coral heads to within 15′ of surface	Boat	60′	Snorkel or dive
CURRENT CUT (Experts only) Between N. Eleuthera and Current Island	41	Narrow deep water pass	Boat 200 yds. hotel dock	65′	Scuba, drift through on fast flow of water
SPANISH WELLS (Experts only)	42	Coral reefs	Boat	120′ – 200′	Dive
CIVIL WAR TRAIN WRECK (18 mi. from Current Club)	43	Wrecked train on coral heads; barge carrying narrow-gauge locomotive and train to Cuba wrecked in 1850s.	Boat	30′	Dive
EGG ISLAND REEF	44	Huge coral heads rising from bottom to within a few feet of surface. Freighter wreck	Boat	10′ – 60′	Snorkel or dive
HARBOUR ISLAND (small island off N.E. coast Eleuthera)	45	Can snorkel off main island or go to other nearby described areas	Boat	Varies	Snorkel or dive

SURF OR CALM	HIGH-LIGHTS	FISHING AND PHOTOS	DANGERS	DIVE FACILITY	ACCOMMODATIONS
Calm	In split—red and yellow sponges, great marine life, fish, grouper, grunt, etc.	Great for photos	Small shark; don't seem dangerous	Eleuthera Water Sports Governor's Harbor, Eleuthera See above; Gardner Young charters fast boats to this area.	Many accommodations on Eleuthera or Gardner Young at Nassau charters boats. See above for address.
Calm	Lovely corals: sea plumes, coral fans, gorgonias; reef fish	Great for photos	None	As above	As above
Rushing water	Big fish, wild fast ride, caves, crevices	Neither	Powerful current, fast water	As above	As above
Calm	Corals, fish	Photos	None	At Lloyds Spanish Wells Bahamas Tel. 299 Romora Club P.O. Box 146 Harbour Island	At Lloyds Spanish Wells Bahamas Tel. 299 also other cottages for rentals At Romora Club P.O. Box 146 Harbour Island other guest houses and small hotels on Harbour Island
Calm	Wheels and wreck; also another ship-wreck.	Photos	None		
Calm	Corals, wreck partly out of water	Photos	None	As above	As above
Calm	Coral reefs, fish; can go to R.R. wreck	Photos	None	As above	As above

BAHAMA ISLANDS CONTINUED

132

PLACE	NO.	DESCRIPTION	ENTRY AND DISTANCE FROM SHORE	DEPTH	SNORKEL OR DIVE
BERRY ISLANDS	46	Shallow reefs, esp. beach in front of Crown Colony Club and Chub Cay	Beach and boat	Shallow	Snorkel or dive
GREAT ABACO ISLAND Sandy Cay Reef	47	Coral reef	Beaches at reef but get there by boat At shore on Sandy Cay	To 25′	Snorkel or dive
GREAT ABACO ISLAND Man-O'-War Reef	48	Coral reef	Beach at cay but go by boat	To 25′	Snorkel or dive
BIMINI N. Cat Cay	49	Coral reefs	Boat	Varies	Snorkel or dive
BIMINI Wreck of the Sapona	50	A concrete shipwreck	Boat 10 min. from yacht club dock	10′–30′	Snorkel or dive
BIMINI Turtle Rocks	51	Coral reef	Boat	10′–200′	Snorkel or dive
BIMINI Huge Blocks	52	Are these rectangular blocks the lost city of Atlantis?	Boat	20′	Snorkel or dive

SURF OR CALM	HIGH-LIGHTS	FISHING AND PHOTOS	DANGERS	DIVE FACILITY	ACCOMMODATIONS
Calm	Great corals, underwater desert, reefs	Photos	None	Charter boat or Chub Cay Marina Chub Cay, Bahamas	Crown Colony Club P.O. Box 223 International Airport Miami, Fl. Chub Cay Marina Hotel Chub Bay P.O. Box 223-I.A.B. Miami, Fl. 33148
Calm	Fish, coral reefs	Photos	None	Elbow Cay Club Hopetown Abaco, Bahamas	Several at varied prices—mostly moderate
Depends on wind	Wreck, reef, fish	Photos	None	As above	As above
Calm	Reef fish, large angels, grouper, snapper	Photos	Strong ebb tide with east wind	Bimini Island Yacht Club Box 646 S. Bimini Tel. (U.S.) 305-688-5685	Bimini Island Yacht Club Box 646 Alicetown S. Bimini Tel (U.S.) 305-688-5685
Calm	Many fish; snapper, jacks, lobsters	Good photos	None	As above	Bimini Hotel Alicetown, Bimini, Bahamas or 1955 Harding Ave. Surfside, Miami Beach, Fl. and others
Calm	Grouper at 50'–60'; caves, reef fish, fans, corals	Photos	None	As above	As above
Calm	Blocks, some on columns	Photos	None	As above	As above

BAHAMA ISLANDS CONTINUED

134

PLACE	NO.	DESCRIPTION	ENTRY AND DISTANCE FROM SHORE	DEPTH	SNORKEL OR DIVE
CAY SAL BANKS (70 mi. off Florida Keys; 30 mi. from Cuba) (Experienced only)	53	A group of rocks & reefs; blue holes and drop-offs and an abandoned light-house	Boat (large)	20' – 120'	Dive
CAY SAL BANKS Paddle Wheel Wreck at Elbow Cay light-house (Experienced only)	54	A stern wheeler sunk in the Civil War	Boat (large)	23'	Dive
GRAND BAHAMA Deadman's Reef the Boiling Hole (Expert only)	55	Blue hole 50' in diameter	Boat ½ mi. off S. shore Grand Bahama	40' at main opening then 15' more to 120'	Dive
GRAND BAHAMA Silver Pt. wreck	56	Shipwreck	Boat ½ mi.	Shallow	Snorkel or dive
GRAND BAHAMA Pillar Corals	57	Part of coral reef; un-usual coral forms	Boat 15 min. 1 mi.	65' – 75'	Dive
GRAND BAHAMA Deep Reef	58	Beautiful, clear coral reef	Boat 20 min.	45' – 80'	Dive

SURF OR CALM	HIGH-LIGHTS	FISHING AND PHOTOS	DANGERS	DIVE FACILITY	ACCOMMODATIONS
Calm areas and rough ones	Black coral, fish, drop-offs, grottos, wrecks, lobsters	Photos	Shark, but don't seem dangerous	Florida Crusty Dutchman, Inc. Box 144 Key Largo, Fl. 33037 Tel. 305-451-0353	Uninhabited
Calm	Paddle wheel with spokes; sponges, gorgonia, fish	Photos	Shark, but don't seem dangerous	Ms. Pat Anderson P.O. Box 487 Islamorada, Fl. 33036	Uninhabited
Calm	Walls of hole covered with red and yellow gorgonia; many fish; grouper, parrot, etc.	Photos	Don't get lost. Watch strong tides. For qualified cave divers only	Underwater Explorer's Club Box F. 2433 Freeport, Grand Bahama Tel. 373-1244 or 1148 N.E. 48 St. Pompano Beach, Fl. 33064 Tel. 305-942-3974	Scubahamas Victoria Inn and Scuba Club P.O. Box F 1261 Freeport Grand Bahama Tel. 31000 and many other accommodations at varied prices
Calm; can chop	Ballast rock, brass nails, glass, shale	Photos	None	Grand Bahama Hotel and Country Club (on w. end)	
Calm	Reefs, fish, shells, fans	Photos (collecting only)	None	Scubahamas Victoria Inn and Scuba Club Box F 1261 Freeport Grand Bahama Tel. 31000	As above
Calm; can chop	Grouper, jacks, other fish; hard and soft coral	Photos	None; shark once in a while but do not seem dangerous	As above	As above

BAHAMA ISLANDS CONTINUED

136

PLACE	NO.	DESCRIPTION	ENTRY AND DISTANCE FROM SHORE	DEPTH	SNORKEL OR DIVE
GRAND BAHAMA Cinderella Reef	59	Part of shallow coral reef	Boat 15 min. 1 mi.	3'−8'−15'	Snorkel
GRAND BAHAMA Shallow Fringing Reef	60	Lovely coral gardens	Boat 10 min. ¼ mi.	5'−25'	Snorkel or dive
GRAND BAHAMA Peterson's Cay	61	A cay a few hundred yds. from shore; coral gardens	Boat 20 min. Beach when you get there	Varies, surface to 20'	Snorkel or dive
GRAND BAHAMA Rocky Creek	62	Blue Holes	Go by car; snorkel to Blue Hole	3'−over 100' in Blue Hole	Snorkel or dive
GRAND BAHAMA McLeanstown	63	Shallow reefs	Go by car and snorkel to reefs	5'−20'	Snorkel or dive

SURF OR CALM	HIGH-LIGHTS	FISHING AND PHOTOS	DANGERS	DIVE FACILITY	ACCOMMODATIONS
Calm; can chop	Reefs, fish, shells, fans	Photos (collecting only)	None	As above	As above
Calm; can chop	Corals, all tropical fish	Photos	None	As above	As above
Calm; can chop	Great corals, fish, fans, gardens, turtles, rays, shells	Photos	None	As above	As above
Calm	Blue Holes	Photos	None; scuba divers should be qualified cave divers	As above	As above
Calm	Shallow coral reefs, fish	Photos	None	As above	As above

137

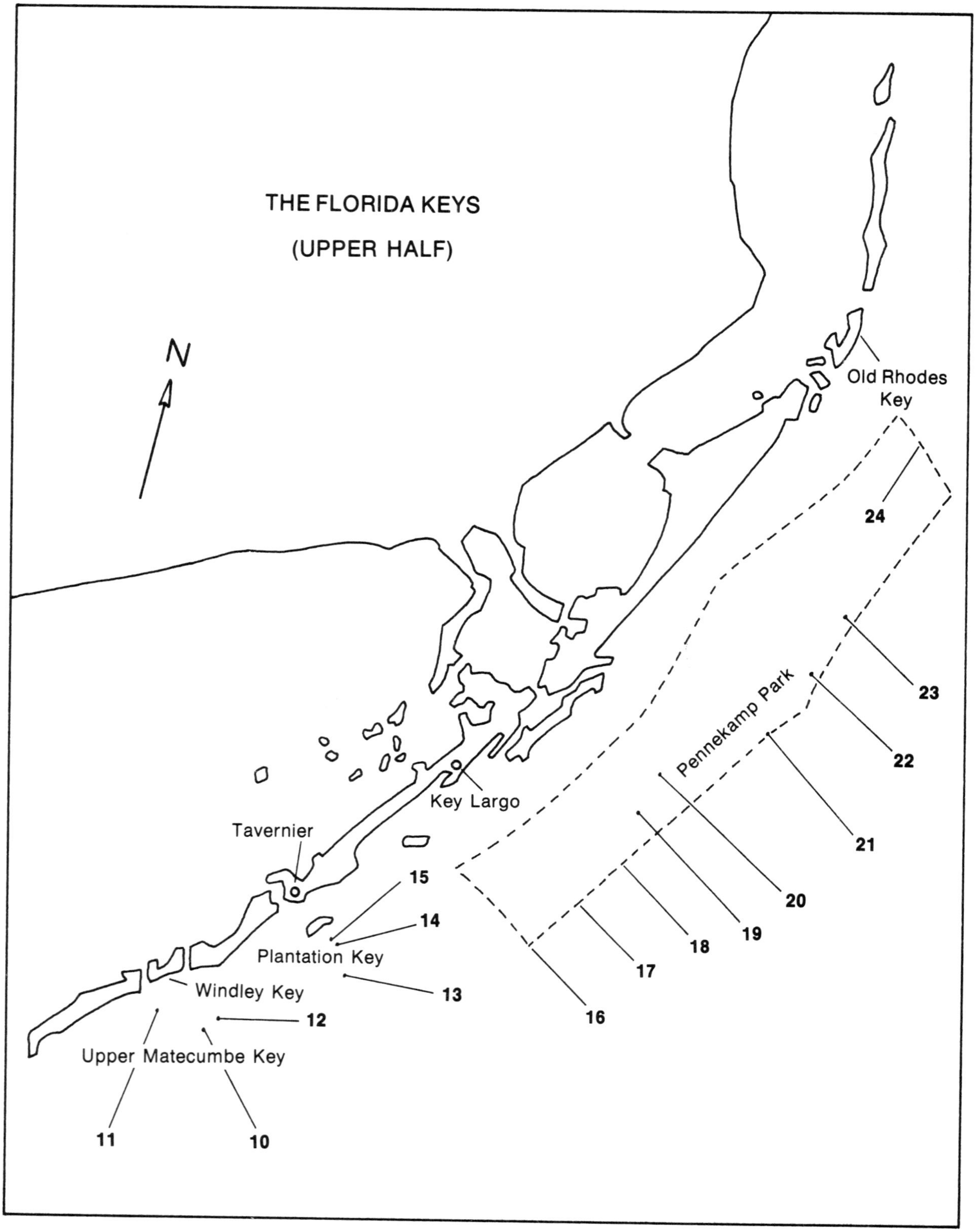

THE FLORIDA KEYS

(UPPER HALF)

N

Old Rhodes
Key

24

23

22

Pennekamp Park

21

20

19

18

17

16

Key Largo

Tavernier

15

14

Plantation Key

13

Windley Key

12

Upper Matecumbe Key

11

10

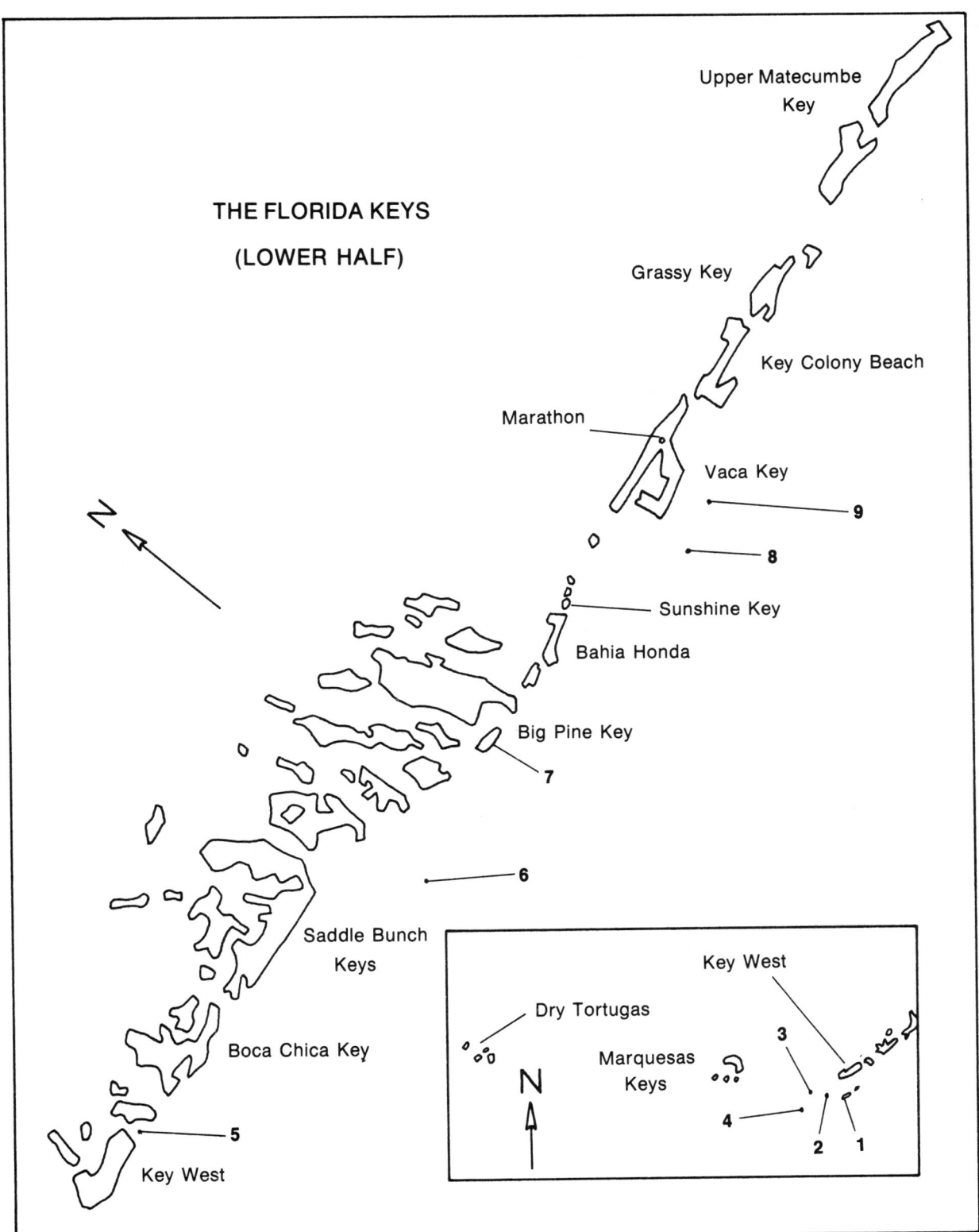

THE FLORIDA KEYS

(LOWER HALF)

Upper Matecumbe Key

Grassy Key

Key Colony Beach

Marathon

Vaca Key

9

8

Sunshine Key

Bahia Honda

Big Pine Key

7

6

Saddle Bunch Keys

Boca Chica Key

5

Key West

N

Key West

Dry Tortugas

3

Marquesas Keys

N

4

2   1

140

A pair of butterfly fish play beneath the sea whips or gorgonias. (Janet Viertel)

THE FLORIDA KEYS

Without a doubt the most dived area in the world is the Florida Keys. Not only is this area popular, it is a sentimental favorite with many divers because it is the site where sport-diving vacations really began—setting up facilities as long ago as the late nineteen-forties. In addition, it is the only "Caribbean-type" dive area accessible by car or trailer from the United States; and it boasts a wide range of hotels, trailer camps, and camp-sites, many of them with remarkably reasonable prices. The Keys are extremely informal and fun, particularly for a vacation with children, who normally become addicted to the fried shrimp and key lime pie that abound on land. Fishing from the bridges between the keys is recommended not only for the catch (plentiful and delicious) but for the characters who fish next to you, many of whom can entertain you all afternoon. The weather is unfortunately unreliable during the winter and on and off can be rough and cold, ruining your snorkeling or diving plans. During the other three-quarters of the year, however, it is quite consistently good; and the farther south in the Keys you go, the more reliable it is, even in winter.

The diving is varied, and it is still excellent despite the threats of pollution and tourist over-population. There are dive spots from off Key West, in the south, all the way north to the upper reaches of Pennecamp Park and the Fowey Rocks. There is no beach diving to speak of; but many of the reefs can be reached by boat in a half-hour, and there are many fine snorkeling areas at about the same distance. There are also boats to take you on overnight or week-long dive charters to areas like the Cay Sal Banks (see Florida Keys Chart).

The underwater scenery is similar to that of the Caribbean; coral heads, reef fish, sponges, and soft coral. Spearfishing is permitted in some areas.

Treasure hunting has become an industry in the Keys. There is no question that treasure is to be found on the wrecks there, but it is not for the sport diver. Most of the wreck location is done with air-planes, which spot sunken ships that are then brought up with professional equipment—not a plausible way to spend your two-week vacation.

The beaches are pleasant, if unspectacular, and care should be taken to avoid the Portuguese man-of-war, a blue, stinging jellyfish that appears in the water from time to time.

For the beginning diver the Keys might be a perfect place to start your exploration, particularly if you are part of a family that doesn't share your enthusiasm. It is easy to pick up other divers, charters are common, and the area is a popular family vacation spot—giving the others in your party a chance to meet people and do other things while you are out over the reefs.

Florida Keys

Water Temp.: 72°–80°

Regulations: Spearfishing is prohibited. Public bathing beaches, fishing piers, bridge catwalks, jetties: Illegal to spear snook, striped bass, porpoises or manta rays. Bag limits same as for sports fisherman. Prohibited entirely in Upper Keys from

PLACE	NO.	DESCRIPTION	ENTRY AND DISTANCE FROM SHORE	DEPTH	SNORKEL OR DIVE
EASTERN DRY ROCKS (2 mi. E. Sand Key 5 mi. S. Key West)	1	A steel beam marks the center; large mounds of coral; remains of wreck	Boat 2 mi. E. Sand Key	2'–60'	Snorkel or dive
ROCK KEY (1 mi. E. Sand Key)	2	A steel beam in back center of reef; reef with deep cracks; 2 wrecks	Boat 20 min.	25'	Snorkel or dive
SAND KEY (6 mi. S. Key West)	3	Lighthouse in middle of small island marks reef with good snorkeling.	20 min. by boat; beach on Sand Key	15'–45'–70'	Snorkel or dive
TEN FATHOM BAR (½ mi. S. Sand Key)	4	Magnificent drop-off	Boat	25'–130'	Dive
WESTERN SAMBO (4 mi. S. out of Boca Chica Channel and a turn E. Pole is on E. end of reef)	5	Mile-long reef; dive on W. end of a lovely reef	Boat 20 min.	25'	Snorkel or dive

Visibility: 75'–100'   **Best Season:** Spring, summer, fall

Dade Monroe County Line to lower end Long Key Bridge, and for a 3-mile limit either side U.S. 1. This includes Pennekamp Park. Unlawful to have equipment in limits of state park.

SURF OR CALM	HIGH-LIGHTS	FISHING AND PHOTOS	DANGERS	DIVE FACILITY	ACCOMMODATIONS
Varies	Lobstering, shelling for conch in shallow water	Fishing, photos	None	Reef Raiders Dive Shop U.S. Hwy 1 Stock Island Key West, Fla. 33040 Franco and Georgeann Piacibello Tel. 305-294-0660	Many at Key West at all prices
Calm	Lobsters in shallow water; wreck on S.W. end of reef; At 15' end is a tile wreck; some artifacts still on wrecks	Lobsters, photos, spearfishing	Only urchins	Key West Pro Dive Shop 1990 Roosevelt Blvd. Key West, Fla. 33040 Tel. 305-296-3823	As above
Always calm on one side or other	Reef ledges, grouper, fish	Fishing, photos	Only urchins	Key West Tennis and Scuba Ctr. Key Wester Inn & Villas 1901 S. Roosevelt Blvd., P.O. Box 331 Key West, Fla. 33040 Lynne Sweeney, Manager Tel. 305-296-5671	As above
Varies	Feeding grouper and snapper; rays, corals, sponges	Great visibility, photos, fishing	Strong current first 30' of dive		As above
Calm; can chop in winter	Corals, lobsters, helmet, shells, porkfish, reef fish, queen conch	Fishing and photos	None	As above	As above

FLORIDA KEYS CONTINUED

144

PLACE	NO.	DESCRIPTION	ENTRY AND DISTANCE FROM SHORE	DEPTH	SNORKEL OR DIVE
LOOE KEY (9 mi. off Big Pine Key)	6	Magnificent reef with wreck of British frigate H.M.S. *Looe* and drop-off ½ mi. S. of key	Boat 9 mi. from Big Pine Key	2′ – 40′ and ¼ mi. S. 50′ – 90′	Snorkel or dive
NEWFOUND HARBOUR KEYS	7	Great coral reef	Boat 8 mi. then beach ½ mi.	5′	Snorkel
SOMBRERO LIGHT (8 mi. S.W. Key Colony Beach— 142′ light tower)	8	Best diving is on S. side of light; magnificent reef	Boat 8 mi.	30′	Snorkel or dive
EAST WASHERWOMAN (6 mi. S.W. Key Colony Beach marked by 36′ tower)	9	Coral reef	Boat 6 mi.	10′ – 18′	Snorkel or dive
CROCKER REEF (5½ mi. S.E. Windley Key)	10	Coral reef	Boat 5½ mi.	35′ – 100′	Dive

SURF OR CALM	HIGH-LIGHTS	FISHING AND PHOTOS	DANGERS	DIVE FACILITY	ACCOMMODATIONS
Varies	Great corals, shells, lovely marine life; some artifacts may still be found from wreck, but it has been "worked over."	Photos; spearing legal 1 mi. from Hwy 1	None at Looe Key but strong current at drop-off	Aqua Center Holiday Inn Trav-L-Park RR 1 Box 790L Sunshine Key, Fla. 33043 Ed Davidson, Pres. Tel. 305-872-2400	Holiday Inn Trav-L-Park P.O. Box 1028 Sunshine Key, Florida 33050 and many other motels on Keys in this area, especially Marathon Campgrounds on Sunshine Key, Knight Key, and and Bahia Honda State Park
Calm	Close in corals, lovely marine life	Great photos and careful fishing	None	Underseas, Inc. U.S. Hwy 1 P.O. Box 319 Big Pine Key, Fla. 33043 G. and M. Rockett Tel. 305-872-2700	
Varies	Corals, gorgonias, tropical fish	Great photos	None	Hall's Dive Shop 1688 Overseas Hwy. Marathon, Fla. 33050 B. and L. Brayman, Tel. 305-743-9474	
Varies	Corals of all sorts, fans, sponges	Photos	None	Divers Headquarters 11511 Overseas Hwy. Marathon Shores, Fla. 33052 Art McDermott, Tel. 305-743-4501	As above
Varies	Staghorn corals, gorgonias, fish, sponges	Photos	None	Key Colony Divers Key Colony Beach Causeway P.O. Box 754-D Key Colony Beach, Fla. 33051 Frank Lea, Owner Tel. 305-289-1141 The Diving Site 12565 Overseas Hwy. P.O. Box 3386 Marathon Shores, Fla. 33052 Ditmar Biller, Tel. 305-289-1021 Coral Lagoon Dive Shop 12399 Overseas Hwy. Marathon, Fla. 33050 Dick Goss, Owner Tel. 305-289-0123	As above

145

FLORIDA KEYS CONTINUED

146

PLACE	NO.	DESCRIPTION	ENTRY AND DISTANCE FROM SHORE	DEPTH	SNORKEL OR DIVE
ISLAMORADA CORAL GARDENS (2½ mi. E. Windley Key—¾ mi. off Plantation Key)	11	Underwater coral gardens; 2nd set of gardens, 3 mi. S.S.W. of Windley Key	Boat 3 mi.	8′ – 12′	Snorkel
DAVIS REEF (3 mi. S.S.E. of Hens and Chickens Tower; 5 mi. from Islamorada)	12	Coral reef	Boat 20 – 30 min. 3 mi.	25′ – 35′	Dive
HENS AND CHICKENS REEF (3 mi. E.S.E. Windley Key)	13	Reef with impressive brain corals and a sunken barge	Boat 3 mi.	20′ – 28′	Snorkel or dive
OUTER CONCH REEF (few hundred yards S. Inner Conch) (Experienced divers)	14	Coral reef with great marine life	Boat 2 mi.	60′ – 100′	Dive
INNER CONCH REEF (2 mi. N. Davis Reef; 5 mi. from Islamorada)	15	Lovely coral reef with fishes	Boat 35 – 40 min. 5 mi.	16′ – 25′	Snorkel or dive

SURF OR CALM	HIGH-LIGHTS	FISHING AND PHOTOS	DANGERS	DIVE FACILITY	ACCOMMODATIONS
Varies	Corals, fans, shells, lobsters	Photos, lobster collecting	None	Holiday Isle Dive Center P.O. Box 588 Islamorada, Fla. 33036 Tel. 305-664-2321, ext. 611	Many accommodations on various keys
Varies	Great corals covered with marine life; enormous schools of tiny fish, sea fans; all tropical fish	Photos, spearfishing	None	Joe Havel The Reef Shop Dive Center P.O. Box 575 Islamorada, Fla. 33036	As above
Varies	Coral tunnels, morays, 20'– high brain corals, soft corals, tropical fish; wreck of a brick barge from W.W. II	Excellent for photos	None	Carl Gage Dive Center P.O. Box 38-111 Key Largo, Fla. 33037 Tel. 305-852-5764	As above
Varies	Large fish, rays, angelfish	Great visibility for photos; spearfishing, collecting	Slight current	As above	As above
Varies	Stunning coral formations, elkhorn corals, pillar coral, fans, soft corals, sponges	Great for photos, spearfishing, collecting	None	As above	As above

FLORIDA KEYS CONTINUED

148

PLACE	NO.	DESCRIPTION	ENTRY AND DISTANCE FROM SHORE	DEPTH	SNORKEL OR DIVE
MOLASSES REEF AND WINDLASS WRECK (5 mi. S. of S. cut off Key Largo; 45' steel light tower)	16	Magnificent reef with archways and tunnels; fish and corals, wreck of schooner	Boat 5 mi.	5' – 40'	Snorkel or dive
FRENCH REEF SEA GARDENS (1 mi. N.E. of steel tower on Molasses Reef; 7½ mi. from Largo)	17	Great coral reef; canyons and fish	Boat 7½ mi.	30'	Snorkel or dive
BENWOOD WRECK (sometimes called Brentwood)	18	A wreck of W.W. II freighter	Boat	25' – 55'	Snorkel or dive
GRECIAN ROCKS (marked by 3 ft. White Buoy)	19	Coral reef with many fish	Boat	5' – 10' – 25'	Great to snorkel or dive
CHRIST OF THE ABYSS (STATUE) AT KEY LARGO DRY ROCKS (6 mi. E.N.E. of S. cut off Key Largo; 3' white buoy)	20	A 4000-lb, 11' statue of Christ with his arms upraised	Boat 6 mi.	5' – 20' – 25'	Snorkel or dive

SURF OR CALM	HIGH-LIGHTS	FISHING AND PHOTOS	DANGERS	DIVE FACILITY	ACCOMMODATIONS
Varies	Corals, arches, tunnels, sea fans, reef fish, wreck 25—30 yds. e. of tower (good night dive); angelfish	Good visibility for photos	None, but watch for fire coral and urchins	John Pennekamp Coral Reef State Park Key Largo, Florida 33037 Available: Glass-bottom boat tours, snorkel tours (rental equipment available), no experience necessary. Must have certification card with you.	Camping reservations: J.P. State Park, Box 487, Key Largo, Fla. 33037 Tel. 305-451-1202
Varies	Many fish, many corals, canyons, caves	Good photos	None		As above
Varies	Weird wreck with fish of every size living around it	Good photos	Some shark	Boat rentals, dockage, scuba instruction PADI (28-hr. 4-day course). Rental equipment. Scuba gear requires certification card to rent.	As above
Varies	Innumerable species of tropical fish, esp. parrotfish; old Spanish cannon	Photos	None	As above	As above
Varies	Statue, tropical fish, skates, rays	Great photos	None	As above	As above

149

FLORIDA KEYS CONTINUED

150

PLACE	NO.	DESCRIPTION	ENTRY AND DISTANCE FROM SHORE	DEPTH	SNORKEL OR DIVE
ELBOW REEF LIGHTHOUSE (8 mi. E.N.E. of the S. cut off Key Largo 36' steel tower)	21	Coral reef with wreck	Boat 8 mi.	5' – 20'	Snorkel or dive
H.M.S. WINCHESTER WRECK (S.E. of Carysfort Light)	22	Wreck of a British ship (wreck 1695)	Boat	28'	Snorkel or dive
CARYSFORT REEF LIGHT (12 mi. N.E. of the S. cut off Key Largo on outside of Park. 100' steel tower)	23	Coral reef fish, shallow areas and deeper ones	Boat	4' – 6' then 30' – 40''	Snorkel or dive
FOWEY ROCKS TO N. END PENNEKAMP AT WHISTLE BUOY (about 20 mi. spearing area in all) (Experts only)	24	An area for spearing fish. You can drag behind boat until you spot prey.	Boat	40' – 100'	Snorkel and free dive without scuba

SURF OR CALM	HIGH-LIGHTS	FISHING AND PHOTOS	DANGERS	DIVE FACILITY	ACCOMMODATIONS
Varies	Elkhorn corals, fishes, wreck in 20' of water	Photos	None	As above	As above
Varies	Wreck with coral growing over it	Photos	None	As above	As above
Varies	Great elkhorn coral; crevices in reef; much marine life	Photos	None	As above	As above
Varies	Large fish: grouper, snapper, amberjack, barracuda, cubera snapper	Spearfishing	Shark, esp. Jan. – May	As above	Many in the Miami area

152

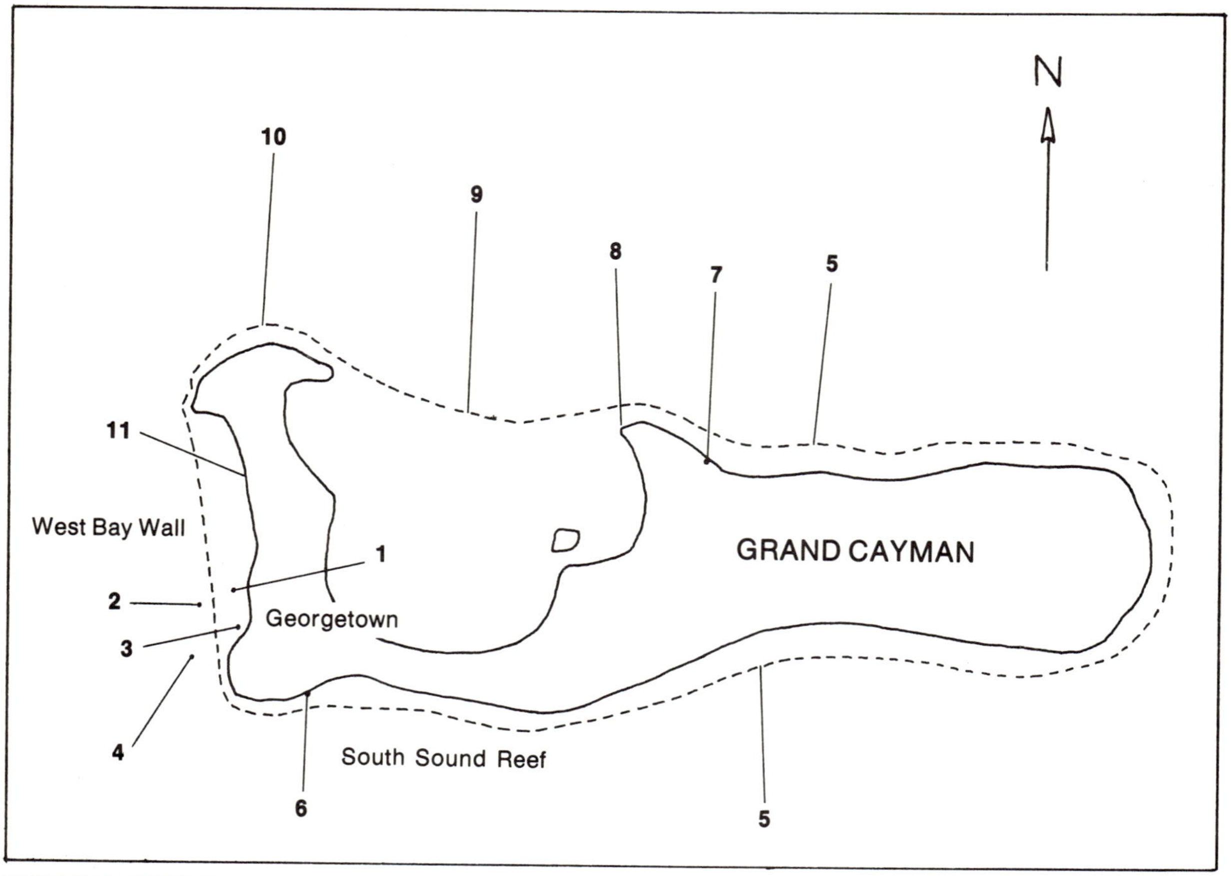

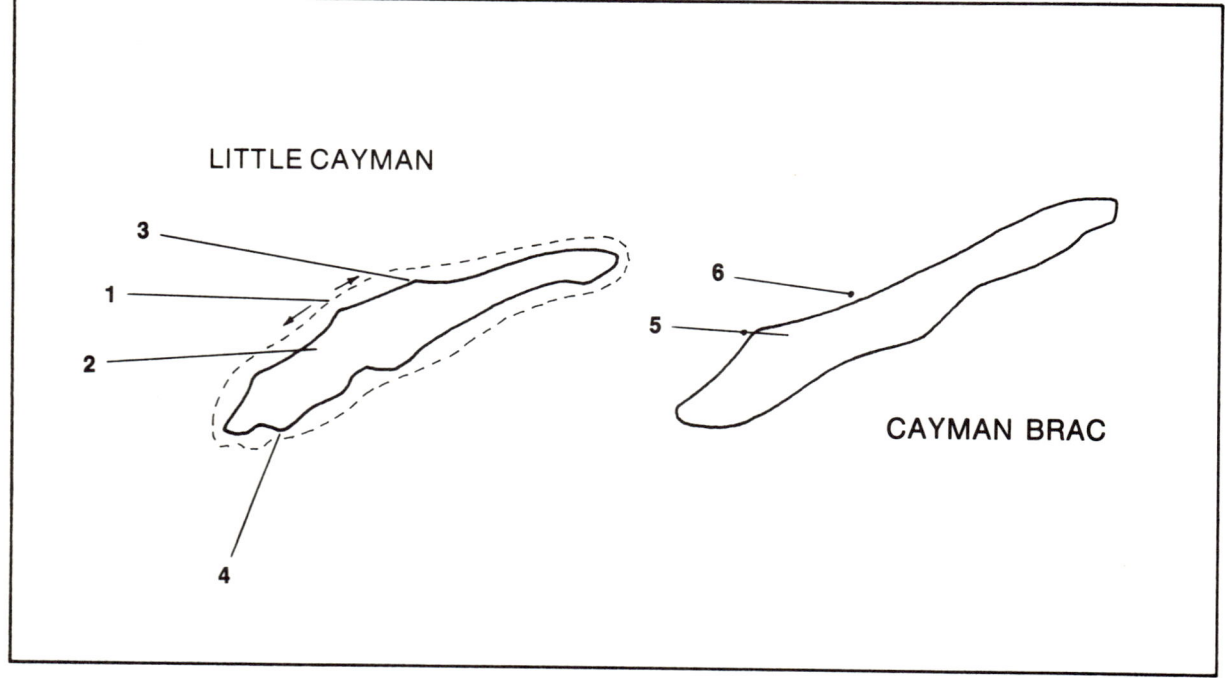

N

10

9

8

7

5

11

West Bay Wall

1

Georgetown

2

3

4

6

South Sound Reef

5

GRAND CAYMAN

LITTLE CAYMAN

3

1

2

4

6

5

CAYMAN BRAC

THE CAYMAN ISLANDS

One hour's plane flight from Miami, just south of Cuba, the Cayman Islands offer a broad spectrum of diving and snorkeling experiences, considered by many to be unmatched for variety. There are reefs and wrecks at depths to suit the beginning as well as the experienced diver—there is one of the most magnificent drop-offs in the hemisphere. The water has a near-perfect record for clarity, and the air temperature averages seventy-five to eighty degrees. In addition to all of the natural factors, the man-made facilities are excellent and include complete diving tours by boat, as well as hotels with diving arrangements and daily reef and wreck tours on party boats that will pick you up at your hotel.

There are three Cayman Islands, of which Grand Cayman is the largest and by far the most developed. Its small town, called Georgetown, is a traditional island metropolis gradually giving way to the vigorous international banking industry of the Caymans, but the nearby seven-mile stretch of beach on which many of the hotels, motels, and rental cottages are built remains undisturbed and ideal for the kind of flop-in-the-sun-with-an-afternoon-rum-punch vacation that's called for when urban or suburban living becomes intolerable.

For the most part, snorkeling from the beach is fairly fruitless here, although there are occasional coral heads and lobster holes, particularly on the public beach near the governor's mansion. Much more

A diver at 140 feet on the Grand Cayman drop-off. (Jack McKenney/Skin Diver Magazine)

rewarding are the twice-daily boat trips, usually one boat for snorkelers only and another for divers. These boats will pick you up at a large hotel and take you to various spots of interest, usually to explore the wrecks and lovely marine life in Georgetown Harbor. The North Sound is another marvelous area to explore. If you wish to snorkel or dive privately, there are charter boats available that will cater to your needs, including night dives if you wish (see Dive Facility column on the Cayman Chart).

The other two Cayman Islands, Little Cayman and Cayman Brac, qualify as real hideouts. Little Cayman, seventy-four miles from Grand Cayman, has only about twenty residents and no dive facil-

ities, although there are spectacular sights to be seen there. To explore the reefs off Little Cayman you can go on a charter boat from Grand Cayman or take a plane from Grand Cayman to the third island, Cayman Brac, and stay at the Buccaneer's Inn, which offers fishing as well as diving charters. The island is more populated than Little Cayman, but still a genuine refuge, and perfect for people who enjoy the isolation of an undiscovered area. Take a book.

The three islands provide some of the best diving spots in the world, but they are tiny and ecologically delicate. Great care should be taken not to damage the reef, as the influx of snorkelers, divers, and industry are bound to be traumatic to the ecosystem.

Cayman Islands

GRAND CAYMAN

Water Temp.: 81°

Regulations: Diver's flag and float required by law. No capturing fish or lobster with scuba. Free-diving spearfishermen can

154

PLACE	NO.	DESCRIPTION	ENTRY AND DISTANCE FROM SHORE	DEPTH	SNORKEL OR DIVE
WRECK OF THE CALI	1	Wreck, fish	Boat	15'	Snorkel or dive
WRECK OF THE BALBOA (Several hundred yards off "Tropical Shipping Co." container dock on Church St., Georgetown)	2	Wreck, fish, corals	Boat	30'	Snorkel or dive
WRECK OF THE ARBUTUS (100 yds. S. of Balboa)	3	Wreck, fish	Boat	30'	Dive
EDEN ROCK	4	Large coral reef	Boat	10'–20'	Snorkel or dive
DROP OFF WALL ALL AROUND ISLAND	5	Spectacular drop off	Boat	To 75'	Dive
WRECK OF THE PALLAS	6	1903 wreck partly above surface of water	Beach Walk to wreck Few yards	7'	Snorkel
CAYMAN KAI (You can snorkel to Rum Point)	7	Barrier reef	Beach Near shore	7'	Snorkel or dive the drop off

Visibility: 100′   **Best Season:** Anytime; April 1–October 1 best

take 3 fish **or** lobsters with no eggs. Lobster season closed Feb. 1–July 31. Collecting and spearfishing discouraged.

SURF OR CALM	HIGH-LIGHTS	FISHING AND PHOTOS	DANGERS	DIVE FACILITY	ACCOMMODATIONS
Calm	Huge anchor tilted up in sand near wreck	Photos	None	Bob Soto Upper Church Street Grand Cayman, B.W.I. Surfside Water Sports at Galleon Beach on 7 mi. Beach Tel. 9-2724 or 9-2252 Spanish Bay Reef Resort Box 800 Grand Cayman, B.W.I. Tel. 9-3493 or reserve through Bay Travel 2435 E. Coast Hwy. Corona Del Mar, Calif. 92625 Tel. 714-675-4320	Many at various prices. Spanish Bay Reef Box 800 Grand Cayman, B.W.I. Tel. 9-3493 Bob Soto's East End Lodge Grand Cayman, B.W.I. Attn: Dave Woodward Tortuga Club P.O. Box 496 Grand Cayman, B.W.I. Tel. 2284
Calm	Wreck with sponges, fish, gorgonias, flower corals	Photos	None		
Calm	Was a wooden vessel; only ballast stones and an occasional artifact	Photos	None		
Calm	Reef with fissures and caves; fish of all sorts	Photos	None		As above
Calm	Wall of living coral, sponges, gorgonians, crevices, arches, caverns, fish (jacks, yellowtail, grouper, etc.)	Photos	None	As above	As above
Calm, but watch current	Wreck, coral heads, fish inside, esp. angelfish	Photos	Fire coral in area. Beyond wreck toward sea, watch current.	As above	As above
Varies	Reef life, fish, shells (queen conch)	Photos	None	As above	As above

GRAND CAYMAN CONTINUED

156

PLACE	NO.	DESCRIPTION	ENTRY AND DISTANCE FROM SHORE	DEPTH	SNORKEL OR DIVE
RUM POINT	8	Barrier reef	Beach Near shore	7'	Snorkel or dive the drop off
NORTH SOUND REEF AND WALL (especially ⅓ of way across North Sound from west)	9	Coral reefs	Boat 10 min. trip	6' reef, 75' wall	Snorkel on reef, dive on wall
SPANISH BAY REEF	10	Coral reef with fish and lobsters	Boat or swim from Spanish Bay Reef Resort	30'	Snorkel or dive
PUBLIC BEACH (Next to Governor's Residence) (S. end)	11	Tropical reef	Beach 100 yds.	6'	Snorkel

LITTLE CAYMAN   Water Temp.: 68°–71°

Regulations: See regulations for Grand Cayman. Coral collecting and spearfishing discouraged.

PLACE	NO.	DESCRIPTION	ENTRY AND DISTANCE FROM SHORE	DEPTH	SNORKEL OR DIVE
DROP OFF WALL (goes all around island)	1	Very steepsided with deepwater drop off; adjacent to shallow coral gardens	Boat 200 yds.	15'–720'	Snorkel shallow, dive deep
BLOODY BAY (along drop off wall, 2 mi. from west end)	2	Steepsided, deepwater drop off; adjacent to shallow coral reef	Boat 200 yds.	15'–720'	Snorkel shallow, dive deep

SURF OR CALM	HIGH-LIGHTS	FISHING AND PHOTOS	DANGERS	DIVE FACILITY	ACCOMMODATIONS
Varies	Reef life, fish	Photos	None	As above	As above
Varies	Magnificent reefs with green coloring; lots of fish, esp. angels	Photos	None	As above	As above
Varies	Beautiful tropical reef; fish, lobsters	Photos	None	As above	As above
Calm	Corals, small fish	Photos	None	As above	As above

Visibility: 100'–200'   **Best Season:** Anytime; April–October 1 best

SURF OR CALM	HIGH-LIGHTS	FISHING AND PHOTOS	DANGERS	DIVE FACILITY	ACCOMMODATIONS
Varies	Breathtaking view, beautiful marine life, esp. sponges	Photos	None	At Cayman Brac: Buccaneer's Inn Box 68 Cayman Brac Cayman Islands, B.W.I. Boat: Cayman Diver from Grand Cayman See Bob Soto (above) Can be rough trip	On Cayman Brac: Buccaneer's Inn Box 68 Cayman Brac Cayman Islands, B.W.I.
Varies	Fish of all sorts, black coral trees, sponges	Photos	None		

LITTLE CAYMAN CONTINUED

PLACE	NO.	DESCRIPTION	ENTRY AND DISTANCE FROM SHORE	DEPTH	SNORKEL OR DIVE
JACKSON'S POINT (1 mi. east of wall)	3	Steepsided, deepwater drop off; adjacent to shallow coral gardens	Boat 200 yds.	15' – 720'	Snorkel shallow, dive deep
SOUTHWEST POINT	4	Steepsided, deepwater drop off: adjacent to shallow coral gardens	Boat 200 yds.	15' – 720'	Snorkel shallow, dive deep

CAYMAN BRAC   Water Temp.: 68° – 71°

Regulations: See regulations for Grand Cayman. Coral collecting and spearfishing discouraged.

PLACE	NO.	DESCRIPTION	ENTRY AND DISTANCE FROM SHORE	DEPTH	SNORKEL OR DIVE
CAYMAN BRAC (directly off Buccaneer's Inn)	5	Drop off in front of hotel	Boat 5 min. 100 ft.	80'	Snorkel or dive
CAYMAN BRAC (7 mi. E. of Buccaneer's Inn)	6	Coral reef with caves	By car Walk into water 100 ft.	75'	Snorkel or dive.

SURF OR CALM	HIGH-LIGHTS	FISHING AND PHOTOS	DANGERS	DIVE FACILITY	ACCOMMODATIONS
Varies	Anchor in a coral cave	Photos	None	As above	As above
Varies	30'–60' corals, coral canyons & tunnels	Photos	None	As above	As above

Visibility: 100'–200'   **Best Season:** Anytime; April–October 1 best

Calm or waves to 3'	Fish, reefs, caves	Photos	None	As above	As above
Calm or waves to 3'	Fish, reefs, caves	Photos	None	As above	As above

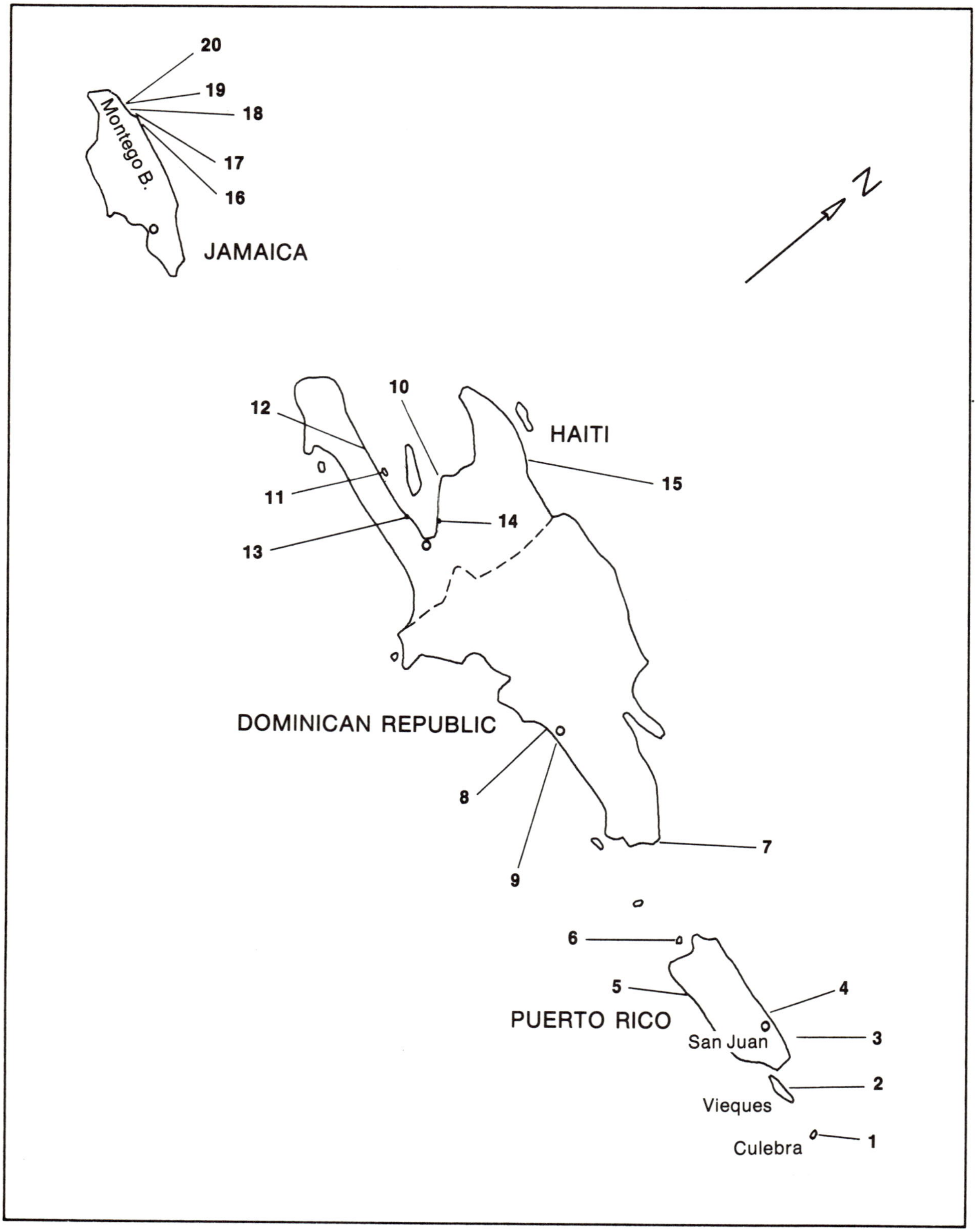

20

19

18

Montego B.

17

16

JAMAICA

N

10

12

HAITI

11

15

13

14

DOMINICAN REPUBLIC

8

9

7

6

5

4

PUERTO RICO

San Juan

3

2

Vieques

Culebra

1

THE GREATER ANTILLES

**(PUERTO RICO/THE DOMINI-
CAN REPUBLIC/HAITI/
JAMAICA)**

Along the Bahamas, the Greater Antilles offer the type of holiday
possibilities most often associated
with a "Caribbean vacation." Lush,
fabulous landscape, potent and
inexpensive rum, native dancing,
tropical cuisine, noisy, darkened
night clubs, and gleaming, quiet
beaches make these islands ideal
for a party that includes some
nondivers, who will never be bored
while the rest of you are out on the
reef. The diving itself is plentiful,
although not as prodigious as in
areas such as Bonaire. The islands
are very easily reached from the
United States, and as a result, are
quite developed, particularly Puerto
Rico, where San Juan has become
a bustling metropolis. The quiet,
hidden resort has not disappeared
from this part of the West Indies,
but it is getting to be a rarity.

In Puerto Rico there is offshore
diving from San Juan, but it tends to
be choppy in the winter. Better
diving is usually available at Fa-
jardo on the northeast coast or
from the south shore near Ponce.

The Dominican Republic offers a
few dive spots reachable by boat,
but very little beach snorkeling or
scuba.

Haiti, which is just coming back
into its own as a tourist area after a

*Divers coming and going to the underwater sights off San Juan, Puerto
Rico.* (Caribbean School of Aquatics, San Juan, Puerto Rico)

period of political unrest, has quite
a few good dive spots reachable by
boat and some good beach areas.
In addition, it is a fascinating and
exotic island to explore on land.

Jamaica's Montego Bay offers excellent snorkeling and diving, both
from beaches and boats, with good
facilities on land. Near Kingston, on
the other end of the island, the
legendary pirate city of Port Royal,
which sunk under the sea in the
earthquake of 1692, is being ex-
cavated, and many fascinating remains and artifacts may be seen.

Most of the snorkeling and diving in
the Greater Antilles is mild, although Jamaica offers a reef drop-
off of 200 feet for the very experienced diver. The sights are spectacular but not unusual for the
Caribbean—fish, coral, fans,
sponges, black coral, some caves,
and a few wrecks. The water is not
as clear as it is in areas further
south, but most of the time it is
perfectly acceptable, tending to be
at its worst in winter and its best in
the summer months.

Greater Antilles

PUERTO RICO

Water Temp.: 75°–80°

Regulations: Please do not break or remove coral. Spearfishing permitted.

162

PLACE	NO.	DESCRIPTION	ENTRY AND DISTANCE FROM SHORE	DEPTH	SNORKEL OR DIVE
CULEBRA (military restrictions)	1	Coral reefs	Boat	3'–150'	Snorkel or dive
VIEQUES (military restrictions)	2	Coral reefs	Boat	3'–100'	Snorkel or dive
FAJARDO Icacos Island	3	Lovely coral reefs	Boat	3'–25'	Snorkel or dive
SAN JUAN Underwater Gardens	4	Inside reefs shallow, with corals and tropical fish; outside reefs deeper and varied types; big boulders, caves, large fish	Boat ½-day trip 1½ mi.	3' and down	Snorkel or dive
GUAYANILLA BAY Reefs at mouth	5	Coral reefs	Boat	60'–80'	Dive
MONA ISLAND (45 mi. W. of Mayaguez) (Expert)	6	Lovely, remote island with reefs and marine life; drop-off	Go by boat; beach when you get there	3'–150' and down	Snorkel or dive

Visibility: 25'–100'   **Best Season:** Spring, summer, fall

SURF OR CALM	HIGH-LIGHTS	FISHING AND PHOTOS	DANGERS	DIVE FACILITY	ACCOMMODATIONS
Calm	Lobster, big fish, clear water, coral	Photos and spearing	Some local strong water currents	The Caribbean School of Aquatics Hyatt Hotel San Juan, P.R. Tel. 809-723-6090 Capt. Greg Korwek	Many accommodations at all prices in San Juan
Calm	Lobsters, reef, fish, shells	Photos and spearing	None		Punta Aloo Box 207 Culebra, P.R. 00645
Calm	Corals, reef fishes, fans, gorgonias	Photos; (sport fish have been fished out)	None	The Puerto Rico Sheraton Caribbean Water Sports San Juan, P.R. Tel. 809-724-6161, ext. 1317	Seafarer's Inn Culebra, P.R. 00645 Tel 809-742-2851

Parador Lacasa de Frances Vieques Tel. 809-741-3751 |
| Depends on weather | Corals, wrecks, caves, fish | Photos and spearing | None in good weather; can be rough | San Juan Hotel, Wonderful World of Watersports San Juan, P.R. Tel. 809-791-1100, ext. 1224 | El Conquistador Hotel Fajardo, P.R. Tel. 809-863-1144 and Hotel Delicias Fajardo, P.R. Tel. 809-863-1818 |
| Calm | Grouper, large fish | Photos and spearing | None | At Puerto Chico Marina, Fajardo (Rt. 987, Km. 2.3) Capt. Jack Becker offers picnic day's sail to Icacos Island. Tel. Fajardo 129-863-1905

Palmas del Mar Humacao Capt. Yost Tel. 809-852-3450 | Hotels at Parguera, Ponce, and Mayaguez |
| Depends on weather | Wrecks, big fish, turtles, lobster, drop-offs, coral | Photos (great visibility), spearing, collecting | Shark, very deep | Charter from Caribbean School of Aquatics (see above) | Uninhabited None |

DOMINICAN REPUBLIC   Water Temp.: 75°–80°

Regulations: Spearfishing prohibited in national park.

164

PLACE	NO.	DESCRIPTION	ENTRY AND DISTANCE FROM SHORE	DEPTH	SNORKEL OR DIVE
PUNTA CANA CLUB	7	Coral reef, shallow; there are corals and fish, and deeper there are caves.	From beach in zodiac boat 700 yds., 5–15 min.	10'–60'	Snorkel or dive
SANTO DOMINGO	8	Lovely bay with coral reef	Boat and then from shore 100'	10'–200'	Snorkel or dive
CAMERA REEF (Expert only)	9	Coral reef	Boat Near	50'–200'	Dive

HAITI   Water Temp.: 75°–80°

Regulations: Spearfishing in some areas.

LES ARCADINS	10	Beautiful coral reefs	Boat 30 min. 5–7 mi.	5'–50'	Snorkel or dive
CATHEDRAL GARDENS	11	Coral reef with fish	Boat 15 min. then beach 25'	25'	Snorkel or dive
LOBSTER WALL	12	Coral reef with fish	Boat 6 min. then beach 25'	25'	Snorkel or dive

Visibility: 25′ – 100′   **Best Season:** July-March

SURF OR CALM	HIGH-LIGHTS	FISHING AND PHOTOS	DANGERS	DIVE FACILITY	ACCOMMODATIONS
Waves and surf	Fish, three wrecks, reefs, caves, walls, arches	Photos	None	At Punta Cana Club P.O. Box 1083 Santo Domingo, D.R. Tel. 565-3077 New dive facility being built: Scuba Dominicana C por A Apt. 1671 Centro Comercial Texaco Prol Bolivar Tel. 532-2600 Jim Olsen & Steve Wieland	Punta Cana Club (Resort) P.O. Box 1083 Santo Domingo, D.R. Tel. 565-3077 and many others in Santo Domingo
Calm	Reefs, fish, dolphins	Photos only	None	Aquaventures P.O. Box 1816 Max Henriquez Ureha #89 Santo Domingo, D.R. Tel. 566-7608 Ruben Carrica	As above
Calm	Dolphins	Photos only	None		As above

Visibility: 25′ – 100′   **Best Season:** Fall, winter, spring.

SURF OR CALM	HIGH-LIGHTS	FISHING AND PHOTOS	DANGERS	DIVE FACILITY	ACCOMMODATIONS
Usually calm; best in a.m.	Schools of small reef fish; black coral at 15′ in coral heads	Photos	None	Trip to Sand Cay Gaston Baussan. Departs from International Casino Docks in downtown Port au Prince. Float on inner tubes with masks, or snorkel. No other known facilities.	All in Port-au-Prince and Petionville
Calm	Lovely reefs with fish	Spearing, photos, collecting	None		
Calm	Reefs with fish	Spearing, photos, collecting	None		

HAITI CONTINUED

166

PLACE	NO.	DESCRIPTION	ENTRY AND DISTANCE FROM SHORE	DEPTH	SNORKEL OR DIVE
SAND CAY REEF	13	Marvelous marine gardens, off-shore reef	Launch from waterfront Port au Prince 10 mi.	Shallow	Snorkel
IBO BEACH ON CAIQUE ISLAND	14	Fair to poor snorkeling	Boat then beach 10'–50'	Shallow	Snorkel
CAP HAITIEN	15	Great wreck-diving (poor visibility)	Boat ½ mi.	25'–100'	Dive

JAMAICA   Water Temp.: 75°–80°

Regulations: No damaging or collecting of coral. Spearfishing discouraged.

PLACE	NO.	DESCRIPTION	ENTRY AND DISTANCE FROM SHORE	DEPTH	SNORKEL OR DIVE
OLD AIRPORT REEF	16	Small wall running parallel with shore 18" high	Boat 200 yds.	25'–50'	Snorkel or dive
POUND HOUSE REEF (MONTEGO BAY)	17	Lovely coral reef	Boat	50'–120'	Dive
CHALET CARIB REEF	18	Drop-off	Beach 200 yds.	50'–220'	Dive
POINT REEF (Experienced only)	19	Drop-off; excellent dive	Boat	70'–360'	Dive
MONTEGO BAY (5½ mi. toward Negril) 100 yds.—W. shore	20	Coral reef with great pillar corals	Boat or swim from beach 100 yds.	15'–25'	Snorkel or dive

SURF OR CALM	HIGH-LIGHTS	FISHING AND PHOTOS	DANGERS	DIVE FACILITY	ACCOMMODATIONS
Calm, a.m. best	Lovely corals, fish, pillar coral	Photos	None	No known dive facility	As above
Calm in a.m.	Some fish	Photos, spearing	None	None	Can stay on beach in cottages.
Rough	Ruins and many wrecks	Neither	Dirty water, heavy tides	None	3-4 hotels

Visibility: 25' – 100'   **Best Season:** Spring, summer, fall.

SURF OR CALM	HIGH-LIGHTS	FISHING AND PHOTOS	DANGERS	DIVE FACILITY	ACCOMMODATIONS
Calm in a.m.	Caves, crevices, and tunnels in wall	Photos	None	Sea Crabs Diving School at Chatham Beach Hotel Montego Bay	Many at all prices
Calm	Fans, black coral, sponges, caves	Photos	Watch for urchins and fire coral in caves and tunnel.	Montego Reef Divers at Chalet Carib Hotel 6 mi W. Montego Bay	As above
Calm	Colored sponges, fans, black coral, crevices, canyons	Photos	Depth: narcosis	Port Royal Water Sports Kingston Negril Sundowner Hotel	As above
Calm	Huge sponges, fans, fish	Photos	Current	As above	As above
Varies	All corals, especially pillar	Photos	None	As above	As above

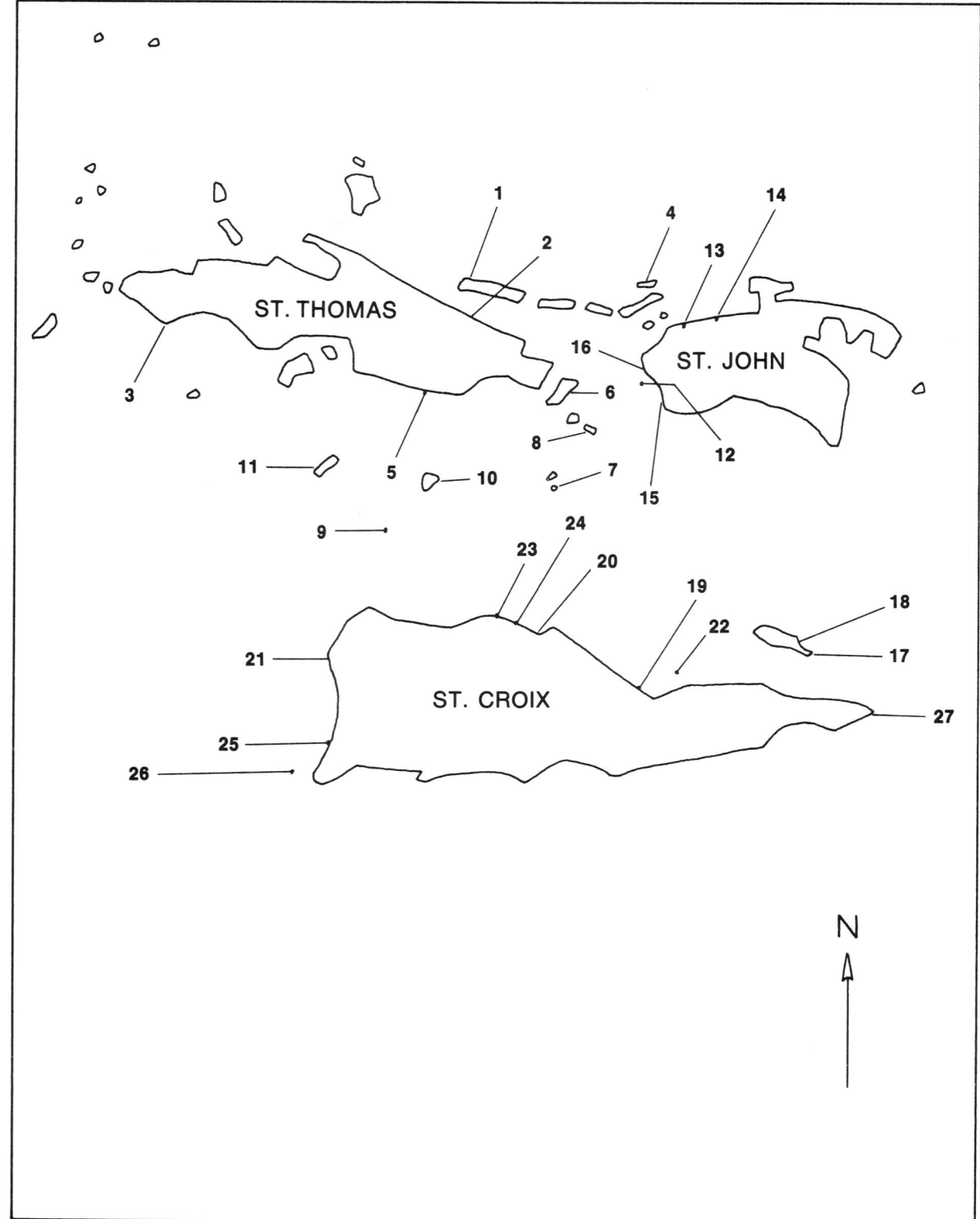

ST. THOMAS

ST. JOHN

ST. CROIX

N

THE U.S. VIRGIN ISLANDS

(ST. CROIX/ST. THOMAS/ST. JOHN)

St. Croix, St. Thomas, and St. John are island possessions of the United States, and as a result, money, stamps, and language will be no problem. Except for the lilting native accent of the people and the slow, relaxed pace, things are as they are on the mainland. The three islands have distinct personalities: St. Thomas offering the night life and excitement of some of the Bahamas and West Indies; St. Croix luring stateside vacationers to become permanent residents with its quiet, stately charm; and St. John providing a haven for the traveler who wants to get away from it all, with its limited development and enormous National Park.

Student divers enjoy a peek at the shy squirrelfish. (Janet Viertel)

Snorkeling and diving are excellent on all three islands. Weather is consistently good, and although the winter can bring choppy waters, reefs are almost never undiveable. The greater part of the activity may be done with snorkel equipment, although there are some deep reefs for the experienced diver.

St. Croix, the largest and most southerly of the islands, boasts the famous Buck Island underwater trail, a national park and monument, with underwater markers identifying the various corals and fish, leading the snorkeler to a spectacular antler-coral forest at the trail's end. In addition to the trail, there are plenty of coral heads surrounding the area where your boat will be moored, and one can snorkel this park endlessly, discovering fresh sights. The collection of fish at Buck Island is nearly unmatchable. Many boats are available to take you to the island trail—about forty-five minutes by sail, shorter by power. For the adventurous snorkeler there are beach entry reefs along the north and west shores of the island.

The snorkeling and diving on St. Thomas are varied. In addition to the reefs, there are wrecks and volcanic rock formations covered with plant life and coral. The best diving is from boats, although there are some good small reefs accessible from the beach. St. Thomas also serves as a jumping-off point for boat trips to the dive spots off the British Virgin Islands, through the Sir Francis Drake Channel. The dive facilities are excellent, and night diving is available for those who are up to it.

St. John, the smallest of the three islands, is taken up primarily by the National Park, and so remains unspoiled and primitive. There are countless small reefs ringing the island and good facilities providing boat trips as well as recommendations for beach dives, particularly Trunk Bay, a marked underwater trail for snorkelers.

All three islands have excellent hotel facilities, reliable weather, good photo possibilities both over and under water. In general they provide excellent vacation spots of varying moods.

U.S. Virgin Islands

ST. THOMAS

Water Temp.: 71º – 83º

Regulations: No restrictions on spearing or collecting except in national parks.

PLACE	NO.	DESCRIPTION	ENTRY AND DISTANCE FROM SHORE	DEPTH	SNORKEL OR DIVE
THATCH CAY	1	Swim through island in tunnels	Boat	60' – 65'	Dive
COKI BEACH	2	Coral reef	Public beach At shore	3' – 10' – 60'	Snorkel or dive
FORTUNA BAY	3	Rocky bottom running parallel to beach with coral formations	Shore 20'	5' – 22'	Snorkel or dive
CONGO CAY (Expert only)	4	Arches and fish	Boat	30' – 55'	Snorkel or dive
SECRET HARBOR	5	Coral reef	Beach 15'	1' – 20'	Snorkel or dive
ST. JAMES ISLAND	6	Coral reefs	Boat to a rocky coral beach. 25 min. St. Thomas	40'	Snorkel or dive
COW AND CALF ROCKS	7	Two rocks around which you can dive	Boat 3 miles	25'	Snorkel or dive
DOG ISLAND E. Dog Rocks W. Dog Rocks (Experienced only)	8	Coral reefs	Boat 10 – 15 min.	50' – 60'	Snorkel or dive
FRENCH CAP CAY OR BAY (Expert only)	9	Fairly shallow to deep reef. Forests, rocks, ridges, alleys	Boat	10' – 90'	Snorkel or dive

Visibility: 50′–85′ **Best Season:** Spring and summer best, but anytime is good.

SURF OR CALM	HIGH-LIGHTS	FISHING AND PHOTOS	DANGERS	DIVE FACILITY	ACCOMMODATIONS
South calm, north surge	Tropical fish, urchins, barracuda, shark	Spearfishing or photos	Shark, but do not seem dangerous	Joe Vogel Box 2091 St. Thomas, V.I. 00801 Tel. 809-774-2321 on waterfront at Sebastian's Restaurant	Many, at all prices
Calm	Coral reef fish	Photos only	Slight current at drop-off	John Hamber P.O. Box 2432 Sapphire Bay St. Thomas, V.I. 00801 Tel. 809-775-0755	As above
Calm or rough	Corals covering rocky bottom, huge boulders	Photos, spearing, collecting	Rough shore entry		As above
N. side varies, S. side calm	Boulders, lava arches, lots of fish	Photos, spearing	None	Undersea Centers Corp. Box 7100 St. Thomas, V.I. 00801 Tel. 809-774-3992	As above
Calm	Corals, fish, marked underwater trail	Photos only	None	Aqua Action Secret Harbor St. Thomas, V.I. 00801 809-775-3275	As above
Calm	Coral-covered rocky reef, sea whips, sea fans, caves, ledges, boulders	Photos only	None	As above	As above
Calm	Corals, fish, caves	Photos	Variable currents	As above	As above
Calm or very rough	Reef, tunnels, caves, fish, corals, sponges, lobster	Collect only, photos	Dangerous when rough	As above	As above
Calm	Large elkhorn corals and sponges	Photos	Shark come easily when spearing	As above	As above

ST. THOMAS CONTINUED

172

PLACE	NO.	DESCRIPTION	ENTRY AND DISTANCE FROM SHORE	DEPTH	SNORKEL OR DIVE
CAPELI ISLAND	10	Wreck dive	Boat	10'–50'	Snorkel or dive
BUCK ISLAND	11	Coral reef	Boat	Varies, 20'–80'	Snorkel or dive
STEVENS CAY	12	Coral reefs	Rocky coral beach reached by boat. 30 min. St. Thomas	5'–60'	Snorkel or dive

ST. JOHN

Water Temp.: 78º–83º

Regulations: No spearing of fish or collecting in National Underwater Park. You can take 2 lobsters a day at park.

PLACE	NO.	DESCRIPTION	ENTRY AND DISTANCE FROM SHORE	DEPTH	SNORKEL OR DIVE
HAWKSNEST BAY	13	Coral reefs	Beach Off shore	To 20'	Snorkel
TRUNK BAY	14	Coral reefs	Beach Off shore	0'–15'	Snorkel
DEEVER'S BAY	15	Coral reefs	Boat or beach. By boat 5 min. from Cruz Bay	40'–55'	Dive
TURNER BAY	16	Coral reefs	Boat	15'–30'	Snorkel or dive

SURF OR CALM	HIGH-LIGHTS	FISHING AND PHOTOS	DANGERS	DIVE FACILITY	ACCOMMODATIONS
Calm	Wreck of Boat Wye. Not too much left	Photos	None	See page 171.	See page 171.
Calm	Corals, fish, wreck	Photos or spearfishing	None	As above	As above
Calm	Fish, reefs, ledges, wreck	Photos only	None, slight current	As above	As above

Visibility: 50′–100′   **Best Season:** Anytime; can be in water every day of year

Calm	Fish, corals	Photos only	None	All at: International Dive Club Box 161 Cruz Bay St. John, U.S.V.I. 00830 Tel. 809-776-6256 Mr. Nose	All. Wide range, from expensive Caneel Bay Plantation to camping sites
Calm	Public underwater marked trail; lifeguards; fish, corals, marine life	Photos only	None		
Calm	Fish, reefs	Photos only	None	As above	As above
Calm	Fish, reefs	Photos only	None	As above	As above

ST. CROIX

Water Temp.: 78°–83°

Regulations: Spearing and collecting permitted except at Buck Island National Monument.

174

PLACE	NO.	DESCRIPTION	ENTRY AND DISTANCE FROM SHORE	DEPTH	SNORKEL OR DIVE
BUCK ISLAND	17	Magnificent national underwater park	By boat ½ hr. St. Croix. Sailboats from Christiansted Harbour	15'	Snorkel
N. CUT BUCK ISLAND	18	Part of #17. Tall coral pinnacles	See #17	2'–40'–75'	Dive
SALT RIVER DROP OFF	19	Drop-off	Boat	20'–1000'	Dive
CANE BAY DROP OFF	20	Drop-off	Boat or beach	60'–70' then deep	Dive
BLUE CHIPS AND NORTHSIDE LEDGE	21	Shallow coral reef	From rocky shore At shore	0'–15'	Snorkel
WHITE HORSE REEF	22	Reef on site of several shipwrecks	Boat 200 yds.	15'–25'	Snorkel or dive
DAVIS BAY	23	Drop-off	Beach or boat Off shore 200' from beach	40'–70'–3000'	Snorkel or dive

Visibility: 50′ – 100′   **Best Season:** Anytime; you can dive any day in the Virgin Islands.

SURF OR CALM	HIGH-LIGHTS	FISHING AND PHOTOS	DANGERS	DIVE FACILITY	ACCOMMODATIONS
Calm	Elkhorn coral (giant), colorful tropical fish, gorgonias	Photos	None	All available at V.I. Divers The Pan Am Pavillion Christiansted St. Croix, V.I. 00820 Attn: Bret Gilliam Tel. 809-773-6045	All of every price and description
Calm	Turtles, porpoises, coral structures, fish	Photos	None		As above
Calm	Big reef, fish, black coral trees	Photos, spearing	None	The Salty Dogs 59 Kings Wharf Christiansted St. Croix, V.I. 00820 Tel. 809-773-2678	As above
Calm	Coral mounds, black coral, large fish, giant turtles	Photos, spearing	None	Snorkel only Sea Rovers Sea Shop Pan Am Pavillion Christiansted St. Croix, V.I. 00820 Tel. 809-773-1355	As above
Very calm	Monks bath carved out of lava, fish, shells	Photos	None	As above	As above
Light breaking surf	Reef, artifacts, caves, elkhorn corals, fish	Photos, spearfishing	None	As above	As above
Calm, can be waves near shore	Rock and coral mound structure	Photos, spearing	None; be careful of beach entry.	As above	As above

ST. CROIX CONTINUED

PLACE	NO.	DESCRIPTION	ENTRY AND DISTANCE FROM SHORE	DEPTH	SNORKEL OR DIVE
NORTH STAR WALL	24	Drop-off	Boat 150'	40' – 75' – drop off	Dive
FREDERICKSTED PIER	25	Great marine life at bottom of pier	Ladder on pier Under pier or boat	25' – 40'	Dive
WRECK OF THE VICTORY	26	Wreck of fishing trawler	From boat or swim from Fredericksted pier 200 yds.	100'	Dive
LANG BANK	27	Unexplored reef, large fish	Boat	45' – 60'	Dive

SURF OR CALM	HIGH-LIGHTS	FISHING AND PHOTOS	DANGERS	DIVE FACILITY	ACCOMMODATIONS
Calm	Coral formations, sea fans, lobster, snapper, grouper, yellowtail	Photos, spearing	None	See page 175.	Many on island.
Calm	Sponges, coral forms, fish, lobster, shrimp, artifacts, bottles	Photos, collecting	None	As above	As above
Calm	Wreck and another wreck, grouper, parrotfish	Photos, spearing	None	As above	As above
Calm	Snapper, grouper, reefs, dolphin, wahoo, tuna	Photos, spearing	None	As above	As above

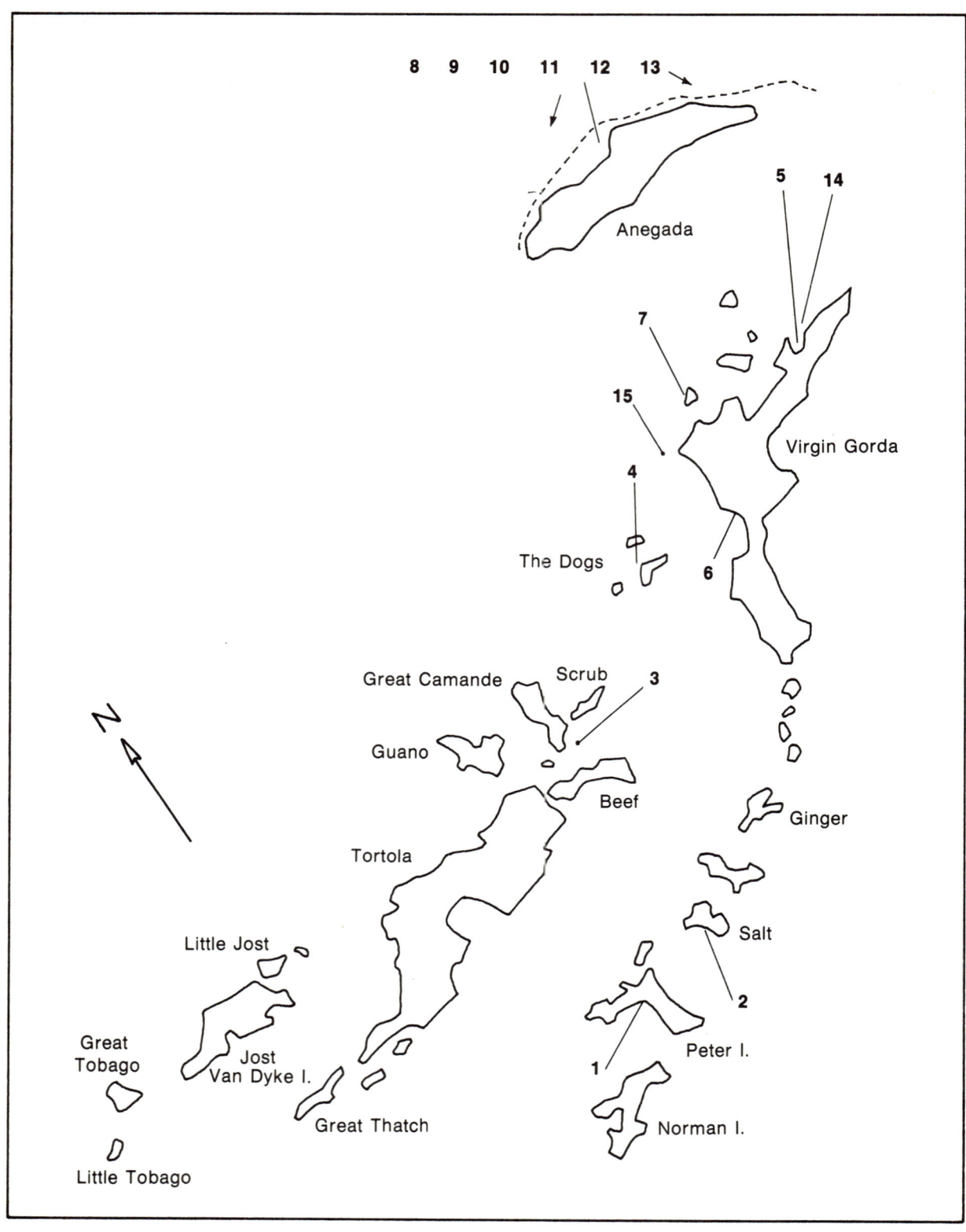

8 9 10 11 12 13

Anegada

5 14

7

15

4

Virgin Gorda

The Dogs

6

Great Camande   Scrub   **3**

Guano

Beef

Ginger

Tortola

Little Jost

Salt

2

Great
Tobago

Jost
Van Dyke I.

1   Peter I.

Little Tobago

Great Thatch

Norman I.

N

THE BRITISH VIRGIN ISLANDS

**(TORTOLA/VIRGIN GORDA/
PETER ISLAND/NORMAN
ISLAND/AND SEVERAL SMALL
ISLANDS AND ISLETS)**

The British Virgin Islands are not as developed as the American Virgins, and therefore, they are good hide-aways for an inactive vacation. The area is studded with reefs, and particularly with wrecks for the advanced scuba diver. Boats are available to carry you from Tortola and Virgin Gorda out to reefs or small cay beaches where you dive and snorkel from shore. St. Thomas, in the American Virgins, also provides a good deal of boat service to the reefs and wrecks of the British islands.

The wreck diving here is legen-dary—there are over 200 wrecks on the Anegada Reef alone, but most of them are in deep enough water to require a good deal of scuba experience, and unfortunate-ly the shark is a frequent visitor to these areas.

The reefs provide a good deal of spectacular scenery in comfort and safety, however, and there are thousands of tame fish, as well as artifacts from the wrecks that get

Lobsters hide in crevices and holes and can be caught by the skin diver with a wire lariat. In the interest of protecting the species, it's best not to take females. (Janet Viertel)

washed over the ocean floor. Like the American Virgins, these reefs tend to be consistently clear and calm. They do become a little unreliable during the winter, but rarely to the point where they are undiveable.

In addition to the standard reef diving, Virgin Gorda offers an area called the baths, where snorkelers can swim out from inlet pools through rock arches into the open ocean.

Living is simple on these islands, but that may be exactly what you are looking for. They are acces-sible, there are hotels of varying prices, and dive facilities are avail-able. Away from the high-power tourism of the other islands, the British Virgins provide an excellent honeymoon spot, or a retreat for the world-weary city dweller.

British Virgin Islands

Water Temp.: 77° – 80°

Regulations: No spearfishing.

PLACE	NO.	DESCRIPTION	ENTRY AND DISTANCE FROM SHORE	DEPTH	SNORKEL OR DIVE
PETER ISLAND Great Harbor	1	Coral reefs and fish which can be hand-fed	Beach or boat 10 min. from dock 30' from shore	25' – 40'	Snorkel or dive
SALT ISLAND Wreck of the Rhone	2	Shipwreck 1876—steel steam-driven mail packet	Boat 20 min. from Tortola 30 min. from Virgin Gorda	35' – 88'	Snorkel or dive
MARINA CAY	3	Lovely coral reef	Beach At shore	5' – 30'	Snorkel or dive
THE DOG ISLANDS	4	Coral reefs with fish	Go by boat. Beach when you get there	10' – 25'	Snorkel or dive
OILNUT BAY	5	Coral reef	Go by boat. Beach when you get there	20' – 40'	Snorkel or dive
VIRGIN GORDA BATHS	6	Arches and tunnels	Beach At shore	3' – 6'	Snorkel
MOSQUITO ISLAND Drake's Anchorage	7	Shallow coral reef	Beach	Shallow	Snorkel or dive
ANEGADA REEF (200 Wrecks) Wreck of the Rocas	8	Shipwreck with animal bones (cargo, horse and cattle); sunk 1919 or 1929. 380' long	Boat	35'	Dive

Visibility: 75'–100'   **Best Season:** Anytime; spring & summer best

SURF OR CALM	HIGH-LIGHTS	FISHING AND PHOTOS	DANGERS	DIVE FACILITY	ACCOMMODATIONS
Calm, sheltered	Protected reef many tame fish	Photos only	None	Bert Kilbride c/o Little Dix Bay Hotel Box 40 Virgin Gorda, B.V.I. Tel. 5-5555 Bring own vests. See above for address.	Of all sorts on many islands Peter Island Yacht Club Box 211 Roadtown, Tortola, B.V.I. Attn: T.G. Loberg
Calm, waves to 2'. Can be rough in winter	Shipwreck artifacts, cannon, many tame fish	Photos only	Currents at times		Little Dix Bay Hotel Resort Box 70 Virgin Gorda, B.V.I. Tel. 5-5555
Calm	Reef fish	Photos only	None	Marina Cay Hotel Frank & Mike Giacinto Marina Cay P.O. Box 76 Tortola, B.V.I. Bring own regulator.	
Calm summer, rough sometimes in winter	Coral reefs and tropical fish	Photos only	None if calm; can be rough		Marina Cay Hotel Marina Cay P.O. Box 76 Tortola, B.V.I. Tel. Roadtown, Tortola 4-2174
Calm	Coral reef fish	Photos only	None	B.V.I. Aquatic Centers Box 108 Roadtown, Tortola, B.V.I. Peter Island Aquatic Ctr. Peter Island Tel. 4-2839 or from St. Thomas See American Virgin Island charts: Joe Vogel John Hamber	As above
Calm	Snorkel through tunnel out into sea	Photos with artificial light	None		As above
Calm	Fish reefs	Photos	None		As above
Varies	Wreck, antler coral, fish	Photos	None Can be shark	As above	As above

BRITISH VIRGIN ISLANDS CONTINUED

PLACE	NO.	DESCRIPTION	ENTRY AND DISTANCE FROM SHORE	DEPTH	SNORKEL OR DIVE
ANEGADA REEF Wreck of Paramatta	9	Shipwreck; sunk 115 years ago. A sidewheeler sunk on maiden voyage	Boat	35'	Dive
ANEGADA REEF H.M.S. Astrea on outside of reef	10	Shipwreck; sunk 1808. 32-gun frigate	Boat	15'	Snorkel or dive
ANEGADA REEF 1776 Wreck (Expert)	11	Shipwreck; sunk in 1776	Boat	Shallow	Snorkel or dive
ANEGADA REEF The Carronade Wreck (Expert)	12	Shipwreck; sunk about 1800	Boat	10'	Snorkel or dive
ANEGADA REEF The French Wreck (Expert)	13	Shipwreck, possibly the Rosembleau, sunk 1791	Boat	40'–50'	Snorkel or dive
ANEGADA REEF The Invisibles (Expert)	14	Large rock formations rising from 50'–3' under surface	Boat	50'	Dive
ANEGADA REEF Van Rhyns Rock (Expert)	15	Many fish	Boat 5 min. Virgin Gorda	15'–45'	Dive

182

SURF OR CALM	HIGH-LIGHTS	FISHING AND PHOTOS	DANGERS	DIVE FACILITY	ACCOMMODATIONS
Varies	Great elkhorn coral; lots of fish	Photos	None Can be shark	See page 181	See page 181
Varies	Wreck, anchors, cannons and cannon balls	Photos	Surge. Can be shark	As above	As above
Varies	Anchors, cannon and round ballast stones	Photos	Shark	As above	As above
Varies	Cannon balls, ballast bars, artifacts	Photos	Shark	As above	As above
Varies	Artifacts	Photos	Shark	As above	As above
Varies	Big fish, great visibility	Photos	Current	As above	As above
Can chop	Lots of fish	Photos only	None	As above	As above

184

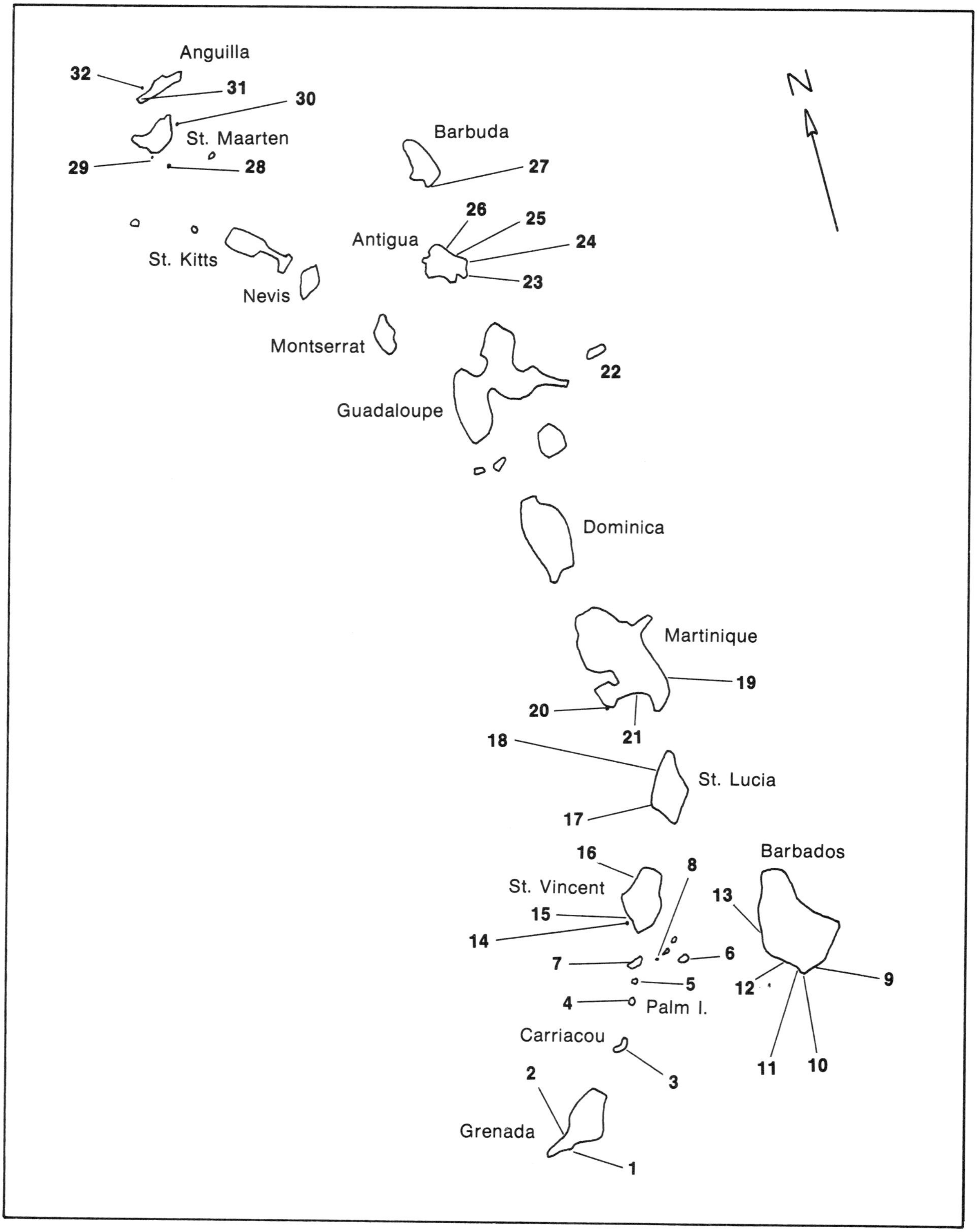

Anguilla

32 **31** **30**

St. Maarten

29 **28**

Barbuda

27

26 **25**

Antigua **24**

23

St. Kitts

Nevis

Montserrat

22

Guadaloupe

Dominica

Martinique

19

20

21

18

St. Lucia

17

16

8

Barbados

St. Vincent

13

15

14

7 **6**

5

9

4 Palm I. **12**

Carriacou **11** **10**

2 **3**

Grenada

1

N

THE LESSER ANTILLES

Forming the eastern border of the Caribbean Sea is a string of islands—some independent, some protectorates of European countries—known as the Lesser Antilles. These islands offer among the finest and most varied diving experiences to be had anywhere in the world. The coral reefs are justly famous, and the hobbyist will find a plentiful selection of shells, and other collectables as well. Underwater photo spots abound. In addition, spearfishing is legal in many areas, although frowned upon by more and more members of the diving community. There is no legal protection for the coral, either, but this should always be left undisturbed.

Due to the sandy bottoms and reduced plankton count (plankton are minute forms of sea life that float in the water and serve as food for fish), the water is a stunning, light turquoise color. The lack of plankton also serves to slightly reduce the number of sea creatures, but the reefs still abound with multicolored fish of various shapes and sizes as well as lobsters and sea turtles. They swim through a veritable fairyland of coral gardens, sea fans, whips, and richly hued sponges that make this area a must for the photographer as well as the casual sightseer. Happily, many of the reefs are shallow enough for snorkeling.

St. Maarten's reefs, protected bays, and covers provide scuba diving for novice and veteran alike. (Helen Marcus/Sontheimer & Co.)

There are countless reefs, many of them not marked on the map, but several of the islands have neither reefs nor facilities, so read the charts with care. As usual, the weather is at its worst in the winter, but as you travel south, the visibility and calm become more and more constant.

Since several nationalities are represented in the chain, the "personalities" of the islands vary, but many of them offer superior shopping, quiet resorts, and native customs and cuisines. Your travel agent will be able to fill in the details.

Lesser Antilles

THE GRENADINES

Water Temp.: 80º

Regulations: Check individual islands.

PLACE	NO.	DESCRIPTION	ENTRY AND DISTANCE FROM SHORE	DEPTH	SNORKEL OR DIVE
GRENADA SOUTH COAST REEFS	1	Coral reefs shallow and deep	Boat ½ hr.	6' and down	Snorkel or dive
GRENADA MOLINET POINT	2	Coral reefs, wrecks	Boat (1-hr. sail from Grand Anse)	20' and down	Snorkel or dive
CARIACOU SANDY ISLAND	3	Lovely protected reef	Boat	Shallow	Snorkel or dive
PALM ISLAND	4	Thirteen dive spots within a 3-mi. radius	Beach or boat	From surface down	Snorkel or dive
MAYERO ISLAND	5	Wreck of the *Poruna*	Boat 20 min.	40'	Dive
MUSTIQUE	6	Coral reef at Brittania Bay	Beach 10 yards	20'	Snorkel or dive

Visibility: Varies to 100′   **Best Season:** Anytime

SURF OR CALM	HIGH-LIGHTS	FISHING AND PHOTOS	DANGERS	DIVE FACILITY	ACCOMMODATIONS
Calm in summer, can be rough in winter	Marvelous corals and fish	Spearfishing and photos	None	Aquatic Sports at Grand Anse Grenada Water Sports Grand Anse Beach Tel. 4239 ext. 191	Secret Harbor Grenada, W.I. also others of varying prices
Calm	Wreck of *Bianca* (594′ long) at 150′ large fish	Spearfishing and photos	None		As above
Calm	Spectacular coral reef with fish	Photos only	None	As above	In Grenada or write Carriacou Tourist and Development Board, Carriacou, Grenada
Calm	Shallow and deep reefs, cliff walls, wrecks, caves, blue hole (unexplored), lobster, fish, conch, turtle	Spear only what you can eat. Photos	None	Scuba Shack Palm Island W.I. Everything available	Scuba Shack, Palom Island St. Vincent, W.I. (a small cottage-type hotel) John and Christie Caldwell
Calm in summer, can be rough in winter	100′ British gunboat; fish, lobsters, bottles, etc.	Spear only what you can eat. Photos	Getting caught in wreck	As above	As above
Calm	Fish, reefs	Photos only	None	No equipment. Zodiac boat and air compressor	The Cotton House Mustique Grenadines, W.I.

THE GRENADINES CONTINUED

188

PLACE	NO.	DESCRIPTION	ENTRY AND DISTANCE FROM SHORE	DEPTH	SNORKEL OR DIVE
BEQUIA FRIENDSHIP BAY	7	Some snorkeling areas; mostly a place for sailing	Not known	Not known	Snorkel
TOBAGO CAYS	8	Horseshoe reef	Boat 25 min. Beach when you get there, 200 yds.	10' – 20'	Great snorkeling for miles

BARBADOS   Water Temp.: 80°

Regulations: Spearfishing permitted.

PLACE	NO.	DESCRIPTION	ENTRY AND DISTANCE FROM SHORE	DEPTH	SNORKEL OR DIVE
COBBLER REEF (Expert only)	9	Coral reef that is a graveyard for old shipwrecks	Boat	70' – 200'	Dive
ASTA REEF	10	Coral reef	Boat 10 min. from dock 300 yds. of rough water from beach	25' – 120'	Snorkel or dive
HILTON REEF	11	Coral reef with a wreck	Hilton Beach or 3 min. by boat to reef 100 yds. calm shallow swim	20' – 80'	Snorkel or dive
CARLISLE BAY	12	Wreck on a coral reef	Boat	15' – 35'	Snorkel or dive
WEST SIDE Shallow and deep reefs	13	Coral reefs	Boat up to ½ mile	15' – 35' Shallow 70' – 200' deep	Dive

SURF OR CALM	HIGH-LIGHTS	FISHING AND PHOTOS	DANGERS	DIVE FACILITY	ACCOMMODATIONS
Not known	Not known	Photos	None	Not known	Sunny Caribbee Bequia, St. Vincent Grenadines or Friendship Bay Hotel Bequia, St. Vincent, Grenadines Capt. Niels Peter Thompsen
Calm; slight current toward shore	Lovely coral gardens, fish, conch, fans, lobsters, shells	Spear only what you can eat. Photos	None	All at Scuba Shack on Palm Island (see above)	By boat. No accommodations

Visibility: Varies to 100′   **Best Season:** Anytime

SURF OR CALM	HIGH-LIGHTS	FISHING AND PHOTOS	DANGERS	DIVE FACILITY	ACCOMMODATIONS
Surf varies	Wrecks, corals, fish	Spearfishing, photos	Currents rough	Scuba Safari Hilton Dr. St. Michael Barbados, W.I. att: Paki Degia (fully equipped dive shop)	Half Moon Beach Hotel Barbados, W.I. and many other accommodations at various prices
Calm when you get there	Corals, tropical fish	Spearfishing, photos (50′−60′ visibility)	None		
Calm	Reef, wreck, artifacts	Photos and spearfishing.	None	As above	As above
Calm	German W.W. I wreck, tropical fish, corals	Spearfishing, photos	None	As above	As above
Calm	Fish, corals, turtles, sponges	Photos and spearfishing, but not too near Coral Reef Club	None	As above	As above

189

ST. VINCENT
Water Temp.: 80°

Regulations: Spearfishing permitted.

190

PLACE	NO.	DESCRIPTION	ENTRY AND DISTANCE FROM SHORE	DEPTH	SNORKEL OR DIVE
YOUNG ISLAND	14	A mini-coral reef on S.E. and a deeper reef on S.W. corner	Beaches S.E. 35' S.W. 250'	3' and down	Snorkel or dive
INDIAN BAY CANASH	15	Coral reefs, fish, marine life	Beach 5 yds.	To 90'	Snorkel or dive
LEEWARD COAST	16	Coral reefs and fish at N. and S. end of coast	Boat; beach when you get there 10 yds.	To 150'	Snorkel or dive

ST. LUCIA
Water Temp.: 80°

Regulations: Spearfishing permitted.

THE SEA OFF ANSE CHASTENET HOTEL	17	A coral reef (diving off St. Lucia is relatively unexplored)	Beach 10'	7'–250'	Snorkel or dive
THE SEA OFF CARIBLUE HOTEL	18	Coral reef	Beach 100'	7'–100'	Snorkel or dive

Visibility: Varies to 100'   **Best Season:** Anytime

SURF OR CALM	HIGH-LIGHTS	FISHING AND PHOTOS	DANGERS	DIVE FACILITY	ACCOMMODATIONS
Calm	Fish and lovely coral reefs	Photos. Spearing in deeper area of S.W.	None	Snorkel equipment on Young Island	Young Island St. Vincent, W.I. att: Mr. Ralph Locke 315 E. 72 St. New York, N.Y. 10021 Tel. 212-628-8149
Calm	All tropical marine life, lots of fish	Spearfishing, photos	None	Bill Miller at Mariner's Inn	Mariner's Inn Villa Beach P.O. Box 868 Kingstown, St. Vincent, W.I. Several others
Calm	Coral, fish	Spearfishing or photos	None	All available c/o Bill Miller at Mariner's Inn, Villa Beach	

Visibility: Varies to 100'   **Best Season:** Anytime

| Calm | Coral reef, fish | Spearing or photos | None | Local divers will take parties out. Contact: Mrs. Beverly Pringle Carib Cruises Ltd. P.O. Box 188 Castries St. Lucia Tel. 3754 | Inexpensive. Several hotels: Anse Chastanet Beach Hotel Soufriere, St. Lucia

and many others including an air conditioned Holiday Inn

Cariblue Hotel St. Lucia, W.I. |
| Calm; once in a while a long swell | Coral reef, fish | Spearing or photos | None | | |

MARTINIQUE Water Temp.: 80°

Regulations: Spearfishing without scuba gear.

192

PLACE	NO.	DESCRIPTION	ENTRY AND DISTANCE FROM SHORE	DEPTH	SNORKEL OR DIVE
PONT EST (and other spots on island)	19	Coral reef	Beach 200′	2′ and down	Snorkel
DIAMOND ROCK	20	Lovely reefs and caverns	Boat 45 min.	10′–70′	Snorkel or dive
COAST FROM DIAMOND ROCK W. TO CLUB MEDITERRANEE	21	Reefs, fish	Beach or boat At shore	Shore and deeper	Snorkel or dive

GUADELOUPE Water Temp.: 80°

Regulations: No spearfishing.

PLACE	NO.	DESCRIPTION	ENTRY AND DISTANCE FROM SHORE	DEPTH	SNORKEL OR DIVE
PIGEON ISLAND	22	Reef, fish	Beach, but go by boat (10 min.) 1 mi.	10′–200′	Snorkel or dive

Visibility: Varies to 100′   **Best Season:** Anytime

SURF OR CALM	HIGH-LIGHTS	FISHING AND PHOTOS	DANGERS	DIVE FACILITY	ACCOMMODATIONS
Calm	Coral, anemones, schools of fish, fans	Photos, spearing	None	Martinique at Club Méditerranée Buccaneer's Creek Ste. Anne Martinique, F.W.I. and at several hotels	Many hotels here including: Club Méditerranée Buccaneer's Creek Ste. Anne Martinique, F.W.I. or N.Y. Representative Club Méditerranée 40 W. 57th St. N.Y. 10019 Tel. 212-977-2121
Calm one side or other	Reef, fish, caverns	Photos or fish without tanks	None		
Calm in many places	Reef, fish	Photos, spearing without tanks	None	As above	As above

Visibility: Varies to 100′   **Best Season:** Anytime

SURF OR CALM	HIGH-LIGHTS	FISHING AND PHOTOS	DANGERS	DIVE FACILITY	ACCOMMODATIONS
Calm	Tropical fish, marine life	Photos only	Currents sometimes	Dive at Club Méditerranée 97180 Sainte Anne Guadeloupe F.W.I.	Holiday Inn Gosler Guadeloupe F.W.I.

ANTIGUA
Water Temp.: 80°

Regulations: Spearfishing permitted.

194

PLACE	NO.	DESCRIPTION	ENTRY AND DISTANCE FROM SHORE	DEPTH	SNORKEL OR DIVE
HALF MOON BAY (Halfway between Long Bay and Nelson's Dockyard)	23	Coral reefs, fish	Beach Off shore	5'–50'	Snorkel or dive
LONG BAY	24	Coral reef	Beach or boat At shore	2'–30'	Great snorkeling and diving
ANTIGUA HORIZONS	25	Coral reefs off beach in front of hotel	Beach Off shore 50'	6'–40'	Snorkel or dive
GREEN ISLAND	26	Coral reefs	Boat 15 min. then beach 50' from shore; easy swim	2'–50' and a second reef to 200'	Great snorkeling and diving

BARBUDA
Water Temp.: 80°

Regulations: Spearfishing permitted.

BARBUDA	27	Coral reefs	Beach At shore	Shallow	Snorkel or dive

Visibility: Varies to 100′   **Best Season:** Anytime

SURF OR CALM	HIGH-LIGHTS	FISHING AND PHOTOS	DANGERS	DIVE FACILITY	ACCOMMODATIONS
Calm	Great elkhorn corals and caves	Spearing, photos	None	All at Long Bay Hotel Box 442 Antigua, W.I. Tel. 32005 Att: Jacques E. Lafaurie	Antigua Horizons Hotel, Antigua, W.I. Holiday Inn Antigua, W.I. Tel. 31015
Calm	Fish, reefs	Photos, spearing	None	Charter boats out of Nelson's Dockyard	Curtain Bluff Hotel Antigua and W.I. Many others
Calm	Fish, corals, huge parrot fish, lobsters	Photos, spearing	None	As above	As above
Calm	Fish and reefs	Photos and spearing	None	As above	As above

Visibility: Varies to 100′   **Best Season:** Anytime

Calm	Reefs and shipwrecks	Photos and spearing	None	At Coco Pt. Lodge	Coco Pt. Lodge small inn (very expensive)

ST. MAARTEN   **Water Temp.:** 80°

Regulations: Spearfishing without scuba gear.

196

PLACE	NO.	DESCRIPTION	ENTRY AND DISTANCE FROM SHORE	DEPTH	SNORKEL OR DIVE
GROUPER ROCKS	28	Coral reef	Boat 45 min.	Shallow then 15'–50'	Snorkel or dive
MAN-O'-WAR WRECK ON PROSELYTE REEF	29	Wreck	Boat 15 min.	15' 60'	Dive
GREEN CAY	30	Mature coral reef	Boat 10 min., beach on Cay Reef near beach	35'	Snorkel or dive

ANGUILLA   **Water Temp.:** 80°

Regulations: Spearfishing permitted.

COVE BAY (Reefs almost encircle Anguilla)	31	Coral reef	Boat	Varies	Snorkel or dive
SANDY ISLE	32	Coral reef	Boat 1 hr. At shore of Sandy Isle	Shallow	Snorkel

Visibility: 10′ – 100′　　　　　　**Best Season:** Anytime

SURF OR CALM	HIGH-LIGHTS	FISHING AND PHOTOS	DANGERS	DIVE FACILITY	ACCOMMODATIONS
Rough in winter, calm in summer	Reef, fish	Photos, no scuba to spear, visibility often poor	None	Underwater Research Ctr. P.O. Box 234 St. Maarten, N.A. (Netherland Antilles)	Many, at varied prices
Rough	Reef, wreck, cannons, anchors, fish	Visibility can be 10′ – 100′. photos; no scuba spearing	Rough and current	Maho Water Sports Mullet Bay Beach Hotel St. Maarten, N.A. att: Jeff and Ann Klein	As above
Calm to rough	Fish, coral, lobsters, shells	Photos and shells	None	As above	As above

Visibility: Varies to 100′　　　　　　**Best Season:** Anytime

Calm	Lots of fish, shells, coral reefs	Photos, spearing	None	None Arrange boats through hotel.	Several hotels, inexpensive
Calm	Lovely reef, fish	Photos, spearing	None	As above	As above

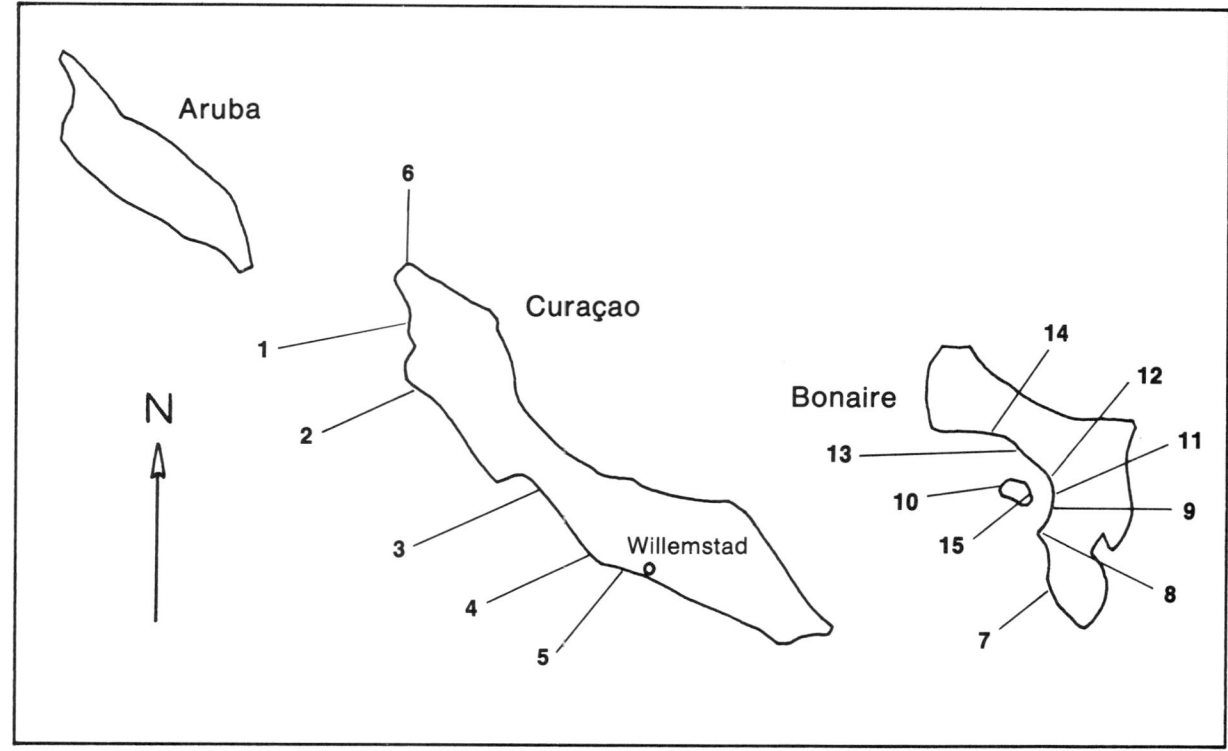

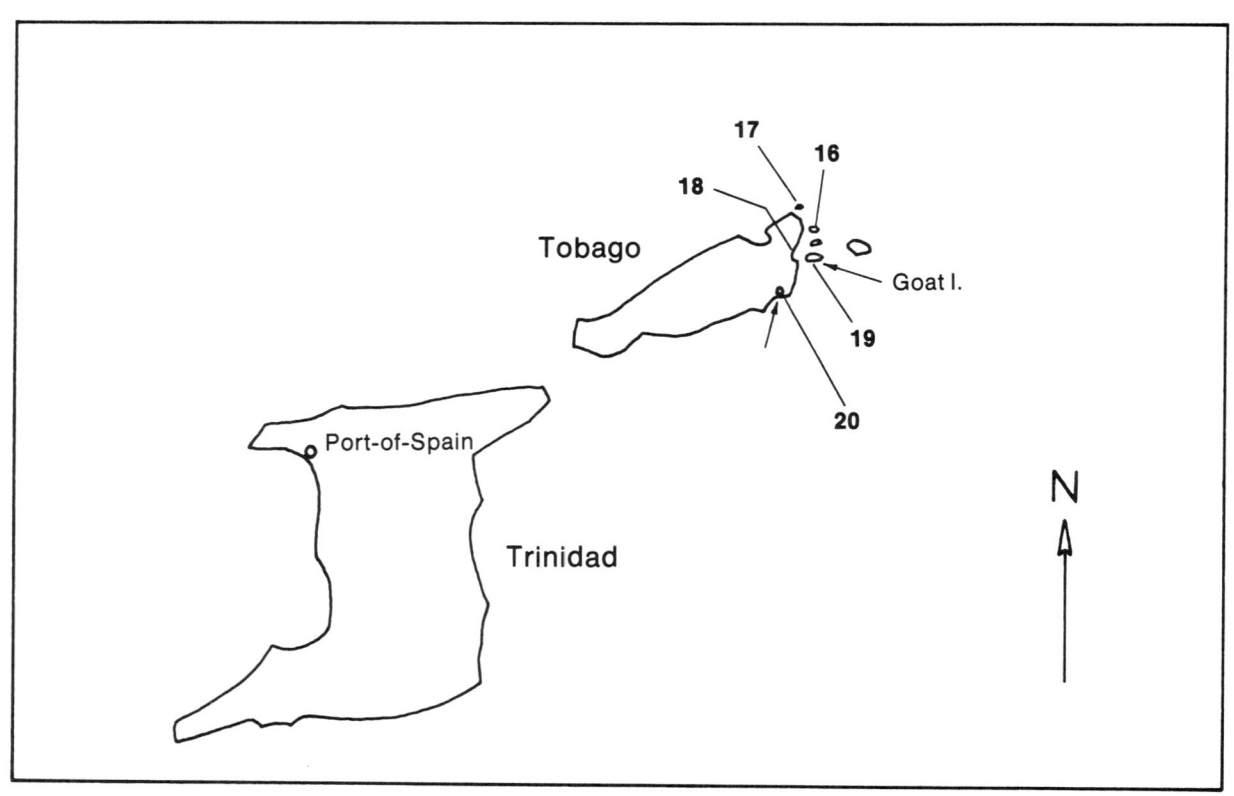

THE NETHERLANDS' ANTILLES: ARUBA, CURAÇAO, AND BONAIRE

These three islands—Aruba, Curaçao, and Bonaire—are owned by the Netherlands and, as a result, are quite different from most other islands in the Caribbean. They are far down the Lesser Antilles chain, only thirty-five miles from the coast of Venezuela, and the weather is consistently excellent. Aruba has only one wreck, and not much other diving available, and so it is not considered in the maps and charts of this book.

Curaçao and Bonaire, however, are thriving dive spots and charming vacation areas as well. Curaçao is very much a bit of Holland, architecturally speaking. And it offers remarkable shopping values, interesting topography and sights, and has top-flight hotel accommodations as well as good commercial hotels for the budget-minded traveler. The people of Curaçao are legendarily friendly, perhaps due in part to the equally legendary liqueur that is distilled and imbibed on the island. Dive facilities are excellent, and there are many reefs to explore. Most diving is done directly from the beach, but despite this the snorkeling is not great. The land drops off so severely that even a short swim from the beach puts you in fifty feet of water, and many of the reefs descend from there to one hundred feet or more. If you are a scuba diver, this should be no problem, and the sights at these depths can be spectacular. Visibility is excellent.

Diver hand-feeds a school of tropical fish swimming about a coral pillar on one of Curaçao's colorful offshore reefs. (Lee Turcotte/Atlantis Safaris)

Bonaire, which is much smaller than Curaçao, nonetheless boasts a casino, discotheque, and luxury hotel, and a stretch of reefs that is quickly making the island's reputation as a diver's paradise. The twenty-one-mile reef is tightly packed with fish, sponges, sea horses, and an incredible variety of other sea life and has many entry points from the beach. Tours by specially equipped truck (see Netherlands' Antilles Chart for details) run daily. Each entry point from the beach is marked by a string of floats leading out to the reef, which help the diver in and out of the water. Spearfishing is forbidden, and as a result, the fish are plentiful and friendly. Bonaire is a "must-see" area for the scuba diver. The overwater dive facilities are remarkably complete and well organized, and the reef is equally outstanding. This is one spot that divers flock to, and you should reserve well in advance.

Netherlands' Antilles

CURAÇAO

Water Temp.: 80°

Regulations: Check locally.

PLACE	NO.	DESCRIPTION	ENTRY AND DISTANCE FROM SHORE	DEPTH	SNORKEL OR DIVE
PLAYA LAGUN	1	Coral reef	Beach At shore	20'; farther out 60' – 160' Drop-off ledge 175 yds. from beach	Snorkel or dive
CORAL CLIFF	2	Coral reef and wall	Beach At shore	10' – 50' drop off 100 yds. from beach to 150' and down	Snorkel or dive
VAERSENBAAI	3	Sports Camp. Get permission to dive thru Antillean Scuba Dive Assn. or Curaçao Oxygen Co. Coral wall.	Go down steps from a pier. 160' from shore	150'	Dive
PISCADERA BAY	4	Small coral reef	Boat 5 min. from Hilton	30' – 50'	Dive
RIF (fairly experienced divers)	5	Double reef	Few min. by boat	60' – 90'	Dive
PLAYA KALKI	6	At edge of open sea	Beach and climb down coral bluff 80 yds.	50' – 150'	Dive

Visibility: 80′ – 150′   **Best Season:** August and September very calm. Always good.

SURF OR CALM	HIGH-LIGHTS	FISHING AND PHOTOS	DANGERS	DIVE FACILITY	ACCOMMODATIONS
Calm	Lobsters, marine, tropicals, caves, polyps, sponges	Photos	None	At Holiday Inn and Hilton Hotel John Baldi or Frank Maynard c/o Frommer Hotel	Many hotels including Hilton and Holiday Inn Frommer Hotel Piscadera Bay Willemstad Curaçao, N.A.
Calm	Wall with sponges; coral formations; all fish	Photos	None	As above	As above
Calm	Clouds of reef fish, sponges, marine life	Photos	None	As above	As above
Calm	Sand patches, brain corals, gorgonia, small reef fish	Photos	None	As above	As above
Calm	Beautiful coral formations; sponges	Photos	Slight current	As above	As above
Can be rough	Big fish, manta rays, corals, sponges	Photos	Strong currents	As above	As above

BONAIRE

Water Temp.: 80º

Regulations: No spearfishing, shelling, or removal of corals. Beach entries to dive sites are marked by floats.

PLACE	NO.	DESCRIPTION	ENTRY AND DISTANCE FROM SHORE	DEPTH	SNORKEL OR DIVE
ALICE IN WONDERLAND	7	A double coral reef	Beach 100 yds.	50'	Dive
18″ PALM	8	Coral reef	Beach Reef close to shore	To 80'	Snorkel or dive
TOWN PIER	9	Under main pier in Kralendijk Harbor; pilings alive with marine creatures	Boat At pier	—	Snorkel or dive
CARL'S HILL	10	Coral reef	Boat	30'–150' one area 15' straight to 80'	Snorkel or dive
THE PORCH	11	A reef in front of dive shop (great night diving)	Beach 75'	20'–100'	Snorkel or dive
THE CLIFF	12	Coral reef and drop-off	Boat	30'–75'	Snorkel or dive
THOUSAND STEPS	13	A climb down 67 steps to a coral reef	Steps At shore	—	Snorkel or dive
KARPATA	14	Beautiful coral reef	Boat	20'–100'	Snorkel or dive
KLEIN BONAIRE	15	Beautiful reefs from surface down	Boat	Shore and down	Snorkel or dive

Visibility: 100′　　　　　**Best Season:** August and September very calm. Always good.

SURF OR CALM	HIGH-LIGHTS	FISHING AND PHOTOS	DANGERS	DIVE FACILITY	ACCOMMODATIONS
Varies	Reef covered with great coral bottoms	Photos	None	Aquaventure Dive Shop Capt. Don Stewart Hotel Bonaire Box 88 Netherlands' Antilles	Hotel Bonaire P.O. Box 88 Bonaire, Netherlands' Antilles Flamingo Beach Club and others
Varies	Tube and basket sponges, sand lake with garden eels, fish	Photos	None	As above	As above
Calm	Reef north of pier has artifacts	Photos, especially close-up photography	None	As above	As above
Varies	Great fish, pipe organ sponge, coral pillars	Photos	None, some current	As above	As above
Calm	Coral heads, sponges, sea horses	Photos	None	As above	As above
Calm	Sponges, gorgonias, black coral, fish	Photos	None	As above	As above
Calm	Beautiful corals, great clarity, fish	Photos	None	As above	As above
Calm	Great sea fan, old anchors, black coral	Photos	None, some current	As above	As above
Calm	Great fish, corals, sponges, etc.	Photos	None	As above	As above

TOBAGO

Water Temp.: 78°–82°

Regulations: No spearfishing

204

PLACE	NO.	DESCRIPTION	ENTRY AND DISTANCE FROM SHORE	DEPTH	SNORKEL OR DIVE
ANGEL REEF	16	Coral reef 75 yds. off white house on Goat Island	Boat 5 min. 75 yds.	5'–110'	Snorkel or dive
JAPANESE GARDENS (Experienced only)	17	Coral reef	Boat 7 min.	20'–160'	Dive
BLACK FOREST (Experienced only)	18	Submerged reef marked by 2 black rocks	Boat	20'–110'	Dive
SOUTH POINT (Very experienced only)	19	S. end of Goat Island. A coral reef with 2 opposite currents that permit the diver to ride one way, descend, and ride the other way back	Boat	20'–100'	Dive
BATTEAUX BAY REEF	20	Small coral reef and nearby shipwreck	Beach 200'	20'–55'	Snorkel or dive

Visibility: 10′−50′   **Best Season:** Anytime

SURF OR CALM	HIGH-LIGHTS	FISHING AND PHOTOS	DANGERS	DIVE FACILITY	ACCOMMODATIONS
Calm	Angelfish, sponges, brain coral, many fish	Photos, visibility poor	Some current, fire coral	Teach Tour Diving Co. Batteaux Bay Speyside, Tobago, W.I. att: Peter M. Philp	At Batteaux Bay Teach-Tour Dive Lodge (20 guests) Speyside, Tobago, W.I. and other hotels to the West on Tobago: Arnos Vale, Plymouth, Tobago, Blue Haven, Scarborough, etc.
Rough	All fish and reef life	Photos, visibility poor	Rough waters	As above	As above
Surge	Great black coral, many fish, sponges	Photos, visibility poor	Strong current	As above	As above
Surge	Gorgonias, corals, black coral, sponges, fans, fish. Often good visibility	Photos	Double current; ride it back and forth	As above	As above
Varies	Corals and sponges, fish, anchor, and nearby a wreck known as "Bottle Wreck"	Photos, visibility poor	None	As above	As above

At the outer edge of a reef, the ocean floor may drop hundreds or even thousands of feet below the surface. (Jack McKenney/Skin Diver Magazine)

FOUR

The Various Forms of Sea Life

CORAL REEFS

What you will see underwater will depend on what area of the world you plan to visit. But since a great many people choose to vacation in the tropics, you may well begin by exploring the most complex and beautiful of all underwater sights, the coral reefs. These can be found most often on the eastern coasts of land masses where the water temperature is above sixty-eight degrees. Within the boundaries of the Americas, this means Florida, the Caribbean, and to a lesser extent, Hawaii. There are none off the coast of California, but that state offers many other compelling underwater experiences. You will probably react in two ways to the reef. At first it seems so spectacular a display of color, shape, and movement that it can induce a near panic of excitement. You will want to swim everywhere at once, as if it might somehow all disappear at any moment, before you have had your fill. You will probably rush past the rocks at the reef's edge into the thick of things, particularly eager to pursue the cruising fish.

A shallow reef, teeming with life. (Janet Viertel)

Your second reaction will set in as you make repeated trips into the water, with the realization that the mundane rocks you so blissfully ignored on your first snorkel or dive have enough life going on around them and attached to them to keep you busy for the rest of your days. As you begin to explore the reef in a more relaxed fashion, you will find that the smallest area to which you can confine yourself will keep you endlessly entertained.

The water leading to the reef is usually shallow, and often you can swim out from a beach. As you swim over the reef, you will still be in shallow water—perhaps twelve or fifteen feet deep—but at the outer edge of some reefs the ocean floor may sharply drop hundreds, or even thousands of feet below the surface. These back sides of the reef are fascinating spots to glance at, and exploring them with scuba is an incredible experience.

A slippery dick swims among the corals. (Janet Viertel)

A baby parrotfish peers around soft corals at the photographer. (Janet Viertel)

Hard corals form the basic shape of the reef. Corals, which look like rock, are colonies of animal life. (Janet Viertel)

of animal life, assuming different shapes. The surface of the coral is made up of living polyps, each about the size of a pencil eraser. In the center of each polyp is a hole, through which it eats. It also has tiny tentacles, and with these it guides still smaller forms of sea life into its "mouth." As it reproduces, the new polyps form directly on top of their "parents," and the "parents" die and turn hard, remaining where they are. By this method the reef builds itself. The hard coral assumes different forms, each named by man to suggest what it resembles: brain coral, elkhorn coral, staghorn coral, finger coral, etc. There are also softer forms of corals, which wave back and forth with the current. These function in similar ways to the hard corals, although they resemble plant life and sometimes even seem to be growing from a stem in the ground. These include gorgonias, whips, sea fans, and many others. These magnificent corals take hundreds and sometimes thousands of years to grow. Please do not touch or break them.

There is one so-called coral that will sting you if you touch it. This is fire coral, and it is not—technically speaking—a coral; but it is similar in appearance. Fire coral is easily recognizable and should be avoided, although its "burns" are rarely serious.

On your first trip over the reef you will doubtless see hundreds of unrecognizable things. Therefore, to give you a basis for understanding what everything is and how it functions you should try to first identify the life that makes up the reef itself; and then the fish that swim through and live off of the surroundings.

The basic shape of the reef is determined by growths of hard coral. The coral that makes up the reef's terrain seems to be related to rock, as it is hard and seemingly inanimate; but in fact, it is a colony

Living polyps form the surface of the coral. The tentacles guide tiny forms of sea life into the hole through which the polyp "eats." (Janet Viertel)

Aptly called the brain coral. (Janet Viertel)

Brain coral segment, greatly enlarged, shows tentacles extended and feeding on tiny forms of sea life. (Janet Viertel)

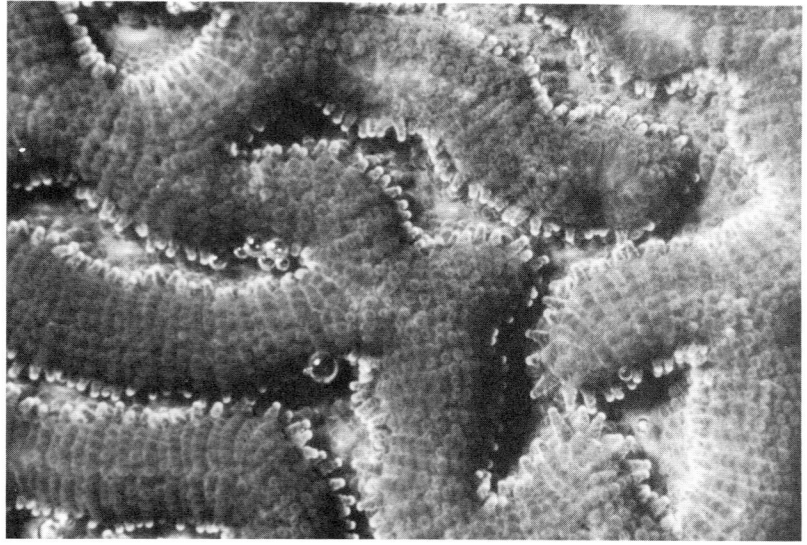

*Delicate staghorn coral is not to be
confused with the larger, thicker
elkhorn coral.* (Janet Viertel)

*Enlarged detail of staghorn coral
showing its beautiful striations.*
(Janet Viertel)

Soft corals—some called gorgonias—wave back and forth with the currents. (Janet Viertel)

A greatly enlarged photograph of a white-spined sea urchin forms a striking design. (Janet Viertel)

Sea fans are one of the most attractive forms of underwater life. They too are colonies of animals and come in various colors—frequently yellow or purple.

Greatly enlarged sea fan. Feeding polyps are visible. (Janet Viertel)

The corals form a landscape in which various weedlike vegetation (forms of algae) grows, lending color to the reef. Tucked in among the crevices and crags of the reef are all sorts of other sea life, much of it overlooked by the casual diver. Sea urchins, with long black, or short white or red spines are tucked among the corals, looking like pin cushions. They are not inviting, and luckily so. Their spines are sharp as porcupine quills and can stick in your skin like splinters, although they are not seriously harmful. Shellfish, such as conch and olive flamingo tongues, "walk" along the bottom of the corals, while lobsters hide in the crevices and holes, waving their long tentacles. Crabs scuttle over the sand, often small and sand colored, so that they are all but invisible until they move. There are slugs, nudibranchs, and sea cucumbers, some of them brightly colored, slinking slowly over the rocks and poking around the corals. These animals are like shellfish without shells. They have no skeleton either inside or out. Indeed, they have no protection from predators except their camouflage.

All of this life can be fascinating, and ultimately you may want to concentrate your interest on the underwater landscape itself, but probably your first interest, on entering the underwater world, will be the multitude of fishes. There are more than six hundred species of fish living on the coral reefs near the United States, the lava reefs of Hawaii, the waters of California, and the inland fresh waters. Naturally it will be impossible to identify so many fish in a book of this size, but we will attempt to deal with as many of the common types as possible.

There are three main types of fish you may see: sharklike creatures (you could easily snorkel for a lifetime without seeing any of these in protected waters, but occasionally you will find babies on the reef—they are not to be feared); scorpion-type fishes, grotesquely shaped and frequently hidden on rocks that camouflage them; and the bony fishes, which we commonly think of as "fish"—snappers, angelfish, and the like. We will concentrate primarily on the last category, since these are the first to be noticed, and by all accounts the most beautiful and plentiful.

There are common "families" of bony fishes—groupers, parrotfishes, snappers, puffers, among others—and endless variation within these families. After a few dives it will be fairly easy for you to identify many of the "family" names, even if you have to come back to look up the specific variety when you are ashore. The fish are of many colors; some are multicolored. Since their colors are probably the most memorable thing about them, the guide that follows classifies them in this rather unscientific manner. Within the color categories, the guide describes many of the fish you are apt to see according to species.

There are certain problems with this system, including the fact that certain fish change color as they change surroundings; and others change color as they grow older. Nonetheless, color seems a simpler constant than size or shape. An alphabetical list would be completely worthless, of course, since you would never know where to begin to look for a particular fish you had seen. We will attempt to give you the approximate size and shape of the fish and any other highly identifiable characteristics. Keep in mind that some fish are called by local names in different places, and they are not always bright enough to keep within their proper size category.

Following the fishes of the coral reef, there will be a list of sport fishes of more northerly areas—fishes of Hawaii and fishes of the California coastal waters. At the end of this listing will be a small compilation of creatures of the waters that can be troublemakers.

TROPICAL FISHES

A. BLUE FISH

A1. Blue-Spotted Cornetfish—three to four feet long. A very thin, pencil-shaped fish, found frequently in grassy areas, where it swims in a horizontal position. A blue filament projects beyond the tail.

A2. Indigo Hamlet—two to six inches long. A blue fish with white bars running vertically over a wide body.

A3. Blue Angelfish—approximately one foot long. Like all angelfish, this is a wide-eyed, small-mouthed fish, extremely wide (from top to bottom). It has a long fin on both top and bottom, which trails almost to the tail. Traces of yellow can be seen on the body, and the tail is partially yellow.

A4. Queen Angelfish—one foot long. Similar to the blue angel, but with a distinctly yellow tail and a dark spot on forehead.

A5. Yellowtail Damselfish (Baby)—one to six inches. These bright blue fish are spotted with aquamarine, when babies, but turn brown or black as they grow to adult size (see D11).

A6. Blue Chromy—five inches long. A brilliant royal blue fish edged in black. It usually swims in groups.

The parrotfish is more easily recognizable by its parrotlike mouth than its color, since these fishes come in an array of colors. (Janet Viertel)

A7. Blue Parrotfish—two to four feet long. Actually many parrotfishes are partially blue, but this one is primarily blue. This is a large family of fish, more easily recognizable by their parrotlike mouth, and their "buck teeth," than by any specific color. Some of them cover themselves at night with a gelatinous cocoon, possibly to protect themselves from predators.

A8. Blue Tang—up to one foot long. This fish is lemon yellow when in infancy, but grows up in colors ranging from pale blue to almost purple. It has a rounded body (slightly similar to the angelfish) and a yellow barb on its tail. Frequently, but not always, it swims in a large school.

A9. Scrawled Cowfish—approximately one and a half feet long. This fish is shaped like a pup tent, wide across the bottom and narrow on top, with a hard shell under its skin. Some species have a spine pointing forward above the eyes. It is quite an odd fish, similar to a trunkfish.

215

The spiny red squirrelfish feeds mostly at night: hence its big eyes. (Janet Viertel)

B. RED FISH

B1. Squirrelfish—six to twelve inches long. These fish are bright red, although on close examination you will find that they are striped with gray. They have large dark eyes, for feeding at night, and spend most of the day hiding under stands of coral. They have a long continuous upper spine and a forked tail.

B2. Blackbar Soldierfish—approximately eight inches long. Similar to the squirrelfish, the blackbar soldier is somewhat squarer in shape. It also hides in the reef, feeding at night, and frequently carries a black parasite on its head. The parasite resembles the body of a shrimp.

B3. Flamefish—two to five inches long. Also a night feeder, the flamefish is recognizable by a horizontal black stripe that runs through its eye. It can be seen during the day under rocks and in crevices.

B4. Barred Cardinalfish—two to five inches long. Very similar to the flamefish, but without the stripe through the eye. Instead, it has two vertical black stripes near its tail.

B5. Glasseye Snapper—approximately one foot. This fish changes color, but it usually has some red in it, and can be completely red. Another nocturnal fish, but distinguishable from the squirrelfish by its flat tail.

B6. Bigeye—approximately fifteen inches long. Similar in almost all respects to the glasseye, this fish doesn't change color as much; it can be a bit larger and has a somewhat lower fin.

B7. Stoplight Parrotfish—up to two feet long. A reddish, checkerboard pattern distinguishes this parrotfish, although the male is primarily blue with red markings and a yellow spot on its tail.

B8. Redband Parrotfish—up to about one foot long. A grayish body with a light red bottom, red tail, and red fins are the usual markings of the redband, but again, the males are primarily blue with the yellow spot on the tail.

C. BROWN FISH

C1. Nurse Shark—can be twelve to fourteen feet long. This brown shark (the young have spots) is often seen lying on the bottom or tucked away beneath large rock stands and ledges. The rear fins are far back, and two whiskerlike barbs ornament the snout. This shark does not normally trouble divers, but do not annoy it or play with it. A misunderstanding between a diver and a shark is never pleasant, and a shark's ability to understand that a diver is "just playing" has been proven unreliable, to say the least.

C2. Spotted Eagle Ray—its "wings" spread to seven and a half feet. This ray has a white underbelly, a brown, spotted back, and can be seen "flying" through shallow waters, trailing its long white tail.

C3. Small (Yellow) Stingray—up to fourteen inches wide. An almost circular ray, this species can sting with its tail, although it is rarely a problem. It can be seen in shallow water as well as on reefs and is related to the Caribbean stingray, which is similarly shaped, paler than the yellow, and grows to four feet in width.

C4. Lizardfish—up to eighteen inches long. Also called a sand diver, this fish sits on the bottom, well camouflaged, and will let you get quite close to it before darting a few feet away. It sits perched on its bottom fin (the fin under its gills), which gives it the same demeanor as a lizard perched on a rock.

C5. Trumpetfish—approximately three feet long. This extremely thin, ribbonlike fish often stands on its head among the gorgonias, probably trying to disguise itself as part of the coral. Its top and bottom fins are set well back toward its tail. It changes color quite easily, but most often retains some brown.

C6. Coney—approximately one foot long. The coney comes in many colors, including brown with blue spots. Its head slopes gently and evenly to a low mouth, and the tail is flat-ended. These fish are also yellow with blue spots, gray with blue spots, and black and white with brown spots.

The spotted eagle ray has "wings" that spread to seven feet. Remora fish are swimming beneath it. (Jack McKenney/Skin Diver Magazine)

The trumpetfish stands on its head among gorgonias, disguising itself as part of the coral. (Janet Viertel)

C7. Graysby—approximately one foot. This is similar to the coney but usually has some shade of brown. It is marked by four or five black or white spots along the upper back, and its tail is curved outward unlike the flat tail of the coney.

C8. Grouper—up to three or four feet, with some deep-water species growing much, much larger. The grouper is an extremely wide-mouthed fish with a flat tail. There are many varieties, some spotted, some striped, and not all of them are brown. They are intelligent and often friendly enough to eat out of a diver's hand.

C9. Dog Snapper—up to over three feet. A white triangle (really a stripe that widens) below the eye distinguishes this brownish fish. Its tail is very slightly forked.

C10. Glassy Sweeper—approximately six inches long. These fish, which swim in schools, are commonly referred to as "hatchet-shaped." Actually they look tremendously pregnant, and their large, silver eye and down-turned mouth add to the general air of discomfort.

C11. Blenny—one to eight inches long. This is a large family of small squarish fish that inhabit grassy areas and algae-covered rocks. Many of them appear sort of hairy and ragged.

C12. Goby—one to six inches long. Another large family of small fish, slightly neater looking than the blennies. They are frequently found in tide pools.

C13. Flying Gurnard—up to eighteen inches long. A square-headed, brown, bottom fish with huge colorful fins, which it keeps tucked to its side until frightened. The flying gurnard scratches at the bottom with its bottom fins. (It is not truly a flying fish, although there have been reports that it does occasionally "fly" out of the water.)

C14. Spotted Scorpionfish—up to eighteen inches long. Dangerous to the touch, this lumpy fish blends perfectly with the rocks on which it hides. Easy to miss unless one keeps a sharp eye. Scorpionfish are found in all tropical and temperate waters.

C15. Ocean Surgeon—up to one and a half feet long. A wide brownish fish (sometimes gray), the ocean surgeon has "pursed lips" and a group of thin blue stripes around the eye. Similar to the doctorfish (but presumably a specialist).

C16. Ocean Triggerfish—over two feet long. A brown or gray wide fish whose fins are set well back toward the tail. The fins are very high. The tail is flat with a slightly protruding point both top and bottom.

D. BLACK FISH (including DARK GRAY-BLACK)

D1. Atlantic Manta Ray—up to twenty-two feet in width. Usually found in deep water, the Atlantic manta ray is not particularly common. Its underside is white, its back blackish gray, and its head fins are curved in front of its mouth, giving it a horned look.

D2. Southern Stingray—up to five feet in width. This ray has a fin on the underside of its tail and usually buries itself in the sand, so that only the eyes and tail are visible.

D3. Black Grouper—see C8. The black grouper can be all black, or can have gray and black stripes and nearly square spots.

D4. Greater Soapfish—approximately one foot long. A spotted black fish with an elongated snout, the greater soapfish hides under rocks, usually without moving at all.

D5. Sharksucker—up to three feet long. A long, narrow fish with a black stripe, bordered with white, running the length of its body, the sharksucker has a suction disc on top of its head, with which it attaches itself to sharks and rays. It has been known to attempt attachment to divers.

D6. High Hat—up to eight inches long. A black- and white-striped, short-faced fish with extremely long top and bottom fins.

D7. Jackknife Fish—up to nine inches long. This looks like a very badly manufactured aquarium angelfish. Its top fin protrudes directly up from its head, and its body almost looks like a bottom fin. It has three black stripes, running more or less vertically.

D8. Spotted Drum—up to about one foot. Similar to the jackknife, the spotted drum has more stripes, as well as white spots. Its tail is almost circular.

D9. Atlantic Spadefish—up to about three feet and twenty pounds. This is a wide, flat-bodied fish with vertical barred stripes, a protruding top fin and a flat tail. It is sometimes found in huge schools.

D10. French Angelfish—approximately one foot long. Shaped like other angelfish (see under blue fish), the French angel is black with yellow edging on its fins and yellow spots on its body. It can frequently be found under rocks but is quite curious and friendly.

D11. Yellowtail Damselfish—up to six inches long. A black or sometimes brown fish with lighter spots along its back and a bright yellow tail.

D12. Threespot Damselfish—up to four and a half inches long. A dark fish with a yellowish cast. The young are bright yellow and tend to nip at divers without doing any harm.

D13. Dusky Damselfish—up to six inches long. The dusky looks a lot like the threespot. The young have a red stripe along the back of their head. It's a little tough to tell one kind of damselfish from another.

D14. Creole Wrasse—up to one foot long. A longish fish with both top and bottom fins set well back on the body and a slightly forked tail.

D15. Midnight Parrotfish—approximately two and a half feet long. The midnight is shaped like other parrots (see A7) but is quite black, with sleek blue markings around its head. Quite glamorous, in a sleazy way.

D16. Black Durgon—approximately two feet long. This coal-black fish has seemingly identical top and bottom fins, and each has a white stripe running along it where it joins to the body.

D17. Smooth Trunkfish—up to one foot long. The trunkfish has a body shaped like a pup tent, with a flat bottom. It maneuvers with short fins that protrude from either side of its body. The smooth trunkfish is black and gray, with white spots and gray hexagons in the center of its body.

D18. Longlure Frogfish—up to four inches long. A rather disgusting little scorpion-type fish, sometimes black, sometimes tan or orange. The longlure sits on the bottom looking like a small black sponge a good deal of the time.

D19. Shortnose Batfish—up to fourteen inches long. Another one of the scorpion-type fishes, the shortnose batfish is entirely black, with wide side fins that look almost like lungs. It has a pointed snout protruding upward from its head and a small "fishing rod" that is attached beneath, which it jiggles to attract the small fish it consumes. It sits on the bottom most of the time, grotesque and uninviting.

E. GREEN FISH

E1. Green Moray Eel—up to seven feet long. Long and snakelike, the green moray hides in holes or beneath coral stands. It is one of the few dangers of the reef, but it will not normally be encountered unless you stick your hands into holes. Once it has bitten something, it seems impossible for it to disengage its jaws. They are rarely seen during the day and are not usually aggressive unless disturbed.

E2. Pearly Razorfish—up to fifteen inches long. A flat-headed greenish-silver fish. The young are much greener, and most specimens are considerably under fifteen inches.

E3. Green Razorfish—approximately four and a half inches long. Greener than the pearly razorfish, the green is frequently seen in grassy areas. The male has a dark spot in the middle of its side.

E4. Blackear Wrasse—up to eight inches long. A streamlined green fish with tan fins and a black mark behind the eye, often seen in grassy areas.

E5. Puddingwife—up to twenty inches long. A greenish-blue flat-tailed fish, its bottom fin is marked with violet horizontal stripes. The young are entirely different in color, pale blue and tan, with pure white bars.

E6. Rainbow Parrotfish—up to four feet long. See yellowtail, below.

E7. Yellowtail Parrotfish—up to one and a half feet long. The rainbow and yellowtail parrots are quite green. The yellowtail sometimes, but not always, has a yellow tail.

F. SILVER OR GRAY FISH

F1. Lemon Shark—up to eleven feet long. It is battleship gray and distinguishable by its two rear fins, upper and lower, which appear to be mirror images of each other.

F2. Bonefish—up to seven feet long. This sleek fish schools in shallow flats and is a legendary fighter for sport fishing.

F3. Gold-Spotted Eel—up to three and a half feet long. A gray eel, it winds through grassy areas along the bottom, looking like a snake with large gold spots.

F4. Needlefishes (Redfin, Houndfish, and Ballyhoo)—fifteen inches to five feet long. These fish swim inches under the surface, sometimes in small schools. They are easy to miss, as one is usually looking down. Some of them have red spots on the edge of the long "needle" that protrudes from the front of the head.

F5. Great Barracuda—up to ten feet long (rarely over five feet, however). A long, sleek fish, sometimes marked by black spots, the barracuda has vicious teeth and will watch you as you snorkel. Barracuda attacks, however, are extremely rare. There is more danger in dangling fingers or feet over the side of a moving boat, where they may look like a small school of fish, than in being fully visible to the fish.

F6. Mullet—up to three feet long. A nondescript silver fish with a short, rounded face and slightly surprised-looking eyes.

F7. Coney—up to one foot long (see C6). Some conies are silver-gray.

F8. Sand Tilefish—up to about two feet long. A long, slender fish with a square, yellow face. Its tail is curved and comes to a point both on top and bottom.

Needlefishes (ballyhoo) swim just below the surface of the water. (Janet Viertel)

F9. Bar Jack—up to nearly two feet long. An extremely forked tail carries the blue and black stripe that originates on the back of this schooling jackfish.

F10. Blue Runner—up to two and a half feet long. Another jackfish, marked by the forked tail, the blue runner has a bluish back and silver-blue body.

F11. Horse-Eye Jack—up to two feet long. Similar to the blue runner but with a much larger eye, a slightly higher forehead, and a yellow tail.

F12. Greater Amberjack—up to five and a half feet long, sometimes longer. A large jackfish with an amber stripe running from its eye through its tail.

F13. Palometa—approximately one foot long. Marked by extremely long, narrow top and bottom fins, this square-looking schooling fish has three vertical bars on its body.

F14. Yellowfin Mojarra—up to about fifteen inches long. Vertical bars and a black-tipped tail mark this silvery fish, as does a slightly protruding lower lip. Its fins are yellow.

F15. Mahogany Snapper—up to fifteen inches long. There are many snappers, as likely to greet you on a restaurant menu as underwater. This one has a black spot beneath its top fin.

The great amberjack grows up to five and a half feet long and is commonly found on tropical reefs. (Janet Viertel)

F16. Gray Snapper—up to approximately three feet long. The gray snapper has a blackish stripe running through its eye.

F17. Mutton Snapper—up to approximately three feet long. The mutton can be gray or brown and has thin, light-blue markings above its head and around its eye, as well as a spot below its upper fin.

F18. Margate—approximately two feet long. A steep-headed fish with a black tail and sometimes a black back.

F19. Black Margate—approximately two feet long. Very similar to the margate above, but darker colored, with a black, wide bar running vertically behind its gills.

F20. Jolthead Porgy—up to over two feet long. A grayish fish with darker gray vertical stripes, a large eye, and a forked tail. The jolthead can change color.

222

F21. Silver Porgy—approximately one foot long. A very wide silver fish with a black spot at the base of its tail.

F22. Goatfish—up to approximately one foot long. This fish is easily identified by two "whiskers" (barbels) that hang from under the mouth. Some species have three spots along the back, some have a vertical stripe.

F23. Yellow Chub—one and a half to two and a half feet long. A moderately wide fish, silvery with yellow horizontal stripes or white spots.

F24. Hogfish—up to three feet long. These fish have three spines, which look like single hairs, extending from the front of their top fin. They are long-snouted and can be brown or blue as well as silver.

F25. Balloonfish—up to twenty inches long. A square-faced fish with spines over all of its body, it can puff up to look like a ball.

F26. Porcupinefish—up to three feet long. Like the balloonfish, the porcupine has spines and is inflatable. It has a spotted, rounded tail, and a slightly less square head.

The peacock flounder lies flat on the bottom of the sea and frequently adds to its disguise by changing color or covering itself with sand. (Janet Viertel)

G. MULTICOLORED FISH

G1. Peacock Flounder—up to one and a half feet long. This gray flatfish has blue circles all over its body but frequently lies covered in the sand so that only its outline can be seen. Both of its eyes are on the top of its head, and it has a small rounded tail.

G2. Fairy Basslet—approximately three inches long. A tiny fish with a purple front half and a yellow back half. It can be found anywhere from the shallows to 200 feet down.

G3. Banded Butterflyfish—up to six inches long. A nearly circular fish, except for its pointed mouth, it has black vertical bands, one of them through the eye, covering a silver body.

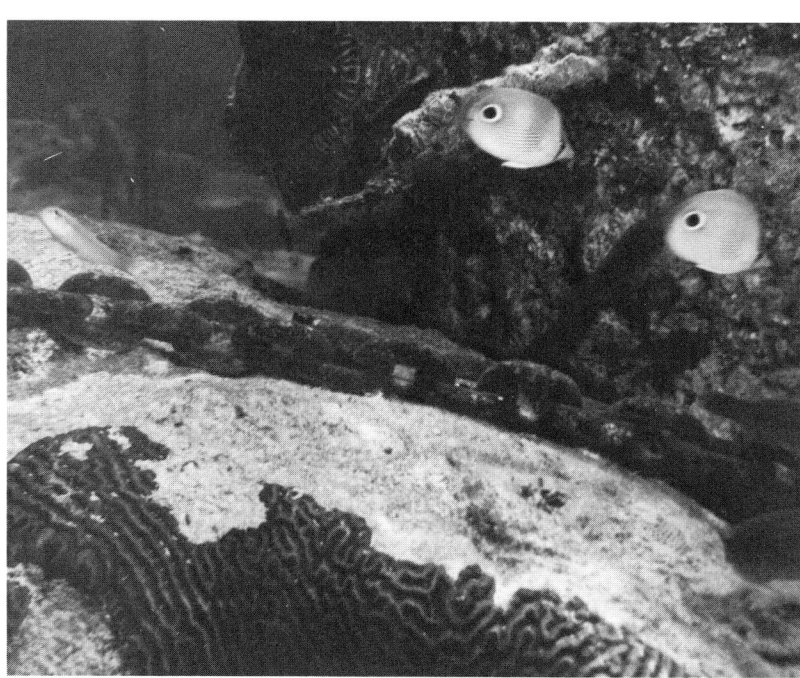

The four-eyed butterfly fish is tiny. Note the anchor chain for an indication of size. It has a "black false eye" near its tail. (Janet Viertel)

G4. Four-Eyed Butterflyfish—up to six inches long. Similar to above, but without the bands, and with a black "false eye" near the tail. The "false eye" is thought to be inducement to predators to strike at the tail, rather than the head of the fish.

G5. Beaugregory—up to four inches long. A blue top and a yellow bottom, including the tail, distinguish this fish, which is of the damselfish family.

G6. Cocoa Damselfish—up to four inches long. Similar to above, but with a spot in the somewhat lighter blue top.

G7. Wrasse—up to eight inches long. There are many varieties of this moderately thin fish. Some are colored like the parrotfish, some are yellow, or yellow and black.

G8. Spanish Hogfish—up to two feet long. Similar to other hogfish but without the three "hairs" and somewhat sleeker in shape. The Spanish hogfish is usually orange with a blue top, although some are almost entirely blue.

G9. Slippery Dick—under nine inches long. A silver wrasse, with a black stripe running horizontally through the eye and all the way to the tail. It sometimes has other stripes as well.

G10. Parrotfish—many are multi-colored (see A7).

G11. Queen Triggerfish—up to two feet long. Perhaps the most spectacularly colored of all the reef fish, the queen trigger has two light blue stripes behind its mouth, running diagonally toward its gills, and whiplike protuberances extending from its top fin and both ends of its tail. It is a very wide (top to bottom) fish, with a narrow "neck" between the body and the tail.

G12. Scrawled Filefish—approximately one and a half feet long. A slightly misshapen gray fish with blue broken-striped markings covering its body. It has a dart over its eye and a snoutlike mouth. It swims with its tail folded.

G13. Honeycomb Cowfish—up to one and a half feet long. Shaped like a trunkfish (see D17) but colored like the scrawled filefish (above). These fish can be caught, cleaned, and eaten, using their shell like the shell of a baked potato.

224

H. ORANGE OR YELLOW FISH

H1. Coney—up to one foot long. This fish is sometimes yellow, with blue spots.

H2. Schoolmaster Snapper—up to two feet long. A yellow-gold snapper with a light-blue horizontal line running under the eye, and lighter yellow vertical stripes.

H3. Yellowtail Snapper—up to two feet long. A silvery snapper fish with a yellow stripe running the length of its body and broadening to include a forked tail. It also has yellow markings above and below the stripe.

H4. French Grunt—up to one foot long. A very common reef fish, seen in schools under coral heads, it drifts back and forth with the current. It has passably horizontal yellow and light-blue stripes and a forked tail. So named for the sounds it makes by grinding its jaws together.

H5. Blue-Striped Grunt—up to one and a half feet long. Similar to the above, but with a black top fin and tail.

H6. Porkfish—approximately one foot long. The back half of this fish is marked exactly like the French grunt, but the head is white with two black vertical stripes, one through the eye. It is wider (top to bottom) than the grunts.

H7. Rock Beauty—approximately one foot long. Shaped like a medieval shield lying on its side, the rock beauty has an orange-yellow head and tail and a black body. Its tail and fins all come to protruding points.

H8. Queen Angelfish—up to fourteen inches long. See A4.

H9. Spotfin Butterflyfish—up to eight inches long. See G3. Slightly darker in color than the other butterflyfishes, the spotfin has three dark spots on the rear of its body.

H10. Reef Butterflyfish—up to six inches. The reef butterfly is somewhat yellower than the spotfin and has a black border around its rear edge.

H11. Orange Filefish—up to two feet long. See section G12. The orange filefish has little orange spots instead of blue markings.

H12. Blue Tang (Baby)—see A8. The young are shaped like the adult but are colored bright yellow.

SPORT FISH

If you dive in areas other than reefs, your main interest in fish will most likely be sport. Following is a list of fish commonly hunted. Since they are all gray to black in color, they are listed alphabetically. There are so many varieties of these fishes that further reading would be required for accurate definition (see Bibliography). Where their geographical range is limited, we have so indicated. They are all good eating fish, except where indicated.

J1. Bass—up to twenty pounds, with sea bass much larger. There are many, many species of bass—white, black, largemouth, and smallmouth. They are found in all areas of the country, and it is best to check with your local sportfishing shop to identify the types in your area.

J2. Buffalo—a large fish of the sucker family. A rather common fish in the Mississippi Valley, commonly shaped, with a slightly forked tail. There are many varieties. Lake carp is also a form of buffalo.

J3. Bullhead—approximately one foot long. A form of catfish with a very large head. It has a whiskered mouth.

J4. Carp—up to forty pounds. A soft-finned fish that lives in lakes and streams and tends to destroy the plant life. It has a large top fin and a slightly forked tail.

J5. Catfish—one to two pounds in weight but can be bigger. A bull-headed, bewhiskered bottom fish that fights ferociously when caught. Their mouths and teeth are said to be catlike. Recently gaining tremendous popularity as a food fish.

J6. Cod—approximately ten pounds. One of the most important food fishes in the world. These soft-finned fish live in water twenty to forty fathoms deep. There are many varieties.

J7. Flounder—a name given to all flatfish, consequently it is difficult to predict the size. The bream is also a flounder. These flatfishes lie on the bottom a good deal of the time. Both of their eyes are on the same side of their head. Although they are excellent eating, catching them has been described as the only foolproof cure for insomnia.

J8. Freshwater Gar—some species are about four or five feet, others grow to eight feet. Commonly found in the eastern and central United States, the gar is an elongated fish with shiny round scales. It is not very good eating, although edible.

J9. Haddock—usually under ten pounds. Similar to the cod, the haddock has a small mouth. A black line runs horizontally down its back, and a small black spot is situated just behind the gills.

J10. Halibut—fifty to two hundred pounds. A huge flatfish. Common south of Massachusetts.

J11. Jewfish—normally about six feet in length, some species much larger. The jewfish is a form of grouper, usually dusky green in color. Found in deep water in warm seas.

J12. Muskellunge, commonly called MUSKIE—up to six feet long. An elongated fish with a wide mouth and a broad stomach, the muskie is a form of large pike. A yellow-olive variety, spotted with black, is found in the Great Lakes. A variety with vertical bars is found in Lake Chatauqua, and other kinds are found in the lakes of Wisconsin and Minnesota.

J13. Perch—usually less than a pound but can grow to about two pounds. A spiny freshwater fish found in lakes and streams. Various colors, mostly dark, are common. Some species have spots or stripes.

J14. Pike—from two to fifteen pounds. An elongated fish with spiny fins, similar to the pickerel and muskie.

J15. Salmon—approximately fifteen pounds. A large, soft-finned fish, living in the sea near coasts, but ascending into streams for the purpose of spawning. Famous as both a game and food fish. It is of variable color.

J16. Trout—under ten pounds. There are many varieties of this freshwater fish. They have down-turned mouths, many have speckles and a line running along the middle of their bodies.

J17. Walleye—this is a form of pike (see J14, above) having large, prominent eyes.

B. HAWAIIAN FISH

In Hawaiian waters many fish are the same or similar to those of the Caribbean—but here are a few that are typical of Hawaii.

K1. Aholehole (Mountain Bass)—up to seven inches. A bright *silver* fish with a somewhat ratty, forked tail and a large eye, indicating that it is a nocturnal feeder.

K2. Alaihi (Indianfish)— approximately four pounds. The Indianfish is *red* with a sloping head and a pointed top fin set quite a ways back on its body. The tail is slightly forked and a barb emerges from the gill plate, to further distinguish this friendly member of the squirrelfish family.

K3. Kala (Unicornfish)— approximately four pounds. As indicated by their name, these fish have a small "horn" emanating from their heads. They are a dull *greenish* color, and their nearly flat tails appear to be too small for their bodies.

K4. Lionfish (Firefish)—approximately six inches long. A beautiful but extremely poisonous fish, whose long, spindly spines emanate from all of its fins. The lionfish is normally *reddish brown* in color, with white or yellow bands and a speckled tail. It is not a common fish, but should be avoided, although admired at a distance.

K5. Lauwiliwili (Long-Nosed Butterflyfish)—up to six inches. A *yellow* fish with a black upper head and tail, the long-nosed butterflyfish is similar in most respects to the other members of its family, except for a long, pointed snout, with which it pokes into crevices for food.

K6. Mu (Porgi)—approximately six pounds. These *silver* fish are easily distinguishable by their red lips and humanlike teeth. They are most frequently found on the deeper portions of the reef.

K7. Menini (Convict Tang)—up to six inches. The convict tang has a wide, *yellow* body, pursed lips, and is marked by vertical "prison" stripes, from which it gets its name. One stripe runs directly through the eye. A shallow-water fish.

K8. Nenue (Chub)—approximately five pounds. A slightly "pushed together" look characterizes the otherwise innocuous chub, a *silver* or *dark gray* fish that schools in middle depths. When threatened, they tend to group closely with their backs to the coral. This makes no sense in terms of survival, but try telling that to a chub. This fish's best defense is simply that it has a rather terrible taste.

K9. U'u (Menpachi)—approximately seven inches. The menpachi is a pug-nosed member of the squirrelfish family, highly prized for food in Hawaii. It is *red* with the large squirrelfish eye and a short, sloping, spined top fin. Its tail is slightly forked. Scarce during the day, the menpachi travels the reef by night feeding on small reef animals and plant life.

B. CALIFORNIA FISH

Off the coast of California, various species of fish are commonly found, such as:

L1. Black Sea Bass—up to seven feet long, frequently much smaller. The *black* sea bass has a nearly flat tail and a "frowning" mouth. The larger ones have grayish spots along the back. Characterized by a spiny top fin and a look of almost shocking stupidity, the black sea bass tends to live along rocky bottoms in anywhere from twenty to sixty feet of water.

L2. Calico Bass—approximately two to three pounds. A pop-eyed fish of *reddish brown* color with a spiny top fin of pronounced slope and a nearly flat tail, it tends to live in kelp at depths from one and a half to sixty feet.

L3. Halibut—from five to twenty pounds. A flatfish, similar to a flounder, with both eyes on the same side of its head, it lives in sandy areas, usually in fairly shallow water, although some are found in depths of two hundred feet. The halibut is gray with a white bottom fin.

L4. Opaleye—approximately nine inches long. A pug-nosed fish with a *green* body, two white spots beneath its top fin, and a nearly flat tail. The opaleye is found in, and feeds off of, kelp beds, and its depth is determined by the depth of the kelp.

L5. Sheepshead—approximately one and a half feet long. A square-faced, sharp-toothed fish with a curved tail. The males are *black* with a *red or pink midsection,* and the females are completely dark red. Found in all depths in kelp and on rocky shoals.

L6. White Sea Bass—approximately two and a half feet long. Longer and narrower than the other sea bass, this fish has an extended lower jaw and a dark stripe running along its belly. It has a flat tail. Found in varying depths, usually in kelp beds.

L7. Yellowtail—up to three feet long. A *silvery* fish with an extremely forked yellow tail and a yellow stripe running the length of its body into the tail, it has small, pointed top and bottom fins and is rather sleek-looking. Found at varying depths, usually outside kelp in the open water.

B. OTHER KINDS OF SEA LIFE

In addition to fish there are a few odds and ends of sea life, some in the tropics, some in northerly areas and off the coast of California.

M1. Abalone—The abalone has a flattened, oval shell, perforated with a line of holes. The shell covers the animal like a roof as it clings to rocks with its open side. They must be pried off the rock with an abalone pry, and only certain kinds are good to eat. They are classified by color. Most common off the coast of California, they are already being fished out because of their popularity in local restaurants.

M2. Conch—Mostly found in the West Indies, the conch is a large, spiral-shelled marine animal. The meat is good and the shell is commonly used as a large ornament, doorstop, or paperweight, although it is not always easy to find a shell in good condition. In the north they are often called winkles.

M3. Crabs—A creature with a broad, short flat shell, its abdomen is tucked under the shell. There are "feelers" on the head and legs on the sides of the shell. It can walk in any direction, but usually moves sideways on land.

M4. Kelp—A form of seaweed common off of California, kelp grows in enormous entangled forests in which sea creatures live and feed. Many diving accidents are caused by divers panicking as they become entwined in kelp. It breaks rather easily, and the patient diver should have no trouble cutting his way out of it (*but if you have never gone kelp diving before, do not do so without someone who is experienced in it*).

M5. Lobster—These shelled animals are, of course, prized as food in almost every country that has them available. There are two main types. The Northeast or "Maine" lobster has claws, but the Caribbean or Pacific lobster does not. The lobster hides in holes but can be taken with a wire lasso. Do not take females, recognizable by the egg sacs under their abdomen, since the lobster population is diminishing at an alarming rate and lobster farming is in its infancy. The males can be recognized by their forked claw (see illustration).

M6. Scallops—These shelled marine creatures are shaped like a fan. They move by flapping their shells. The muscle portion of the animal is used as seafood. The whole animal can be eaten, but since the shells do not close tightly, the animal tends to die and spoil much more quickly than clams or oysters.

M7. Shells—The collecting of shells can be a full-time job. They can be found almost anywhere, and there are literally thousands of types. In the Bibliography you will find several books listed that deal with the collecting, identifying, and preserving of shells.

M8. Octopus—This eight-armed creature has been the subject of much horror fiction, but it is actually not dangerous to man and is quite timid. It is also apparently quite intelligent. It has a saclike body, and each tentacle is covered with two rows of suction cups, with which it clings to rocks, coral, etc. Octopuses generally live in holes on the bottom among rocks and eat shelled animals. If you encounter a hole in the bottom with discarded shells around it, the chances are that you have found the home of an octopus.

M9. Miniature Fish Specimens— Certain tropical fish remain miniature, and these can be collected with the use of a slurp gun. The collected fish can be kept, if properly handled, in plastic bags for limited periods until transferred to a domestic fish tank. Several books on miniature fish are available at pet stores that sell tanks and fish food for such home aquariums. However, the fish tend to die, and it is a questionable hobby from the point of view of conservation of the seas.

TROUBLESOME CREATURES

There are a very few forms of underwater life that can present problems for the snorkeler or diver. For the most part these creatures can be avoided and with sensible care should cause no problem. After all, there are vastly more people damaged by the automobile than by creatures of the sea. Most common are:

Sea Urchins—colored black, white, or red, they look like pin cushions, and if you touch them, the spines remain in your flesh like splinters. They will remain for a few days. Look at what you are touching, where you are going, and especially where you put your feet down. They are most sedentary and do not come after you.

Fire Coral—is a mustard-colored "hydroid" that is smooth and, if touched, can burn and sting. Its wounds are temporary. It does not move.

Portuguese Man-of-War—is a bluish bubble float on the surface of the water with long trailing tentacles that can cause painful stings. It drifts with the tide. Avoid them.

Sharks—can range from eighteen inches to fifty feet long. If they are not in a feeding frenzy—and if you have not been spearing fish—they will probably swim right by you and not molest you. However, if you do see one—don't panic, don't thrash about, and certainly do not play with it or tease it. They are unpredictable, but rare in shallow reef areas. Quoting Captain Jacques-Yves Cousteau, "Sharks belong to the undersea environment. They rank among the most perfect, the most beautiful creatures ever developed in nature. We expect to meet them around coral reefs or in the open ocean, even if it is with a twist of fear. When their formidable silhouette glides along the populated coral cliffs, fish do not panic; they quietly clear the lord's path and keep an eye on him. So do we."*

Lionfish—See under Fishes of Hawaii.

Spotted Scorpionfish—See under Tropical Brown Fish.

Green Moray Eel—See under Tropical Green Fish.

---

*Jacques-Yves Cousteau and Philippe Diolé, *The Shark: Splendid Savage of the Sea* (Garden City, N.Y.: Doubleday & Co., 1970).

HOBBIES

Aside from the collecting of shells, the collecting of miniature tropical fish specimens, and fish watching, diving can lead you to several interesting hobbies. Spearfishing is frowned upon in many areas but is popular in others, and instruction is needed to begin this sport. A dive shop can sell you equipment and instruct you on its use or advise you as to where such instruction can be found.

Shipwrecks are one of the most gripping of underwater sights. Each wreck is unique. (Be careful not to get caught in the wreck.) Wrecks vary in appearance. There are ancient wrecks from which nothing remains but a few ballast balls and strands of rope, and eerie sunken schooners, lodged in the sand with their riggings swaying in the surge. There are also comparatively recently wrecked barges, some of which have been sunk on purpose, for reasons that vary from collecting insurance to creating an artificial reef to attract fish. But the vast majority of sunken ships were wrecked in storms.

We do not have the space to deal with this subject adequately, but if you wish to pursue shipwrecks and treasure, the Bibliography lists books that will help you. And Chapter 3 will help you find wrecks, some probably near your part of the country.

A diver explores the shipwreck of the Cleveland *in the Great Lakes area of Tobermory.* (Jack McKenney/Skin Diver Magazine)

UNDERWATER PHOTOGRAPHY

Photographing the underwater world can become a consuming passion. Here we can deal only with its rudimentary aspects, in addition to listing books in the Bibliography for those who wish to pursue this hobby. Taking pictures while snorkeling or diving gives pleasure to those who, for one reason or another, can-

not join you underwater, but one of the real advantages to the photographer is that it forces him to examine the underwater world more and more closely, as he looks for subject matter to shoot. This close examination leads to discoveries undreamed of. Before you begin underwater photography you should be comfortably snorkeling or diving, so that almost all of your attention can be devoted to your photographic equipment and subjects. It helps if you are already a

230

photographer, but this is not necessary. If you have no knowledge of photography, you will probably have to learn basic photographic technique and terminology to understand fully the following section. Most of it is simple, however, and if you are planning to use an Instamatic or Polaroid SX-70 camera, you will not need much of the technical data.

To adapt a conventional camera for underwater use, you must enclose it in a waterproof housing that will permit manipulating at least some, if not all, of the controls while underwater. Plastic housings for just this purpose are made by several companies and are available in most dive shops, as well as in some sporting goods stores and large camera shops. Prices for these housings vary from as little at $30, for one that will fit an Instamatic, to as much as $150, for some that are designed for use with the more expensive single-lens-reflex models.

At least one company (Ikelite) also makes kits from which the photographer can assemble his own housing. These range in price from about twenty to eighty dollars and are not at all difficult for the handy person to assemble. Ricoh also makes a special housing, which costs only about twenty dollars, to fit their 35mm. rangefinder camera, which is about fifty dollars.

One camera that requires no housing because it is made specifically for underwater use is the Nikonos, but this costs over $300. Probably the newest underwater housing for a regular camera is one made specifically to fit the new Polaroid SX-70. Costing about $100, it has a plastic pocket into which the finished photos fall; so that when the photographer comes out from the water, his pictures are ready for viewing.

Because underwater light is difficult to estimate, a light meter is essential for those cameras that are not fully automatic. Plexiglass housings are available to fit most separate light meters at prices that range from $30 to $60. There are also a few special light meters designed for underwater photography—one, the Seconic—requires no additional housing and is easy to read underwater. It sells for about $125.

Flash and strobe are helpful when taking underwater pictures, though they are not always essential at shallow depths. Plexiglass housings for flash units are about $20, and for strobe units about $60. Flash bulbs or cubes give considerably more light than strobe, so unless the photographer will be very close to his subject, a rather large unit is necessary when using strobe. The Nikonos flash, like the Nikonos camera for which it is designed, requires no separate housing—but it does cost about $125.

Although almost any kind of film can be used, the higher the speed of the film, the better the chance of getting sharp pictures. When using black-and-white films, look for subjects with great contrast—dark fish over white sand for example. Develop with the sharpest contrast possible. For the Instamatics, V.P. 126 (which has an A.S.A. speed of 125) is fine. With a 35mm. camera, Tri-X has more speed, so a smaller aperture that provides greater depth of field can be selected. Tri-X is made for Instamatics, too, but it is not always available in local stores. Using color, the C 126 film will give good Instamatic prints, and Kodacolor KR 126 is fine for transparencies. For color prints with the 35mm. cameras, use Kodacolor II; for transparencies use Kodachrome 64. High-speed Ektachrome is faster, but it tends to produce bluish results. Since red tones disappear almost at once underwater, it's a good idea to compensate for the loss by using a very light magenta color-correction filter such as the CC30 R. It helps warm the tones of the photograph and makes color look more natural to the viewer's eye.

As with snorkeling, the best place to practice underwater picture taking is in a pool, under relaxed conditions. Shoot a few rolls of black-and-white film of anything—the pool drain, a number on the side of the pool, a foot hanging over the edge, a friend partially or fully submerged. When the pictures are processed, they should be evaluated for errors in aiming and focusing and for sharpness and contrast. After studying them, the photographer should try again—a great deal can be learned by simply shooting a few rolls in this manner under reasonably controlled conditions. Don't forget that the technique is not quite the same as when shooting out of the water—underwater the photographer is not standing still but is often in motion; and underwater distance and perspective is distorted to some degree.

Try to select subjects with contrast, either at eye level or overhead. Photographing in a downward direction is less successful. Try to surface dive, and shoot pictures on the way up, including the surface of the water if possible. It's best to keep the principal subject no more than five feet away, because within the range of the camera, the nearer the subject the better the results.

When photographing a person, suggest that he or she wear a colorful bathing suit, one that contrasts with skin color and the water's color.

In large open bodies of water, look

The play of light on these seals helps make a striking picture. (Jack McKenney/Skin Diver Magazine)

for old pilings or piers. Sea creatures will attach themselves to these places, often in clusters, and fascinating shots can be made of barnacles, anemones, and star fish. When photographing fishes, sprinkle bread or catfood under water to attract them. It is impossible to chase a fish and photograph it properly. If you entice it with food, it is likely to come toward you. When you look through the camera, focus on its eye. A photo with a glistening eye gives the fish "personality." Where underwater visibility is great, try to find an interesting composition of corals or rocks and keep feeding food to the fish to entice them into the composition. Soft or hard coral, rocks, and the play of light on sea creatures can make beautiful underwater photos.

If you plan to take a trip on which you will be doing your first underwater photographing, purchase any new equipment you will be using well in advance and try it out several times near your home in order to have a chance to evaluate your results and to make sure your equipment is working properly. In the world of underwater photography, equipment failure is common, but often traceable to some small human error that results in a waterlogged camera and a hair-tearing diver.

When you're finally ready to wade, jump, or dive in, always pause for a moment to review and check each fitting and connection to be sure it's watertight before taking equipment under water.

FIVE

All about Scuba Diving

For exploration of shallow-water reefs and certain other underwater sightseeing, a snorkel, mask, and flippers may be the only equipment you will ever need. But if the underwater life really intrigues you, you may ultimately want to become a scuba diver. This is not to imply that scuba diving is objectively better than snorkeling; for shallow-reef sightseeing, snorkeling is actually preferable, and it is always pleasant not to have to lug scuba equipment around. But scuba opens up so many new avenues of exploration that once you have seen the sea from the surface with a snorkel, you may well find it an irresistible temptation to go down. The scuba diver glides through the water like a bird in flight, touching down on the ocean floor every now and then to gaze up at the forests of marine life twining toward the surface. Under water your heavy equipment is weightless, and so are you. It is a thrill—one that is absent from snorkeling. In addition to the mere pleasure aspects of scuba over snorkeling, you will find that almost any specialized underwater activity, from photography to commercial diving, requires scuba for best results. The photographer faces so many problems underwater that he must be able to station himself for a period of time to do any serious work; and the same is true for the student of marine biology collecting data, the archeologist, the wreck excavator, and those concerned

with underwater construction. This is not to say that good photos can't be taken while snorkeling, or that interesting undersea artifacts can't be collected. But the hobbyist who is really serious about this activity will ultimately find lack of scuba capability a real handicap.

Although diving requires a special training program and should not be undertaken by the untrained snorkeler, it is not a difficult sport. The following section lists the facts about scuba—its joys and its risks. As you will see, the average person is perfectly capable of obtaining scuba certification and enjoying a long career of trouble-free diving.

There are, however, certain qualifications that must be met before you undertake the training. You should be in good physical health. Of course, there are certain ailments that do not affect your ability to become a scuba diver, and if in doubt, consult your physician to determine whether you are fit to dive. The most critical parts of your body, as far as diving is concerned, are your heart, circulatory system, lungs, sinuses, ears, and nose. In addition, you should not be a regular drug user, a heavy smoker, or an alcohol dependant. You should be in good muscular condition and be willing to maintain that condition, preferably by regular swimming. Scuba diving is substantially more strenuous than snorkeling and can put you in spots where your distress might go unnoticed by those who could help you. A diver quickly fatigued is a danger to himself.

Panic is a frequent cause of diver accidents, and the prospective diver must be of sound and stable mental health as well as in good physical condition. The tendency of some people to panic underwater is understandable. On land one has five senses to warn of danger: sight, smell, touch, taste, and hearing. Once you are underwater, four of the five senses are practically wiped out, and the remaining one, sight, is distorted to the extent that things appear 25 percent larger and closer than they actually are. This deprimation and disorientation of the senses naturally makes one feel less secure in the water, even when there is no danger present. Therefore, even small problems can cause panic in the unstable individual. Many a diver accident is caused by an individual panicking when a cool head would have prevented the mishap. If you tend to panic, don't risk diving.

The physics of diving with compressed air is not particularly complex, but it is essential that it be well understood. For this reason, diving is not recommended as a sport for children under fifteen years of age. About half of your dive course will be taken up with lectures on the effects of gases and

234

pressures on the human body. It should be stressed that any person of normal intelligence can understand the lecture section of a dive course. But a person under fifteen frequently does not have the mathematical and scientific skills to work with even the simple physics of diving. In a particularly safe and shallow area, a certified diver might closely supervise a younger person using scuba, but until the young diver is able to pass the written certification exam, no amount of swimming skill and stamina should convince you to let the young diver scuba dive in an unsupervised situation.

Scuba certification is available through several reputable organizations throughout the Americas. It is awarded after the completion of a thirty-hour course and the passing of both a written examination and an open-water checkout. No one should consider himself a competent diver without having received his certification. Various diving resorts, particularly in the Caribbean and in Hawaii, offer a short scuba course, followed by trips to the reef with an instructor. It is true that at these places, with a conscientious and attentive instructor present, you might have several enjoyable diving experiences. But you should not consider this a satisfactory substitute for taking a dive course for certification for diving in other locations or under less careful supervision.

Kim McKenney, carefully supervised by her father, dives at Guayamas. (Jack McKenney/Skin Diver Magazine)

A dive course leading to certification usually gives you about ten hours of pool diving—in which you learn to use your equipment—and twenty hours of lectures, including dive physics, safety procedures, and information about your local dive area. Usually the course will end with one or more open-water boat dives, and sometimes it includes a beach dive as well.

Among the things you will learn in order to earn your certification are:

1. Understanding and handling of all your equipment.

2. Assembling and disassembling your regulator and tank before and after dives.

3. The safe and proper way to put on your equipment, and how to transport it from place to place.

4. How to enter the water with your equipment, or when preferable, how to don your equipment after you are in the water.

5. How to clean and care for your equipment and the importance of having it regularly checked by professionals.

6. Understanding the effects of compressed air on the body. This includes:
(a) the perils of holding your breath while ascending; (b) the effect of too much bottom time; (c) the importance of calculating the time and depth of each dive in a twenty-four-hour period; (d) how to prevent the "bends"; and (e) the effect of excess nitrogen on the body at depths over thirty feet (nitrogen narcosis or "rapture of the deep").

7. How to assist divers in trouble, and how to get them to the surface with the least risk.

8. What to do in emergencies.

9. Removing all or part of your equipment underwater, and successfully retrieving it and putting it back on. This is essential, in case you should lose any of your equipment while diving.

10. How to dive with a "buddy," and that your "buddy" must be in your sight at all times.

When you have completed your dive course, you will be able to dive with the confidence of one who has been properly trained to meet unusual diving situations, and that confidence is easily worth the time and effort expended in the course. While you will always have to consider the mood of the sea, at least you will know what to expect from her and be able to cope with varying situations.

Your dive course will thoroughly prepare you for diving in your local area; and on your boat-dive "checkout" you will deal with the underwater terrain common to that area. When you travel to different places to dive, it is wise to remember that each area has its own peculiarities, its own pleasures, and its own hazards. If you are unfamiliar with the particular area you want to dive, it is best to go to the local dive shop or club and ask. If possible, go diving with local people, who can show the place off to its best advantage.

For example, the Caribbean diver has the advantage of warm and extremely clear water, but must be familiar with harmful fish and other dangerous marine life—fire coral, stinging jelly fish, sea urchins, etc. The West Coast diver has many large fish to hunt, but must be able to cope with colder, rougher water, entangling kelp forests, and sometimes the necessity of rough beach entries. Cave diving presents special problems, since there is frequently only one way in and out of a cave; and one must bring "pony tanks" and ropes and lights as well. Lake and quarry diving require special care to look out for water-skiers, fishermen and their lines, and boats. Ice diving requires very specialized skills.

In other words, even if you are certified, find out from local authorities about the area you are diving, and take their advice. Apply common sense, and never make a dive to "prove" to yourself or anyone else that you can do it. Diving should always be a pleasure, and while the meeting of a challenge can be extremely gratifying, the diver who attempts more than he is up to is a danger to himself and a pleasure to no one else.

If you have gained certification, you are capable of diving more spots in this world than you could ever get to, and each spot will offer unique rewards. With a cool head to assess each day's dive and a certification to reassure you of your training, you should be in for years of spectacular and trouble-free diving, surrounded by scenery and marine life of unimaginable beauty and variety.

236 Should you wish to take a course in scuba, here are the people you can contact. In all likelihood there are some in your area.

National YMCA Scuba Headquarters
291 Broadway
New York, N.Y. 10007
212-374-2151 National Aquatic Program Director: Robert J. Orozco

There are over 1,800 YMCAs in the U.S. and in eighty-six countries of the world. In addition to the headquarters listed above, here are some of the national and regional scuba commissioners, some of whom may be near your area.

National YMCA Underwater Activities Program Director
Robert W. Smith
1129 Simonton Street
Key West, Florida 33040
305-294-0341

Southeast
Robert Axelrod
Star Route 1, Box 1386
Middleburg, Florida 32068
904-282-5464

Mid-America
Jay Hytone
1702 Keo Way
Des Moines, Iowa 50314
515-288-1122

Pacific
William Athow
16555 Kennedy Road
Los Gatos, California 95030
408-287-2990

Mid-Atlantic
John Geary
10-07 Bellair Avenue
Fairlawn, New Jersey 07410
201-796-0203

Northeast
Walt Hornberger
7161 Spire Falls Road
Gansevoort, New York 12831
518-457-7396

Great Lakes
John Lewis
5000 YMCA Drive
Cincinnati, Ohio 45242
513-791-5000

Southwest
Pat Ryan
4332 Northaven Road
Dallas, Texas 75229
214-357-8431

Maine
Joseph Gallant
41 Belmont Street
Portland, Maine 04104
207-772-7518

NAUI, the National Association of Underwater Instructors is situated at 22809 Barton Road, Grand Terrace (Colton), California 92324 (714-783-1862). There are over 3,000 instructor members in the field. You might contact the headquarters listed above, or refer to the classified listings in *Skin Diver Magazine* (available on the newsstand) in order to find a teacher.

NASDS

The National Association of Skin Diving Schools (NASDS) may be contacted by writing to: P.O. Box 17067, Long Beach, Calif. 90807—tel. (213) 595-5361. Below is a list of local schools and teachers.

ALABAMA
Aquaspace
7250 Governors Dr.
Huntsville, Ala. 35805

Ripp-Tide Diving Center
2805 18th St. South
Homewood, Ala. 35209

Robertson Skin Diving Schools
1605 S. Oates St.
Dothan, Ala. 36301

Southern Water Sports
1284 Hutson Dr.
Mobile, Ala. 36609

ARIZONA
Aqua Sports, Inc.
4230 E. Indian School Rd.
Phoenix, Ariz. 85018

Arizona Aqua
2429 Miami Ave.
Kingman, Ariz. 86401

Havasu Scuba & Sports
1668 McCulloch Bl.
Lake Havasu City, Ariz. 86403

Scuba Sciences
616 S. Myrtle
Tempe, Ariz. 85281

Scuba Sciences, Inc.
2620 W. Butler
Phoenix, Ariz. 85021

Tucson School of Scuba Diving
3575 E. Speedway
Tucson, Ariz. 85716

ARKANSAS
Arkansas School of Diving
426 N. Vine
Harrison, Ark. 72601

Cap'n Frogs of Arkansas
11401 Rodney Parham Rd.
Little Rock, Ark. 72205

The Scuba Hut
3906 Hwy. 71 Rt. 46
Springdale, Ark. 72764

BAHAMAS
The Dive Shop Bahamas Ltd.
San Salvador, Bahamas

BRITISH WEST INDIES
Diving Headquarters
P.O. Box 194
Grand Cayman
British West Indies

CALIFORNIA
Aloha Dive Schools
7626 Tampa Ave.
Reseda, Calif. 91335

Aloha Dive Schools
2910 W. Magnolia
Burbank, Calif. 91505

The Anchor Shack Ventures, Inc.
571 Jackson St.
Hayward, Calif. 94544

The Anchor Shack Ventures
5775 Pacheco
Concord, Calif. 94520

Aqua-Gear
1254 9th Ave.
San Francisco, Calif. 91422

Aquarius Dive Shop
2240 Del Monte Ave.
Monterey, Calif. 93940

Aquarius 11
1025 W. Main St.
Salinas, Calif. 93901

Aquatic Center
4535 W. Coast Hwy.
Newport Beach, Calif. 92660

Aquatic Center
312 N. Harbor Blvd.
Santa Ana, Calif. 92703

Arcadia Pool & Dive
21 W. Duarte Rd.
Arcadia, Calif. 91006

Bob's Dive Shop of Fresno
1312 Blackstone
Fresno, Calif. 93703

California Skin Diving Schools
4420 Holt Blvd.
Montclair, Calif. 91763

California Skin Diving Schools
9762 Magnolia Ave.
Riverside, Calif. 92503

California Skin Diving Schools
1173 E St.
San Bernardino, Calif. 92408

Clendenin Boat Sales
P.O. Box 963
El Centro, Calif. 92243

Coastal Diving Co.
320 29th Ave.
Oakland, Calif. 94612

Colo-Riv-Val Divers School
1920 Rio Vista
Needles, Calif. 92363

Competition Ski & Sports
8958 Huntington Dr.
San Gabriel, Calif. 91775

Dive N' Surf
504 N. Broadway
Redondo Beach, Calif. 90277

Diver's Corner
11200 Old River School Rd.
Downey, Calif. 90241

Diver's Den
22 Anacapa St.
Santa Barbara, Calif. 93101

Diver's Dock
1020 W. El Camino
Sunnyvale, Calif. 94087

Diver's Down Sport & Dive
540 N. Main St.
Ft. Bragg, Calif. 94537

Diving Locker
348 E. Grand
Escondido, Calif. 92025

Diving Locker
1020 Grand Ave.
San Diego, Calif. 92109

Diving Locker
155 S. Hwy. 101
Solana Beach, Calif. 92075

El Camino Skin Diving School
1015 El Camino Real
Mt. View, Calif. 94040

G.E. Monahan & Co.
3142 E. Belmont
Fresno, Calif. 93701

Innerspace
1303 N. Chester
Bakersfield, Calif. 93308

Lodi Skin Diving School
430 W. Lockeford St.
Lodi, Calif. 95240

Monterey Dive Center
763 Lighthouse
Monterey, Calif. 93940

238

Olympic Scuba School
2599 N. Main St.
Walnut Creek, Calif. 94596

O'Neill Dive Shop
2222 E. Cliff Dr.
Santa Cruz, Calif. 95060

Pelican Dive Shop
1645 Broadway
Valejo, Calif. 94594

San Diego Divers Supply
1214 Rosecrans St.
San Diego, Calif. 92106

San Diego Divers Supply
1084 National Ave.
Chula Vista, Calif. 92011

San Diego Divers Supply
4004 Sports Arena Blvd.
San Diego, Calif. 92110

San Diego Divers Supply
7522 La Jolla Blvd.
La Jolla, Calif. 92037

San Jose Divers School
2221 The Alameda
Santa Clara, Calif. 95050

Scuba Tech
1613 W. Garvey Ave.
West Covina, Calif. 91790

Scuba Tech
9422 Alondra Blvd.
Bellflower, Calif. 90706

Sea d Sea
1911 S. Catalina Ave.
Redondo Beach, Calif. 90277

Skip Sports, Inc.
3144 Jefferson St.
Napa, Calif. 94558

Skip Sports, Inc.
34 Bayhill Shopping Center
San Bruno, Calif. 94066

Skip Sports, Inc.
733 4th St.
Santa Rosa, Calif. 94504

Skip Sports, Inc.
Corte Madera Center
Corte Madera, Calif. 94925

South Valley Skin Diving School
3852 Monterey Rd.
San Jose, Calif. 95111

Sports World
2477 Huntington Dr.
San Marino, Calif. 91108

Stan's For Sports
28th & F Sts.
Bakersfield, Calif.

Stan's For Sports
3rd & Grand
San Rafael, Calif. 94901

Stan's For Sports
1620 Mendocino Ave.
Santa Rosa, Calif. 94504

Stan's For Sports
201 E. Millbrae Ave.
Millbrae, Calif. 94030

Stan's Sport Chalet
3303 N. Main St.
Pleasant Hill, Calif. 94523

Underwater Schools of America
1083 N. Harbor Blvd.
Anaheim, Calif. 92801

Underwater Schools of America
2547 Lincoln Blvd.
Venice, Calif. 90291

Underwater Schools of America
11501 Whittier Blvd.
Whittier, Calif. 90601

Ventura County Skin & Scuba
Schools
2805 Palma Dr.
Ventura, Calif. 93003

Visalia Scuba Center
1933B W. Caldwell
Visalia, Calif. 93277

Water Pro
280 Higuera St.
San Luis Obispo, Calif. 93401

CANADA
Aquasport
223 King St. West
Brockville, Ontario, Canada

Aquasport
1175 Provost St.
Lachine, Quebec, Canada

Aquasport
1187 Hurontario St.
Mississauga, Ontario, Canada

Aquasport
Main Square 2575 Danforth Ave.
Toronto, Ontario, Canada

Aquasport
Auberge de la Lanterna
Georgeville Rd.
Magog, Quebec, Canada

Aquasport
Bell Canada Bldg.
Ottawa, Canada

Aquasport
105 Mann Ave.
Ottawa, Canada

Argonauts Scuba Divers School
1294 Lauzon Rd.
Windsor, Ontario, Canada

Argonauts Scuba Divers School
905 Tecumseh RR No. 1
Belle River, Ontario, Canada

Atlantic Diving Service & Supply
245 Waterloo St.
St. John N.B. Canada

Innerspace Adventures
33784 Hazel St.
Abbotsford, B.C. Canada

Island Divers
79 Queen St.
Charlottetown, P.E.I., Canada

Nautilus Sports
1594 Chemin St. Louis
Quebec, Canada

Nautilus Sports
583 St. Jean
Quebec, Canada

Okanagan Scuba Academy
2970 Pandosy St.
Kelowna, B.C. Canada

Pro Dive Store
500 Esplanada St.
Sydney, Nova Scotia, Canada

Russ Reid's Scuba School
1347 Kingsway
Vancouver, B.C., Canada

Scubanautique Limited
5791 Tecumseh Rd. W.
Windsor, Ontario, Canada

Sea Trek Dive Center Ltd.
629 Dunedin Rd.
Victoria, B.C., Canada

Skin Scuba Schools
533 11th Ave. S.W.
Calgary 3, Alberta, Canada

Three Fathoms Divers Supply
163 Henderson Hwy.
Winnipeg, Manitoba, Canada

Thunder Country Diving
986 Memorial Ave.
Thunder Bay, Ontario, Canada

Waddell Aquatics
6044 Cote St. Luc Rd.
Montreal, Quebec, Canada

Waterworld
5246 Blowers St.
Halifax, N.S., Canada

COLORADO
Colorado Divers World
557 Milwaukee Ave.
Denver, Colo. 80206

The Sports Arena
405 W. 8th St.
Pueblo, Colo. 81003

DELAWARE
Delaware Diving Academy
Box 157
Ocean View, Dela. 19970

FLORIDA
Allen's Aquatic Center
3448 W. University Ave.
Gainesville, Fla. 32601

American Diving Headquarters
Rt. 1 Box 274-B
Key Largo, Fla. 33037

Aquatic Associates, Inc.
5831 Hallendale Beach Blvd.
W. Hollywood, Fla. 33023

Aquatic Gateways
15 N. Federal Hwy.
Pompano Beach, Fla. 33062

Blue Water Marine Supplies
3511 S.E. Dixie Hwy.
Stuart, Fla. 33494

Boca Dive Shop
251 N. Federal Hwy.
Boca Raton, Fla. 33432

C & G Sporting Goods
137 Harrison
Panama City, Fla. 32401

Carter's Sporting Goods
3001 W. Tennessee St.
Tallahassee, Fla. 32304

The Diving Locker
295 Sunny Isles Blvd.
Miami Beach, Fla. 33160

Everglades Skin Diving School
310 9 St. S.
Naples, Fla. 32940

Everglades Skin Diving School
1173 Estero Blvd.
Ft. Myers, Fla. 33941

Florida State Skin Diving Schools
4172 Phillips Hwy.
Jacksonville, Fla. 32207

Florida State Skin Diving Schools
1900 N. Mills Ave.
Orlando, Fla. 32803

Ft. Lauderdale Divers, Inc.
33 E. Acre Dr.
Plantation, Fla. 33317

Ft. Lauderdale Scuba Academy
3410 N.W. 9th Ave.
Oakland Park, Fla. 33334

Hatt's Diving Headquarters
2006 S. Front
Melbourne, Fla. 32901

Herb's Dive Shop
2434 S. Atlantic Ave.
Daytona Beach, Fla. 32018

Ideal Sport Shop
Stuart Shopping Center
Stuart, Fla. 33494

Inlet Dive Shop
1940 N. Federal Hwy.
Boynton Beach, Fla. 33435

Key West Pro Dive Shop
1605 N. Roosevelt Blvd.
Key West, Fla. 33040

Mac's Scuba, Inc.
600 Mandalay Ave.
Clearwater, Fla. 33515

Missile Skin Diving
691 Courtney N.
Merritt Island, Fla. 32952

Ocean Reef Dive Shop
Rt. 1, Box 274-B
Key Largo, Fla. 33037

Ocean Sports, Inc.
129 E. Miracle Strip Pkwy.
Ft. Walton Beach, Fla. 32548

P.A.C. Diver's Supply
1754 Drew St.
Clearwater, Fla. 33515

Pelican Swim Center
1010 S. 76 St.
Tampa, Fla. 33619

Polk County Skin Diving School
717 6th St. S.W.
Winter Haven, Fla. 33880

Reef Dive Shop
304 E. Ocean Ave.
Lantana, Fla. 33462

Robertson Skin Diving Schools
Court House Square
Marianna, Fla. 32446

Seaview Divers, Inc.
6826 Gulf of Mexico Dr.
Longboat Key, Fla. 33548

Skippers Diving, Inc.
408 E. Wright St.
Pensacola, Fla. 32501

Suncoast Divers Skin Diving School
5120 Kelly Rd.
Tampa, Fla. 33615

Tackle Shack
7801 66th St.
Pinellas Park, Fla. 33565

Under Sea World
521 N. 4th St.
Ft. Pierce, Fla. 33450

Underwater Unlimited
216 Palermo
Coral Gables, Fla. 33134

Underwater Unlimited
8429 S.W. 132 St.
Miami, Fla. 33143

GEORGIA
Aqua Shop
131 E. Montgomery Crossroads
Savannah, Ga. 31406

Dixie Diving Center
2546 Melville Ave.
Decatur, Ga. 30032

W. Georgia Skin Diving School
2111 Wynnton Rd.
Columbus, Ga. 31906

HAWAII
Aloha Dive Shop
Koko Marina Trade Center
Honolulu, Hawaii 96825

Dan's Dive Shop
1382 Makaloa St.
Honolulu, Hawaii 96814

Island Marine
RR 1, Box 180 B
Luhue, Hawaii 96766

South Seas Aquatics
1125 Ala Moana Blvd.
Honolulu, Hawaii 96814

ILLINOIS
Aqua Center, Inc.
717 Morton Ave.
Aurora, Ill. 60506

Aquatic Sports Center
1703 W. Washington
Waukegan, Ill. 60085

Aquaventure Diving School
Arlington Park Towers
Arlington, Ill. 61312

Aquaventure Diving School
1655 Oakton St.
Des Plaines, Ill. 60018

The Twin Fin Diving Center
81 S. Hennepin
Dixon, Ill. 61021

INDIANA
Aqua Den
705 E. 8th St.
Anderson, Ind. 46012

The Flipper Locker, Inc.
1924 E. Illinois
Evansville, Ind. 47711

IOWA
Iowa State Skin Diving School
216 Euclid
Des Moines, Iowa 50317

KANSAS
Frank's Dive Shop
1226 E. Harry
Wichita, Kansas 67211

LOUISIANA
Louisiana State Schools of Diving
427 Rena
Lafayette, La. 70501

New Orleans Skin Diving School
4417 Dryades St.
New Orleans, La. 70115

MAINE
Aqua Diving Academy
999 Congress St.
Portland, Maine 04102

Skin Diver's Paradise
RFD No. 3 Turner Rd.
Auburn, Maine 04210

MARYLAND
Catalina, Inc.
176 Great Mills Rd.
Lexington Park, Md. 20653

Diver's Den
8105 Harford Rd.
Baltimore, Md. 21234

Diver's World
923 Gist Ave.
Silver Spring, Md. 20910

The Scuba Hut
418 Crain Hwy. S.W.
Glen Burnie, Md. 21061

MASSACHUSETTS
Boston School of Diving
57 Washington St.
Somerville, Mass. 02143

Cape Cod School of Skin Diving
39 Main St.
Fairhaven, Mass. 02719

Eastern Divers Supply
196 Middlesex St.
Lowell, Mass. 01852

Lakeville Divers Supply, Inc.
Bedford St., Rt. 18
Lakeville, Mass. 02346

South Shore Divers
511 Washington St.
Quincy Point, Mass. 02169

MICHIGAN
Divers Supply
G-4142 Fenton Rd.
Flint, Mich. 48507

Michigan School of Diving
1806 E. Michigan
Lansing, Mich. 48912

Michigan Underwater School of
Diving
3280 Fort St.
Lincoln Park, Mich. 48146

Recreational Diving Systems
1247 Rosewood
Ann Arbor, Mich. 48104

Scuba-Ventures Underwater
School of Diving
35 W. Square Lake Road
Troy, Mich. 48084

Scuba-World-Fun
26565 John R. St.
Madison Heights, Mich. 48071

The Skamt Shop
5055 Plainfield Ave.
Grand Rapids, Mich. 49505

The Skamt Shop
1081 Holton Rd.
Muskegon, Mich. 49445

West Michigan School of Diving
347 S. Hancock, Box 141
Pentwater, Mich. 49449

MINNESOTA
Club Scuba
1300 E. Wayzata Blvd.
Wayzata, Minn. 55402

Club Scuba
991 Arcade Street
St. Paul, Minn. 55106
Rochester Skin & Scuba, Inc.
528 S. Broadway
Rochester, Minn. 55901

Sports Craft, Inc.
Rt. #7
Brainerd, Minn. 56401

St. Cloud Dodge & Marine
301 S. 5th Ave.
St. Cloud, Minn. 56301

MISSISSIPPI
Earl's Dive & Sports Shop
401 Bouslog St.
Gulfport, Miss. 39501

Skippers Diving, Inc.
4441 N. State St.
Jackson, Miss. 39206

242

MISSOURI
Divers Equipment & Repair
5800 Barrymore Dr.
Kansas City, Mo. 64134

The Diving Chamber
4047 Grayois
St. Louis, Mo. 63116

John the Diver
SR 1 Box 459 Indian Pt.
Branson, Mo. 65616

John the Diver
110 E. 25th
Joplin, Mo. 64801

John the Diver
2555 S. Campbell
Springfield, Mo. 65807

NEBRASKA
Clemens Mobile Marine
1620 E. Overland
Scottsbluff, Neb. 69361

Sports Corner Lincoln
1217 Que St.
Lincoln, Neb. 68508

Sports Corner
287 Italia Mall
Westwood Shopping Cent.
Omaha, Neb. 68114

NEVADA
Scuba Center
400 W. Sahara
Las Vegas, Nev. 89107

NEW HAMPSHIRE
Atlantic Aqua Sport
522 Sagamore Rd.
Rye, N.H. 03870

Lakes Region Divers Supply
RFD No. 3, Weirs Blvd.
Laconia, N.H. 03246

NEW JERSEY
Professional Divers, Inc.
Neptune City Shopping Center
Hwy. 35
Neptune City, N.J. 07753

The Quarry
Route 517
Hamburg, N.J. 07419

Sea N' Ski
246 Main St.
Lincoln Park, N.J. 07035

Skin Diving Center
1659 Hwy. No. 27
Edison, N.J. 08817

Underwater Schools of S. Jersey
1346 Tilton Rd.
Northfield, N.J. 08225

Underwater Sports of New Jersey
Rt. 17
Rochelle Park, N.J. 07662

NEW MEXICO
New Mexico Divers Supply
623 Amherst N.E.
Albuquerque, N. Mex. 87106

NEW YORK
BFV Pro Dive Shop
175 Fort Hill Ave.
Canandaigua, N.Y. 14424

Central New York School of Skin
Diving
Rt. 12 Rd. 2
Norwich, N.Y. 13815

Central New York School of Skin
Diving
1716 Burrstone Rd.
New Hartford, N.Y. 13413

Cougar Sports, Inc.
3470 Webster Ave.
Bronx, N.Y. 10467

Cove Diving Center
57 Forest Ave.
Glen Cove, N.Y. 11542

Danziger, Inc. Skin Diving School
of Long Island
70 S. Main St.
Freeport, N.Y. 11520

Diving Center of Liverpool, Inc.
504 Old Liverpool Rd.
Liverpool, N.Y. 13088

Kings County Divers Corp.
3040 Ave. U
Brooklyn, N.Y. 11229

Marshall's Professional Diving Service
R.D. No. 3
Trumansberg, N.Y. 14886

National Aquatic Service
1425 Erie Blvd.
Syracuse, N.Y. 13210

North Shore Diving Center
58 Lakefield Rd.
East Northport, N.Y. 11731

Scubar
P.O. Box 475
Canton, N.Y. 13617

South Bay Diving Center
502 Old Sunrise Hwy.
Massapequa, N.Y. 11758

Staten Island Diving College
1149 N. Railroad Ave.
Staten Island, N.Y. 10306

Trydent Diving Associates
876 Hazelwood Ave.
Schenectady, N.Y. 12306

NORTH CAROLINA
Aqua Haven
5212 Holly Ridge Dr.
Raleigh, N.C. 27612

EJW Bicycle & Sport Shop
2204 Arendell St.
Morehead City, N.C. 28557

Underwater Schools of North Carolina
2007 Lejeune Blvd.
Jacksonville, N.C. 28540

Underwater Unlimited, Inc.
2438 Park Rd.
Charlotte, N.C. 28203

OHIO
The Aqua Shack, Inc.
440 E. Dixie Dr.
W. Carrollton, Ohio 45449

Aquarian Diving Center
5232 Market St.
Youngstown, Ohio 44512

Buckeye Diving Schools
46 Warrensville Center Rd.
Bedford, Ohio 44146

Central Ohio School of Diving
3120 Indianola Ave.
Columbus, Ohio 43214

Chafee's Marina
2707 N.E. Catawba Rd.
Port Clinton, Ohio 43452

Dive, Inc.
4615 Park Ave. West Rd.
Mansfield, Ohio 44903

Ka Puka Wai Dive Shop
1506 Whipple Ave. N.W.
Canton, Ohio 44708

Midwest Underwater, Inc.
29006 Lakeland Blvd.
Wickliffe, Ohio 44092

Salem School of Scuba
405 E. State St.
Salem, Ohio 44460

Underwater Specialties, Inc.
338 Northland Blvd.
Cincinnati, Ohio 45246

OKLAHOMA
Gene's Aqua Pro
Rt. 1, Box 324
Ft. Gibson, Okla. 74434

Gene's Aqua Pro Shop
Tenkiller Aqua Park
Gore, Okla. 74435

Oklahoma Divers Supply
909 Q Street S.W.
Ardmore, Okla. 73401

Oklahoma Schools of Diving
5733 E. Admiral Pl.
Tulsa, Okla. 74115

The Scuba Shack
119 N. Broadway
Ada, Okla. 74820

Underwater Sports Shop
2533 N.W. 10th
Oklahoma City, Okla. 73107

OREGON
Cap'n Frogs
312 N. Central
Medford, Ore. 97501

Klamath Basin Divers Supply
1033 Main St.
Klamath Falls, Ore. 97601

Northwest Divers Supply
852 S. Broadway
Coos Bay, Ore. 97420

The Northwest Diver
1677 Coburg Rd.
Eugene, Ore. 97401

Oregon Diving School
525 Edgewater St., N.W.
Salem, Ore. 97304

Trans-Global Divers
5405A North Lagoon Ave.
Portland, Ore. 97217

Tri-West School of Skin Diving
13625 S.E. Powell
Portland, Ore. 97236

Underwater Enterprises, Inc.
2500 W. Harvard
Roseburg, Ore. 97470

Valley Scuba Center, Inc.
10803 S.W. Barbur Blvd.
Portland, Ore. 97219

244

PENNSYLVANIA
B & B Marine Specialties
P.O. Box 277
Hillsville, Pa. 16132

Gilligan's Isle, Inc.
6545 Roosevelt Blvd.
Philadelphia, Pa. 19149

RHODE ISLAND
Rhode Island Academy of Skin
Diving
111 Bellevue Ave.
Newport, R.I. 02840

Rhode Island Academy of Skin
Diving
209 Elmwood Ave.
Providence, R.I. 02907

SOUTH CAROLINA
Aqua Venture Dive Center
4357 Jackson Blvd.
Columbia, S.C. 29205

Aqua Venture Dive Center
2247 Augusta Rd.
Greenville, S.C. 29605

Neptune Dive & Ski
133 Georgia Ave.
N. Augusta, S.C. 29841

SOUTH DAKOTA
Coral Reef
1113½ S. Minnesota Ave.
Sioux Falls, S. Dak. 57105

TENNESSEE
Aquarius School of Skin Diving
6863 Lee Hwy.
Chattanooga, Tenn. 37412

Dive Shop
3149 Poplar
Memphis, Tenn. 38108

Tennessee Divers
4110 Gallatin Rd.
Nashville, Tenn. 37206

TEXAS
Copeland's Specialty Sports
4041 S. Padre Island Dr.
Corpus Christi, Tex. 78411

The Dive Shop
2719 Live Oak St.
Dallas, Tex. 75204

Houston Scuba Academy
13628 Almeda Rd.
Houston, Tex. 77045

Houston Scuba Academy (West)
10134 Long Point Rd.
Houston, Tex. 77043

School of Scuba
1009 Walnut St.
Abilene, Tex. 79601

Skin Diving Schools of Fort Worth
3807 Southwest Blvd.
Fort Worth, Tex. 76116

Texas Divers Co.
Fm Rd. 306 at Canyon Dam
New Braunfels, Tex. 78130

Texas Skin Diving Schools
4320 N. Lamar
Austin, Tex. 78703

Texas Skin Diving Schools
Intersection 2222 Hwy. 620
Austin, Tex. 98703

Texas Skin Diving Schools
803 N. 2nd St.
Killeen, Tex. 76544

Trident Diving Equipment
2110 West Ave.
San Antonio, Tex. 78201

Trident Diving
927 Burr Rd.
San Antonio, Tex. 98209

U.S. VIRGIN ISLANDS
Aqua Action
Wintberg Peak
St. Thomas, V.I. 00801

Virgin Islands Diving Schools
P.O. Box 1704
St. Thomas, V.I. 00820

UTAH
USAFECO Diving School
2909 Washington Blvd.
Ogden, Utah 84401

USAFECO Diving School
3500 S. State
Salt Lake City, Utah 84115

USAFECO Diving School
Elmo, Utah 84521

VIRGINIA
The Dive Shop
2814 Graham Blvd.
Falls Church, Va. 22042

The Dive Shop
9401 Little River Turnpike
Fairfax, Va. 22030

Martens & David Diving Shop
5107 Colley Ave.
Norfolk, Va. 23508

National Diving Center II
7502 Leesburg Pike
Falls Church, Va. 22043

Norfolk Academy of Scuba Diving
Skills
5115 Colley Ave.
Norfolk, Va. 23508

Ski & Dive Shop, Inc.
1545 N. Quaker Lane
Alexandria, Va. 22302

WASHINGTON
Allied Dive Center, Inc.
N. 8029 Division
Spokane, Wash. 99208

Anchor Line Divers
415 W. Wishkah
Aberdeen, Wash. 98520

Aqua Masters
201 Meridian North
Puyallup, Wash. 98371

Aquarius Skin Diving School
20801 Hwy. 99
Lynnwood, Wash. 98036

Ron's Dive Inn
19 W. Yakima Ave.
Yakima, Wash. 98902

Northwest Divers
2720 W. Maplewood
Bellingham, Wash. 98225

Northwest Divers
1342 Old Hwy. 99
Mt. Vernon, Wash. 98273

Northwestern School of Skin Diving
2123 N. 30th St.
Tacoma, Wash. 98403

Scuba Supplies
738 Marine Dr.
Port Angeles, Wash. 98362

Sea Anchor
234 Mission St.
Wenatchee, Wash. 98801

Silent World Divers, Inc.
14444 Sunset Hwy.
Bellevue, Wash. 98007

Whidbey Divers Shop
P.O. Box RR 80 N.W. & 900 W.
Oak Harbor, Wash. 98277

WASHINGTON, D.C.
National Diving Center
1305 Connecticut Ave. N.W.
Washington, D.C. 20015

WISCONSIN
Diving Unlimited
41 W. Maple
Sturgeon Bay, Wisc. 54325

Inland Seas Diving Academy
310 N. Commercial St.
Neenah, Wisc. 54956

On the Rocks
Rt. 1, Box 164
Ellison Bay, Wisc. 54210

Sea N' Ski
4248 N. 76th
Milwaukee, Wisc. 53222

Sea N' Ski
Brookfield, Wisc. 53005

Sea N' Ski
Fox Point, Wisc. 53217

Seaway Sports, Inc.
1255 Main St.
Green Bay, Wisc. 54302

246 PADI

The Professional Association of Diving Instructors (PADI) at P.O. Box 177, Costa Mesa, Calif. 92627—tel. (714) 979-4826—has over 3,500 instructors throughout the world who teach independently in addition to maintaining training facilities. These training facilities are dive stores owned by private owners or instructors that teach scuba according to the standards and ethics of PADI and then certify their students. The following is a list of such facilities.

ALABAMA
Gulf Coast Divers Supply
512 Houston St.
Mobile, Ala. 36606

Southern Skin Divers Supply
506 S. 45th St.
Birmingham, Ala. 35222

BAHAMAS
Nassau Dive Supply
Box N 1658
Nassau, Bahamas

CALIFORNIA
Ed Brawley Skindiving School
598 Foam St.
Monterey, Calif. 93940

Ed Brawley Skindiving School
2147 Hurley Way
Sacramento, Calif. 95825

Ed Brawley Skindiving School
514 S. Bayshore Blvd.
San Mateo, Calif. 94402

Ed Brawley Skindiving School
7831 Thornton Rd.
Stockton, Calif. 95207

Ed Brawley Skindiving School
2756 Camino Diablo
Walnut Creek, Calif. 94596

Scuba Center
8682 Stanton Ave.
Buena Park, Calif. 90620

Scuba Center
2986 Huntington Dr.
San Marino, Calif. 91108

Scuba West
2720 E. Coast Hwy.
Corona Del Mar, Calif. 92625

Scuba West
1162 N.E St.
San Bernardino, Calif. 92410

CANADA
Atlantic Diving Supply & Service, Ltd.
61 Pacific Ave.
Moncton, N.B., Canada

Canada Scuba School, Ltd.
4164 Kingston Rd.
Searborough, Ontario, Canada

Northern Ontario Diving Supplies
Manitoulin Scuba Centre
Little Current, Ontario, Canada

Northern Ontario Diving Supplies
Sub-Aqua Centre
Sudbury, Ontario, Canada

Northern Ontario Diving Supplies
Box 2276, Stn. A
Sudbury, Ontario, Canada

DOMINICAN REPUBLIC
Aquatic Centers International
Max Henriquez Urena No. 89
Santo Domingo, Dominican Republic

FLORIDA
Aqua Mundo, Inc.
P.O. Box 9102
Winter Haven, Fla. 33880

Atlantic Scuba Academy
20 N. Atlantic Ave.
Daytona Beach, Fla. 32018

Bob's Scuba/Sport Center
5527 S. Orange Blossom Trail
Orlando, Fla. 32809

Central Florida Divers
10022 N. 30th St.
Tampa, Fla. 33612

The Dive Shop
155 Knox Merae
Titusville, Fla. 32780

Diveco Diving Systems
50 Royal Palm Blvd.
Vero Beach, Fla. 32960

Diveco Diving Systems
P.O. Box 892
Vero Beach, Fla. 32960

Divers Unlimited, Inc.
4305 Hollywood Blvd.
Hollywood, Fla. 33021

Gulfview Divers Headquarters
101 Bridge St.
Bradenton Beach, Fla. 33510

H & T Dive Shop, Inc.
233 Sixth Ave. North
Jacksonville Beach, Fla. 32250

Hall's Dive Shop
1688 Overseas Hwy.
Marathon, Fla. 33050

Jim Hollis' Scuba World
5107 East Colonial Dr.
Orlando, Fla. 32807

New England Divers
2945 N.E. 2nd Ave.
Miami, Fla. 33157

Professional Diving, Ind.
1693 N. Harbor City Blvd.
Melbourne, Fla. 32935

Sous Marine Enterprises
449 McDonald St.
(P.O. Box 215)
Mt. Dora, Fla. 32757

Surf Sun n' Fun
905 N. Atlantic
Ft. Lauderdale, Fla. 33304

The Tackle Box
1568 Main St.
Sarasota, Fla. 33577

GEORGIA
Airco the Diver
634 Lindbergh Way N.E.
Atlanta, Ga. 30324

Aqua Sport
1766 Green Rd.
Buford, Ga. 30518

Diving Locker
Box 106
Ila, Ga. 30647

HAWAII
Central Pacific Divers
780 Front St.
Lahaina, Hawaii 96761

Hawaiian Divers
P.O. Box 572
Kailua-Kona, Hawaii 96740

Pau Hana Dive, Inc.
33 Nawiliwili St.
Honolulu, Hawaii 96835

IOWA
Chambered Nautilus
7 S. Dubuque St.
Iowa City, Iowa 52240

LOUISIANA
Gulf South Diving Academy
P.O. Box 158
Hammond, La. 70401

MARYLAND
Dynamo, Inc.
8906 Rhode Island Ave.
College Park, Md. 20740

The Scuba Hut, Inc.
418 Crain Hwy. S.W.
Glen Burnie, Md. 21061

MASSACHUSETTS
Cape Cod Skindiving School
39 Main St.
Fairhaven, Mass. 02719

Cape Cod Skindiving School
6 Pine Needle Way
Westport, Mass. 02790

The Scuba Shack, Inc.
1293 Ocean St. Rt. 139
Marshfield, Mass. 02050

MICHIGAN
Lubberts Dive Shop
4389 Chicago Dr.
Grandville, Mich. 49418

N.M.U. Scuba School
North Michigan University
Marquette, Mich. 49855

MISSISSIPPI
The Divers Den
1014 Bowen St.
Ocean Springs, Miss. 39564

MISSOURI
Divers Equipment & Repair Service, Inc.
5800 Barrymore Dr.
Kansas City, Mo. 64134

West End Diving
4714 Bridgeton Station Rd.
Bridgeton, Mo. 63042

West End Diving
11004 Manchester Rd.
St. Louis, Mo. 63122

NEVADA
The Abyss
3021 E. Charleston
Las Vegas, Nev. 89104

Desert Divers Supply
5720 E. Charleston
Las Vegas, Nev. 89122

NEW JERSEY
Four Divers, Inc.
56 Broadway
Point Pleasant Beach, N.J. 68742

NEW MEXICO
New Mexico Marine Supply
5004 San Mateo N.E.
Albuquerque, N. Mex. 87109

NEW YORK
Advanced Underwater Diving
Schools
215 Bert Ave.
Westbury, N.Y. 11590

Brooklyn Divers
2917 Avenue I
Brooklyn, N.Y. 11210

Niagara Scuba Sports
2048 Niagara St.
Buffalo, N.Y. 14207

Night Star Divers
P.O. Box 1
Highland Falls, N.Y. 10928

Skin & Scuba
19 Callingham Rd.
Pittsford, N.Y. 14534

NORTH CAROLINA
Blue Dolphin Dive Shop
2510 English Rd.
High Point, N.C. 27260

Key West Diving Co.
6419 Yadkin Road
Fayetteville, N.C. 28303

Undersea Center
4762 Yadkin Rd.
Fayetteville, N.C. 28304

OHIO
Creelman Diver Supply
2117 Beechmont Ave.
Cincinnati, Ohio 45230

Scuba East Diving School
21950 Lake Shore Blvd.
Euclid, Ohio 44123

Sub Aquatics, Inc.
8855 E. Broad St. RR 1
Reynoldsburg, Ohio 43068

Sub Aquatics, Inc.
10333 Northfield
Northfield, Ohio 44067

Underwater Sports of Ohio
703 S. Main St.
Urbana, Ohio 43078

OKLAHOMA
Gene's Aqua Pro Shop
Rt. 1, Box 324
Ft. Gibson, Okla. 74434

OREGON
Aquarius Underwater Center
7660 S.W. Barbur Blvd.
Portland, Ore. 97219

Deep Sea Bill's
Box 213 South Jetty
Newport, Ore. 97365

PENNSYLVANIA
Sub Aquatics, Inc.
1593 Banksville
Pittsburgh, Pa. 15216

SOUTH CAROLINA
Carolina Divers Center, Inc.
217 Piedmont Hwy.
Greenville, S.C. 29605

Palmetto Divers, Inc.
5541 Shakespeare Rd.
Columbia, S.C. 29204

Palmetto Divers, Inc.
Box 1592
Myrtle Beach, S.C. 29577

SOUTH DAKOTA
Scuba Supply
1607 Saint Joe
Rapid City, S. Dak. 57701

TENNESSEE
Currint Interprises, Inc.
600 Magnolia Ave.
Knoxville, Tenn. 37912

TEXAS
Anderson Scuba School
5800 Diamond Oaks Dr.
Ft. Worth, Tex. 76617

The Dive Shop, Inc.
1426 Ranch Rd. 12
San Marcos, Tex. 78666

J. Rich Sports, Ltd., Inc.
420 Northcross Mall
2525 Anderson Lane
Austin, Tex. 78757

VIRGIN ISLANDS
Virgin Islands Diving School
P.O. Box 1704
St. Thomas, V.I. 00801

WASHINGTON
Eason's Marine Service
8420 Martin Way
Olympia, Wash. 98506

WISCONSIN
Blue Water Divers Supply
Rt. 3
New Auburn, Wisc. 54757

R.S. Diving Supply Co.
109 N. Lake Ave.
Crandon, Wisc. 54520

West Bend Aqua Shop
1829 N. Main St.
West Bend, Wisc. 53095

Bibliography

In addition to individual books listed here, there are book catalogues concerning the marine world. Write:

The Mariner's Press
P.O. Box 540
Boston, Mass. 02117

Underwater Society of America
Ambler, Pa. 19002

PAMPHLETS AND PERIODICALS

Chaplin, C.G. *Fishwatchers Guide to the West Atlantic Coral Reefs.* (Take it with you underwater.) Valley Forge, Pa.: Harrowood Books, 1972.

Ocean's Magazine. Six times a year by Ocean's Magazine Co., 125 Independence Drive, Menlo Park, California 94025.

Sea Frontiers and *Sea Secrets.* Published bimonthly by the International Oceanographic Foundation, Virginia Key, Miami, Florida 33149.

Skin Diver Magazine. Published monthly by the Peterson Publishing Company, Hollywood, California.

Underwater Naturalist. Published as a bulletin for members of the American Littoral Society, Sandy Hook, Highlands, N.J. 07732.

BOOKS

Arnov, Boris, Jr. *Homes Beneath the Sea.* Boston: Little, Brown and Company, 1969.

Berman, Bruce D. *Encyclopedia of American Shipwrecks.* Boston: The Mariners Press, 1972.

Bohlke, James E., and Charles C.G. Chaplin, *Fishes of the Bahamas and Adjacent Tropical Waters.* Wynnewood, Pa.: Livingston Publishing Company, 1968.

Bridges, William. *The New York Aquarium Book of the Water World.* New York: American Heritage Publishing Co., 1970.

Carson, Rachel L. *The Edge of the Sea.* New York: Houghton Mifflin Co., 1955.

Carson, Rachel L. *The Sea Around Us.* New York: Oxford University Press, 1951.

Cooper, Allan. *Fishes of the World.* New York: Grosset & Dunlap, 1971.

Cousteau, Jacques-Yves. *Captain Cousteau's Underwater Treasury.* New York: Harper & Row, 1959.

Cousteau, Jacques-Yves. *Oasis in Space.* New York: World Publishers, 1972.

Cousteau, Jacques-Yves, and Philippe Diolé. *Diving Companions: Sea Lions, Elephant Seal, Walrus.* New York: Doubleday & Co., 1974.

Cousteau, Jacques-Yves, and Philippe Diolé. *Diving for Sunken Treasure.* New York: Doubleday & Co., 1971.

Cousteau, Jacques-Yves, and Philippe Diolé. *Dolphins.* New York: Doubleday & Co., 1975.

Cousteau, Jacques-Yves, and Philippe Diolé. *Life and Death in a Coral Sea.* New York: Doubleday & Co., 1971.

Cousteau, Jacques-Yves, and Philippe Diolé. *Octopus and Squid.* New York: Doubleday & Co., 1973.

Cousteau, Jacques-Yves, and Philippe Diolé. *The Shark: Splendid Savage of the Sea.* New York: Doubleday & Co., 1970.

Cousteau, Jacques-Yves, and Philippe Diolé. *The Whale: Mighty Monarch of the Sea.* New York: Doubleday & Co., 1972.

Cousteau, Jacques-Yves, and Frédéric Dumas. *The Silent World.* New York: Harper & Row, 1953.

Cousteau, Jacques-Yves, with James Dugan. *The Living Sea.* New York: Harper & Row, 1963.

Cousteau, Jacques-Yves, and James Dugan. *World Without Sun.* New York: Harper & Row, 1965.

250

Fricke, Hans W. *The Coral Seas.* New York: G.P. Putnam's Sons, 1973.

Gabrielson, Ira N., and Francesca LaMonte. *The Fisherman's Encyclopedia.* New York: Stackpole & Heck, 1950.

Gotto, R.V. *Marine Animals, Partnerships and Other Associations.* New York: American Elsevier Publishing Co., 1969.

Halstead, Bruce W. *Tropical Fish: A Guide for Setting Up and Maintaining an Aquarium for Tropical Fish and Other Animals.* New York: Golden Press, 1975.

Hannau, Hans W., and Bernard H. Mock. *Beneath the Seas of the West Indies.* New York: Hastings House.

Hardy, Sir Alister. *The Open Sea.* Boston: Houghton Mifflin, 1965.

Herring, Peter S. *Deep Oceans.* New York: Praeger Publishing, 1971.

Hess, Lilo. *Sea Horses.* New York: Charles Scribner's Sons, 1966.

Lomer, Gordon. *Diving Guide to the Bahamas.* Miami: Argos.

Marshall, Norman and Olga. *Ocean Life.* New York: The Macmillan Company, 1971.

Marx, Wesley. *The Frail Ocean.* New York: Ballantine Books, 1967.

Matthiessen, Peter. *Blue Meridian.* New York: Random House, 1971.

McDonald, Kendall. *Fish Watching and Photography.* New York: Charles Scribner's Sons, 1972.

Olney, Ross R. *Oceanography.* Camden, N.J.: Thomas Nelson, 1969.

Ray, Carleton, and Elgin Ciampi. *Marine Life.* New York: A.S. Barnes and Co., 1956.

Reader's Digest. *Secrets of the Seas.* Pleasantville, N.Y.: Reader's Digest Association, 1972.

Ricciuti, Edward R. *Killers of the Seas.* New York: Walker & Co., 1973.

Schroeder, Robert E. *Something Rich and Strange.* New York: Harper & Row, 1965.

Silverberg, Robert. *Sunken History.* Philadelphia: Chilton Books, 1963.

Slosky, Bill, and Art Walker. *Guide to the Underwater.* New York: Sterling Publishing Co., 1966.

Starck, Walter A., II, and Paul Brundza. *Underwater Photography.* New York: American Photographic Book Publishing, 1966.

Stevenson, Robert A., Jr. *The Complete Book of Saltwater Aquariums.* New York: Funk & Wagnalls, 1974.

Stix, Hugh and Marguerite. *The Shell: Five Hundred Million Years of Inspired Design.* New York: Harry N. Abrams, 1968.

Straughan, Robert P. *Exploring the Reef.* S. Brunswick, N.J.: A.S. Barnes Co., 1968.

Straughan, Robert P. *The Salt Water Aquarium in the Home.* S. Brunswick, N.J.: A.S. Barnes Co., 1970.

Street, Donald M., Jr. *A Cruising Guide to the Lesser Antilles.* New York: Dodd, Mead & Company, 1966.

Thorne, Jim. *The Underwater World.* New York: Thomas Y. Crowell Co., 1969.

Ullman, James Ramsey, and Al Dinhofer. *The Official Caribbean Guide Book.* New York: Macmillan Company, 1968.

Viertel, Janet. *Blue Planet.* New York: Grosset & Dunlap, 1973.

Viertel, Janet. *Undersea Garden of the Virgin Islands.* Hollywood, Florida: Dukane Press, 1969.

Wilson, Lloyd R., and James E. Landfried. *Diver's Guide to All the Bahamas and the Turks and Caicos Islands.* Melbourne, Florida: Islands Unlimited, 1972.

Credits

Original information for the maps and charts in Chapter 3 was furnished most generously by the following, and I am most grateful to all of them:

A-1 Diving Center of Waterbury, Conn.; Akumal Club of Juarez, Mexico; Allen Sport Shop of New Rochelle, N.Y.; Anthony's Key Resort of Roatan, Honduras; Anzac Sportsmen Club of Kailua, Hawaii; Aqua Sports Center of Smithfield, Rhode Island; Aquatic Research & Diving Company of Evergreen, Colorado; Aquaventures of Santo Domingo; Avalon Catalina Island Chamber of Commerce, Avalon, California; Atlantic Scuba Academy of Daytona Beach, Florida; Atlantis Safaris of Miami Shores, Fla.; B.G. Divers of Crystal River, Fla.; British Virgin Islands Government and Tourist Board of the British Virgin Islands; Bahama Out Islands Tourist News of Nassau, Bahamas; Bahamas Tourist Office of New York, N.Y.; Bamboo Reef Enterprises of San Francisco, Calif.; Belize Tourist Organization of Belize City, Belize, C.A.; Blue Grotto of Williston, Fla.; Bob Sotos Diving Lodge of Grand Cayman Island; Bonaire Tourist Board of New York, N.Y.; Brawley's Seven Seas Skin Diving Center of Monterey, Calif.; Buccaneer's Inn of Cayman Brac; Buckeye Diving Schools of Bedford, Ohio; Carib Cruises Limited of Castries, St. Lucia; Caribbean School of Aquatics of San Juan, P.R.; Caribbean Tourism Association of Dominica, W.I.; Caribbean Tourism Association of New York, N.Y.; Carl Gage Dive Center of Key Largo, Fla.; Cayman Islands Department of Tourism of Georgetown, Grand Cayman Island; Consulate of Granada of New York, N.Y.; Cougar Sports of Bronx, N.Y.; Coral Beach Hotel of Belize, C.A.; Coral Beach Travel Service of Belize City, Belize, C.A.; Coral Reef Park Company, Inc., of Key Largo, Fla.; Crusty Dutchman of Key Largo, Fla.; Current Club Resort of North Eleuthera, Bahamas; Cutler Ridge Diving Center of Miami, Fla.; Dale Stones Aqua Shack of Branford, Fla.; Dan's Dive Shop of Honolulu, Hawaii; Diver's Paradise of Toledo, Ohio; Diving Locker of North Vancouver, British Columbia, Canada; Diving Unlimited of San Diego, Calif.; Dominica Safaris of Dominica, W.I.; Dominica Tourist Board of Roseau, Dominica; Eastern Caribbean Association of New York, N.Y.; Eden Isles, Cay Caulker of Belize, C.A.; El Pescador of Ambergris Caye, Belize, C.A.; Michael Finn Associates, Inc., of New York, N.Y.; Fish and Game Department of California at Sacramento, Calif.; John Scott Fones, Inc., of New York, N.Y.; Four Fathoms Dive Center of Port Au Prince, Haiti; Go Mexico, Inc., of South Minneapolis, Minn.; Grand Turk Tourist Information of Grand Turk Island, B.W.I.; Half-Moon Beach Hotel of Barbados, West Indies; Hana Maui Hotel of Maui, Hawaii; John Hamber's Diving Center of St. Thomas, V.I.; Hawaii Visitors Bureau of Honolulu, Hawaii; Hawaiian Council of Diving Clubs of Honolulu, Hawaii; Hawaiian-Pacific Divers of Maui, Hawaii; Hawks Nest Fishing and Yacht Club of Cat Island, Bahamas; Heber Springs Boat Dock of Heber Springs, Ark.; Herb's Dive Shop of Daytona Beach, Fla.; International Dive Club of St. John, V.I.; International Diving of Northridge, Calif.; Jamaica Tourist Board of New

252

York, N.Y.; John Pennekamp Coral Reef State Park of Key Largo, Fla.; John the Diver, Inc., of Branson, Mont.; John F. Jorna of Saint Mary's, Ontario, Canada; Woody Kepner Assoc. of New York, N.Y.; Key Colony Divers of Key Colony Beach, Fla.; Key West Pro Dive Shop of Key West, Fla.; Bert & Jacki Kilbride of Virgin Gorda, British Virgin Islands; La Porte's Skindiving Shop of Newbury, N.H.; Long Bay Hotel of Antigua, West Indies; Carmen Lopez of New York, N.Y.; Louisbourg Marine of Louisbourg, Nova Scotia; Lomont Enterprises, Ltd. of Belize City, Belize, C.A.; Maho Watersports of St. Maarten, N.A.; Marina Cay Hotel of Road Town, Tortola, British Virgin Islands; Marine Specialties, Inc., of Provincetown, Mass.; Marler Industries of Road Town, Tortola, British Virgin Islands; McWayne Marine Supply of Honolulu, Hawaii; Bill Miller of St. Vincent, Grenadines; Mexican Tourist Council of New York, N.Y.; Mexico National Tourist Council of Mexico City, Mexico; Montserrat Tourist Board of Montserrat, West Indies; New England Divers of Los Angeles, Calif.; New England Divers of San Diego, Calif.; Niagara Scuba Sports of Buffalo, N.Y.; Norman, Lawrence, Patterson and Farrell of New York, N.Y.; North Carolina Department of Cultural Resources of Raleigh, N.C.; Northwest Divers Supply, Inc., of Coos Bay, Ore.; Oceanic Society of Uxbridge, Mass.; Ohio Council of Skin and Scuba Divers, Inc., of Neward,

Ohio; On the Rocks of Ellison Bay, Wisconsin; Orange City Chamber of Commerce of Orange City, Fla.; Orbit Marine Sports Center of Bridgeport, Conn.; Palm Island Dive Shop of St. Vincent, Grenadines, W.I.; Palmas Del Mar Undersea Center, Palmas Del Mar, P.R.; Paradise House Hotel of Belize City, Belize, C.A.; Peace and Plenty of Georgetown, Exuma, Bahamas; Pirate's Den Hotel of Roatan, Honduras, C.A.; Professional Association of Diving Instructors of Evergreen, Colo.; Professional Diving Instructor College of Monterey, Calif.; Puerto Rico Tourism Development Company of New York, N.Y.; Punta Cana Club of Santo Domingo, The Dominican Republic; The Quarry of Hamburg, N.J.; The Reef Shop of Islamorada, Fla.; St. Kitts-Nevis-Anguilla Tourist Board of Basseterre, St. Kitts, West Indies; St. Lucia Tourist Board E.C.T.A. of New York, N.Y.; St. Mary's and District Chamber of Commerce of St. Mary's, Ontario, Canada; St. Vincent Marine and Yacht Co. of St. Vincent, West Indies; St. Vincent Tourist Board of St. Vincent, West Indies; San Andros Inn and Tennis Club of San Andros Island, Bahamas; Richard A. Scott of Orlando, Fla.; Scubahamas of Freeport, Grand Bahama; Scuba Safari of Barbados, West Indies; Scubalab of Madison, Wisc. Seaview Divers of Longboat Key,

Fla.; Secret Harbour of Granada, West Indies; Ski and Dive of Tinley Park, Ill.; Ski and Dive Shop of Alexandria, Va.; Skin Diver Magazine of Los Angeles, Calif.; Skin Diving Hawaii of Kailua Kona, Hawaii; Small Hope Bay Lodge of Andros Island, Bahamas; Sontheimer & Co. of New York, N.Y.; Spanish Bay Reef of Grand Cayman Island; South Seas Aquatics of Honolulu, Hawaii; Sports Craft, of Brainerd, Minn.; Sub Aquatics, Inc., of Cleveland, Ohio; Captain Don Stewart of Bonaire, West Indies; Sunshine Key Aqua Center of Sunshine Key, Fla.; Teach Tour Diving Co. of Nazareth, Pa.; Teach Tour Diving Co. of Bridgetown, Barbados, W.I.; Teach Tour Diving Co. of Speyside, Tobago; Tementos of Westwego, La.; Tourism and Public Relations National Office of Port-au-Prince, Haiti; Trinidad and Tobago Tourist Board of New York, N.Y.; Undersea Centers Corp. of St. Thomas, Virgin Islands; Underwater Engineering Ltd. of Nassau, Bahamas; Underwater Research Center of Philipsburg, St. Maarten, N.A.; United States Divers Co. of Santa Ana, Calif.; Viking Camera and Dive Shop of Newport, R.I.; Watershed Dive Shop of Carbondale, Ill.; and Young Island St. Vincent, W.I. (information from Ralph Locke).

Index

254

255